S0-BOG-179

333.9100975   78827
H29w

DATE DUE			

WATER RESOURCE INVESTMENT AND THE PUBLIC INTEREST

Water Resource Investment and the Public Interest

An Analysis of Federal Expenditures in Ten Southern States

BY ROBERT H. HAVEMAN

VANDERBILT UNIVERSITY PRESS

Nashville, Tennessee

CARL A. RUDISILL LIBRARY
LENOIR RHYNE COLLEGE

333.9100975
H29w
78827
June/972

Copyright © 1965 by Vanderbilt University Press
International Standard Book Number 0–8265–1077–9
Library of Congress Catalogue Card Number 65–18545
Composed, Printed, and Bound by the Methodist Publishing House
Nashville, Tennessee, U.S.A.
Second printing, 1970

Foreword

ON JANUARY 9, an article by Kermit Gordon, head of the Budget Bureau, on economy in government appeared in the *Saturday Review*. This article stressed the necessity for choice in the expenditure of Federal funds in these words: "The necessity for choice—for a reexamination of existing programs, for a weighing of alternatives—is always an imperative of responsible budget-making." The article went on to say that the necessity for choice is especially compelling in this day of increased demand on the Federal dollar.

This necessity for choice first led me to take an interest in the work that has been done by Professor Haveman in the area of evaluating proposed federal investment opportunities. In fact, the doctoral thesis that forms the basis of this book seemed to be so relevant to the problems I encountered in my efforts to see that Congress made the right choice that I reproduced much of this thesis in the *Congressional Record* late in 1963. I felt that my colleagues should have a chance to examine this evidence that the wasteful practices in evaluating proposed public works projects that I had criticized for so many years represented an inefficient use of the taxpayer's dollars.

Perhaps the single most spectacular instance of Congressional waste in water resource projects that I have encountered during my years in the Senate was the Glen Elder, Kansas, project. It certainly represents an ideal case study of the type of wasteful evaluation procedures so effectively documented in this book.

Twenty-one years ago, Congress passed a major public works bill known as the Pick-Sloan Act. This was authorizing legislation. In other words, it permitted Congress to appropriate funds for the carrying out of any one or a number of the projects mentioned in the Act if Congress so determined. The authorization for the Glen Elder project was buried in the Pick-Sloan Act so deeply that the project is not mentioned by name in the Act itself. It was one of a number of projects included within a one-line blanket reference.

Eighteen years later, appropriations were requested to begin the Glen Elder Dam project. In those eighteen years the situation that existed when construction was first authorized had changed drastically. In the war year of 1944 the need for an increase in productive farm land constituted the principal reason for approving the Glen Elder proposal. The primary objective of the Dam was to provide irrigation in order to step up the production of feed grains. In 1962, while appropriations for the Glen Elder Dam were under consideration, Congress passed a bill intended to take millions of acres of farm land out of production. This country was faced with a large and growing feed-grain surplus that cost the government millions of dollars simply to store. In fact, today a reclamation project must demonstrate that it will not contribute to farm surpluses before it can be approved by Congress. Yet the principal benefit which the Glen Elder project was supposed to provide was an increase in the production of feed grains, a surplus crop.

In these eighteen years the estimated cost of the project had skyrocketed from 17 million dollars to 76 million dollars, the storage capacity estimated as necessary to irrigate the land had increased from 300,000 acre-feet to 800,000 acre-feet, and the area to be irrigated was cut from 26,000 to 21,000 acres. In the years since 1962, when the Glen Elder appropriation was first considered by Congress, the estimated cost has increased again to at least 78 million dollars—five times the original estimate. This means that it will cost $1,729 an acre to bring water to the 21,000 acres involved in the project. Not only is this more than the land is worth, but farmers using the land will pay back only $191 per acre at the rate of $4 a year during the 50-year repayment period.

Despite these facts and in the face of a determined fight on my part to prevent the appropriation of funds for this project, it was approved. How could this sort of project be approved by the members of Congress? Was it a result of pressures from the folks back home? Far from it. Ninety percent of the landowners in the area were vigorously opposed to the project. The following is a typical complaint:

This area had been fighting this dam for 25 years. The dam is neither needed or wanted. Since the project will do none of the things for which it is proposed, and since the majority opposes it, why waste money investigating, surveying it and planning it?

Why indeed? Basically there are two reasons. One is the artificial yardstick used in measuring the cost of public works projects in relationship to their benefits. But perhaps more important is the "you scratch my back, I'll scratch yours" type of political logrolling which is so much a part of the legislative process, whether local or national. In the words of the Milwaukee *Journal* "many of the votes for Glen Elder were cast by Senators who expected, in return, to win support for other federal projects in their own states." I wish that I could point to the Glen Elder case as an isolated example; however, this is far from the truth.

On the other hand, I would not want to give the impression, that inefficient expenditures of Federal funds on water resource projects result solely from a change in conditions between the time the project is authorized and the time funds are appropriated to begin construction. Earlier I mentioned certain flaws in measuring benefits in relation to cost. These flaws are the theme of Professor Haveman's book. They account for the great number of inefficient projects that are supported by the Federal government.

Although I have attempted to correct some of these flaws through a resolution intended to produce a more realistic estimate of project benefits, I have been handicapped in this work because of the paucity of any concrete studies in the area. Professor Haveman has done the tough, vital job of examining the benefit-cost ratio problem with a series of concrete criteria and formulae. He has demonstrated from existing evidence that the present system of computing benefit-cost ratios is inaccurate and misleading.

For example, Professor Haveman has gone into the serious

problem of the inadequate discount rate being used by the Corps of Engineers to determine the present value of future benefits. He has examined weaknesses in the treatment of risk and uncertainty in arriving at the proper amount of benefits. He has consolidated and explored many of the criticisms leveled by Otto Eckstein and other noted economists and has introduced still other considerations.

I only hope that by confronting the people and their lawmakers with facts and figures showing the inadequacy of the benefit-cost ratios being used in approving public works projects, critics can force a change. Certainly this is the best road to travel, for no one can explain away the truth. Professor Haveman, in this excellent book, has performed a valuable service in bringing clarity to the difficult process of evaluating alternative government investments and stimulating further discussion of this little-understood but extremely important question.

WILLIAM PROXMIRE

United States Senate
Washington, D. C.
May 1965

Preface

IN RECENT years, the problems of Federal water resource development have occupied a central position in the evolution of applied or empirical welfare analysis. Beginning in the middle 1950's, several studies have appeared which were concerned with both the economic and the political phenomena associated with Federal water resource development. Prominent in the forefront of these analyses have been the contributions of both economists (e.g., Otto Eckstein, John V. Krutilla, and Roland McKean) and political scientists (e.g., Arthur Maass), whose findings have by now become the essence of any serious discussion in this area. Essentially, all of these studies were concerned with a single key question: With the goal of social economy, what are the processes, the standards, and the criteria which the government should apply in forming basic investment decisions in the water resource field? Consequently, recommendations on the appropriate criteria to be used in project choice, the proper techniques for designing individual projects and for estimating future project effects, and the implementation of effective political and administrative processes have occupied important positions in the discussion.

The present study is derived from these analyses; it draws heavily upon and, hopefully, adds to the stream of progress in this area. What is added is perhaps most simply described as an empirical combination of the two primary determinants of that variable which economists call economic welfare. Although both the size of the national income (economic efficiency) and its distribution have been recognized in the literature as the primary determinants of economic welfare, economists have generally proceeded on the assumption that welfare is but a single-valued function of only the size of the national income. In distinction to this approach, the present study empirically investigates the relationship between these welfare determinants and incorporates both of them into a multidimensional welfare function.

In the first section of the study, Chapters One to Three, the nature of the past Corps of Engineers program is described and evaluated. The stated goals of the program are outlined, and an empirical verification of the operation of these motivations is set forth. In the second and major section of the study, Chapters Four to Six, the two problems of allocative efficiency and income distribution are empirically analyzed in separate chapters and then combined in a final analysis of their inter-relationship. In the final chapter, the Epilogue, both of these concepts are united in a multidimensional welfare function, and through this function, a pair of experiments in welfare evaluation are performed.

In the preparation of the study, I have benefitted greatly from the suggestions, guidance, and encouragement of several friends and colleagues. My special appreciation goes to Professor Rendigs Fels of Vanderbilt University and Dr. John V. Krutilla of Resources for the Future, Inc., who read and commented upon the entire manuscript. Their suggestions and comments were most helpful and substantially improved the study. My appreciation also goes to Professors James W. McKie of Vanderbilt University and Fred M. Westfield of Northwestern University who read and commented upon parts of the manuscript and to Professors John C. Dawson, Robert Voertman, Phillip Thomas, and Kenyon Knopf, all of Grinnell College, and Martin A. Garrett of The College of William and Mary, for both their encouragement and their helpful criticism. Also, I am indebted to various people in the Corps of Engineers for much information and assistance and to the Inter-University Committee for Economic Research on the South which supported the study on two occasions. Finally, I am most grateful to my wife, Sally, who conscientiously typed several drafts of the study and provided much encouragement at innumerable junctures.

I am also appreciative of the permission granted by the *American Economic Review* to reproduce substantial parts of an article which appeared in the May, 1964, issue of that journal and by the University of North Carolina Press for permission to reproduce a portion of an article which appeared in their volume, *Essays in Southern Economic Development* (Chapel Hill: University of North Carolina Press, 1964).

R. H.

Grinnell College
Grinnell, Iowa
May 1965

Contents

1

Introduction: The Setting for Analysis

The Army Corps of Engineers and Water Resource Development—
A Broad View

SINCE 1802 and the origin of the U.S. Army Corps of Engineers, the bulk of the responsibility for the development of the nation's water resources has been borne by the Federal government. From the first humble appropriation of 75 thousand dollars to the Corps of Engineers in 1824 for the "removal of 'snags, sawyers, planters and other impediment of that nature' " [1] from the Ohio and Mississippi Rivers, Federal participation has grown to substantial proportions. By 1963, total Federal investment in water resource projects had reached the sum of 23.5 billion dollars [2] with more than one-half of this amount appropriated since 1950.[3] Of the 23.5 billion dollars, nearly 15 billion dollars or about 65 percent was appropriated to and administered by the Corps of Engineers.[4] Of this 15 billion dollars, approximately 23 percent was allocated to navigation projects, 28 percent to flood control projects (including the Mississippi River project), 24 percent to multiple-purpose (including power) projects, and 24 percent to operation, maintenance, investigation, and other work.[5] To obtain a clearer and more precise concept of the nature of the over-all Corps program, let us first examine the growth of investment in navigation projects and then in turn, flood control and multiple-purpose projects.

From the very inception of Federal activity in the field of river and harbor improvement, responsibility for its administration has

1. W. Stull Holt, *The Office of the Chief of Engineers of the Army*, p. 7. This volume provides a detailed history of the early Corps program.
2. See Table 1.
3. *Ibid.*
4. *Ibid.*
5. Chief of Engineers, U.S. Army, *Annual Report*, 1960, I, vii.

TABLE 1

Appropriations to Federal Agencies for Water Resource Development, 1824 to 1962ᵃ

Agency	Appropriationsᶜ, Millions of Dollars						Percent of Total by Agency	Percent of Agency Total			
	1824–1930	1931–1940	1941–1950	1951–1956	1957–1962	Total		1824–1930	1931–1940	1941–1950	1951–1962
Corps of Engineers	1,646	1,904	3,127	3,241	4,878	14,796	62.8	11.1	12.9	21.1	54.9
Bureau of Reclamation	309	506	1,397	1,149	1,495	4,856	20.6	6.4	10.4	28.8	54.5
Other Department of Interior Agencies ᵇ	48	65	211	380	280	984	4.2	4.9	6.6	21.4	67.1
Tennessee Valley Authority	—	221	456	1,064	859	2,600	11.1	—	8.5	17.5	73.9
International Boundary and Water Commission	—	15	24	40	41	120	0.5	—	12.5	20.0	67.5
Department of Agriculture	—	—	20	45	106	171	0.7	—	—	11.7	88.3
Total	2,003	2,711	5,235	5,919	7,659	23,527	100.0				

a. Basic data for years before 1955 furnished by agencies concerned to the Commission on Organization of the Executive Branch of the Government: data since 1955 computed from U.S. Treasury Department, *Annual Budget Report*, 1955–1960.
b. Includes the Bonneville Power Administration, Southwestern Power Administration, Southeastern Power Administration, and the Bureau of Indian Affairs.
c. Fiscal years.

fallen almost exclusively to the Corps of Engineers. Exceptions to this statement are limited to the Tennessee River basin administered by the Tennessee Valley Authority and the Rio Grande River under the International Boundary Commission. In terms of total appropriations, Corps rivers and harbors projects have constituted the bulk of the entire Federal water resource program. In fact, from 1824 to 1879 when the Mississippi River Commission was established to administer the flood control program in the alluvial valley of the Mississippi River, all Federal appropriations for water resource development went strictly for navigation projects. During this entire period, total Corps expenditures for navigation projects approximated only 7 million dollars or an average of less than 160 thousand dollars per year.[6]

From 1879 on, the Corps navigation program shared appropriations with flood control projects. Until 1928, however, flood control expenditure was limited to the activities of the Mississippi River Commission and, of total water resource appropriations in this period, it accounted for only a very small proportion.[7] River and harbor construction was not only dominant during this period but also grew rapidly. The annual expenditures rose from less than 8 million dollars in 1880 to 18 million dollars in 1900 [8] and to over 50 million dollars in 1928.[9] Not only did the entire program grow during this period but appropriations per project also rose significantly. During this era it became common for annual appropriations for a single navigation project to reach several hundred thousand to a million dollars. By 1928, the Corps was actively engaged in the improvement of 200 harbors, 292 rivers, and 49 canals and other waterways.[10] Rivers and harbors expenditures from 1879 to 1928 totaled 1.2 billion dollars or approximately 86 percent of total Corps investment during that period.[11]

From 1928 until World War II, both navigation and flood control

6. These values computed from a detailed breakdown of Corps expenditures found in Holt, *op. cit.,* p. 136.
7. See page 5.
8. Holt, *op. cit.,* p. 16.
9. Chief of Engineers, U.S. Army, *Annual Report,* 1928, I, 7.
10. *Ibid.,* p. 3.
11. Holt, *op. cit.,* p. 136 and Chief of Engineers, U.S. Army, *Annual Report,* 1923–1928.

expenditures grew rapidly. Navigation projects still formed the bulk of the Corps program during this period but received a declining proportion of total annual expenditures. Of the total Corps expenditures of nearly 2 billion dollars during this period, approximately 1.3 billion dollars was allocated to rivers and harbors projects. This amount was 66 percent of the total expenditure and averaged about 108 million dollars per year.[12] The functions of the Corps remained much the same through this period, and by 1940, the entire Federal rivers and harbors program could point to some 1,000 separate projects scattered throughout the country.[13]

During the war, new construction was halted, and only the minimum necessary maintenance operations were carried on. Immediately after the war, however, construction activity began in earnest. Large river basin surveys were made, and total appropriations and expenditures ". . . expanded like a prairie fire." [14] From 1945 to 1961, total appropriations to the Corps for projects with new navigation work as their only purpose amounted to 1.2 billion dollars or an average of nearly 80 million dollars annually.[15] This appropriation for navigation projects was about 15 percent of the total new construction appropriations for water resource projects administered by the Corps during this period. By 1963, the Corps was actively engaged in new construction work on more than 100 different navigation projects.

Until 1879, flood control was viewed by Congress as a purely local problem and, consequently, an area which the Federal government should refrain from entering. Because of the disastrous flood of 1874 in the Mississippi Valley, however, the opinion that local interests could no longer control the erratic force of the giant stream became widespread. In 1879, Congress, reacting to the growing pressure, put the Federal government into the field of flood control with the passage of a bill creating the Mississippi River

12. Tabulated from Chief of Engineers, U.S. Army, *Annual Report,* 1928–1940.
13. Chief of Engineers, U.S. Army. *Annual Report,* 1941, I, 1.
14. Ben Moreell, *Our Nation's Water Resources—Policies and Politics,* p. 17.
15. Tabulated from Chief of Engineers, U.S. Army, *Annual Report,* 1945–1960. If operation, maintenance, and repair expenditures are included, the expenditure on navigation projects is nearly 2.5 billion dollars or an annual average of 150 million dollars.

Commission. One observer, writing in 1930, claimed this act to be ". . . the most important piece of flood control legislation of our history." [16] Although ostensibly the Commission was set up for flood control purposes, of the 13.5 million dollars which was appropriated to it by 1892, only 4 million dollars was authorized for flood control.[17] From 1892, appropriations to the Commission averaged about 2 million dollars annually, and by 1917 the aggregate appropriations reached almost 83 million dollars.[18]

In the 1917 Flood Control Act, Congress authorized additional projects bearing some 50 million dollars of estimated Federal cost and further stipulated that the laws applying to rivers and harbors projects would also apply to flood control. With this act, the government assumed ". . . undisguised responsibility for protecting a group of its citizens from floods." [19] From 1917 through 1927, flood control expenditures totaled almost 90 million dollars or about 8 million dollars annually, a significant increase over the previous flood control program but still a small proportion of the total Federal government water resource program.[20] Of this amount, 88 million dollars or 97 percent of the total was devoted to flood control along the Mississippi under the control of the Mississippi River Commission.[21]

Notwithstanding the work accomplished along the Mississippi River by 1927, that year witnessed the greatest inundation, loss of life, and physical damage which had occurred since the formation of the Union. Because of this disaster, both Congress and the general public clamored for a comprehensive program designed to protect the Mississippi Valley from the largest conceivable flood. Of the approximately 300 programs submitted, Congress settled on a compromise of the two most important; the Mississippi River

16. A. D. Frank, *The Development of the Federal Program of Flood Control in the Mississippi River*, p. 42.
17. *Ibid.*, p. 148.
18. U.S. Congress, House Committee on Flood Control, *Report on Flood Control Appropriations*, p. 27.
19. U.S. Commission on Organization of the Executive Branch of the Government—Task Force on Water Resources and Power, *Report on Water Resources and Power*, 1955, II, 733.
20. Chief of Engineers, U.S. Army, *Annual Report*, 1917–1927.
21. *Loc. cit.*

Commission plan and the Corps of Engineers plan. The three chief provisions of this compromise were (1) the authorization of an expenditure of 325 million dollars by the Federal government, (2) a resolution which placed the Mississippi River Commission in charge of operations but under the domination of the Corps of Engineers, and (3) the assumption of complete responsibility by the Federal government with no requirement of local contribution.[22]

With the initiation of this new Mississippi River project, both appropriations and expenditures skyrocketed. From 1928 through 1935, flood control expenditures totaled approximately 250 million dollars or an average of 31 million dollars annually.[23] This is nearly a 400 percent increase over average annual appropriations in the previous period. Until 1936, however, the Mississippi River program still constituted *the* flood control activity of the Federal government. Of total Federal flood control expenditures during this period, over 90 percent was administered by the Commission.

In 1936, this situation underwent a radical change. In the Flood Control bill of that year, Congress took the first steps in assuming responsibility for nationwide flood control. "[F]lood control on navigable waters or their tributaries is a proper activity of the Federal government." [24] The act, in its final form, set forth a basic flood control policy for the country; 250 projects and an expenditure of 310 million dollars were authorized for construction. "[T]hus was initiated one of the greatest public work programs the world has ever seen." [25] In 1938, this act was amended to provide that the Federal government should bear the entire cost of flood control improvements. Senator Vandenburg's statement issued as a warning two years before seems almost prophetic now.

Let it not be overlooked that this is the first time in 150 years of American history when it has been proposed to assert that floods upon practically all the rivers of the United States constitute a menace to national welfare and are a Federal responsibility. The moment we have accepted that responsibility, . . . we have accepted it for every navigable

22. Frank, *op. cit.*, pp. 220–243.
23. Chief of Engineers, U.S. Army, *Annual Report*, 1928–1935.
24. U.S. Commission on Organization of the Executive Branch of the Government, *op. cit.*, p. 735.
25. *Ibid.*, p. 737.

stream in 48 states of the Union; and the human imagination can hardly encompass the total extent of the burden and responsibility which is thus laid at the door of the Treasury of the United States by the adoption of this policy.[26]

From 1936 to the end of the war, the flood control program grew rapidly. From its previous position as a small segment of the total Corps program limited to projects on the lower Mississippi, the flood control program proceeded to become the major civil works function of the entire program. In this period, the Mississippi River project remained large, but it became a relatively smaller portion of both the flood control program and the entire Corps program. Of the total appropriations of 1.9 billion dollars during this period, flood control projects received 945 million dollars or 50 percent of the total. Of the total flood control program, Mississippi River flood control expenditures averaged about 94 million dollars annually during this period.[27]

In the period after the war both the flood control and the rivers and harbors program took on a new face. Although appropriations were still made under these two categories, a substantial share was allocated to multiple-purpose projects which had as a major function either flood control or navigation as well as power production. Of the two programs, however, the general flood control sector had the most rapid growth during this period. Projects whose sole purpose was flood control received construction appropriations totaling over 2.5 billion dollars, and those which had flood control as the major purpose, 1.8 billion dollars. Of the 4.3-billion-dollar total, the Mississippi River project received over 600 million dollars or about 15 percent.[28]

Moreover, during this postwar period, the flood control program became the major function of the Corps of Engineers. Whereas up to 1945 only 1.1 billion dollars [29] had been appropriated for flood control, by 1962 this figure had increased to 3.8 billion dollars.[30] In

26. *Ibid.*, p. 736.
27. Chief of Engineers, U.S. Army, *Annual Report*, 1936–1945.
28. Chief of Engineers, U.S. Army, *Annual Report*, 1945–1960.
29. Chief of Engineers, U.S. Army, *Annual Report*, 1945, I, 6 and 10.
30. U.S. Congress, Senate, *Report of the Select Committee on National Water Resources*, p. 99.

1945, the total number of authorized projects totaled 650 with an expected authorized cost of 1.7 billion dollars.[31] By 1955, this had increased to 1,033 projects authorized with an expected cost of 11.1 billion dollars.[32] In 1960, the Corps estimated that to prevent flood damages until 1980 would require an additional expenditure of about 11.5 billion dollars with an expenditure of 300 million dollars annually simply to keep pace with the anticipated growth of flood damage caused by the increased use of floodplains or 500 million dollars annually to reverse the trend of increasing flood damage.[33] In a rough estimate of the ultimate total cost of the flood control program, the Task Force on Water Resources and Power, using 1948 Corps data, stated that the ultimate drain on the U.S. Treasury would be over 41 billion dollars.[34]

Under the authority of the 1936 Flood Control Act, the Corps of Engineers began to propose the installation of power facilities in dams and reservoirs whose major purpose was ostensibly for flood control or navigation. The first of these projects to be put into operation was the Bonneville Lock and Dam in 1938. The cost of this project was more than 80 million dollars and its installed generating capacity is 518,400 kilowatts,[35] which places it even today among the top dozen installations in absolute size. By 1945, four of these multipurpose projects were completed, and the Corps had already spent over 325 million dollars on their construction.[36] By 1950, seven were in operation with an installed capacity of 888,400 kilowatts, representing Corps expenditures of nearly a billion dollars.[37]

In the most recent decade, this phase of the total Corps program has grown with amazing alacrity. In almost all of the years from 1950 to 1960, projects with power facilities received more appropria-

31. Chief of Engineers, U.S. Army, *Annual Report,* 1945, I, 6.
32. U.S. Commission on Organization of the Executive Branch of the Government, *op. cit.,* p. 774.
33. U.S. Congress, Senate, *Report of the Select Committee on National Water Resources,* pp. 99–100.
34. U.S. Commission on Organization of the Executive Branch of the Government, *op. cit.,* p. 776.
35. Chief of Engineers, U.S. Army, *Annual Report,* 1941.
36. Chief of Engineers, U.S. Army, *Annual Report,* 1945.
37. Chief of Engineers, U.S. Army, *Annual Report,* 1950.

tions than either strictly navigation or flood control projects, the supposed heart of the Corps program. Moreover, in five of the ten years, these multipurpose projects received more appropriations than the sum total appropriations going to single purpose navigation and flood control projects.[38] By 1960, over 3.1 billion dollars had been appropriated for the construction of 32 of these projects with an installed capacity of over 6.5 million kilowatts, "20.8% of the hydro-electric generating capacity supplying the Nation's utility systems." [39] Moreover, in 1961, projects having about 4 million additional kilowatts were under construction [40] and by the end of 1962, projects containing a total of 7.4 million kilowatts were in operation.

A Brief Look Ahead

With the importance and size of the entire Corps program presented, a brief summary of what the rest of the volume contains is in order. Essentially, the study is regional in nature, dealing empirically with appropriations to Corps projects in ten southern states in the years since World War II. In general, its structure and content, indeed, its justification, are based upon the validity of a certain presumption and a realization of its implications. That is, with the assumption that such a Federal endeavor must have as its goal the maximization of social welfare [41] and the realization of the necessary implication that such a goal depends upon both the size of the national income pie (economic efficiency) and its distribution (income distribution), this study undertakes to analyze empirically and somewhat theoretically the relationship of these two primary welfare determinants. In particular, it attempts to analyze these forces in both their *ex ante* roles as self-contained

38. This is true primarily because most large river basin projects include some power development even though most of the expenditures are allocated to either flood control or navigation.

39. Chief of Engineers, U.S. Army, *Annual Report,* 1960, I, 25.

40. *Ibid.,* p. 27.

41. "Well-being of all of the people shall be the overriding determinant in considering the best use of water and related land resources."—The President's Water Resources Council, *Policies, Standards, and Procedures in the Formulation, Evaluation, and Review of Plans for Use and Development of Water and Related Land Resources,* p. 2.

goals which determine the allocation of water resource appropriations and their *ex post* roles as effecters of changes in social economic welfare.

In the second chapter, the formal process of project evaluation is described along with some recent statements concerning goals and criteria for future evaluation. It is shown that in the past, Congress, the Bureau of the Budget, and the Corps have acted mainly on the grounds of expediency, political or otherwise, and that while paying lip service to pure economic efficiency (the benefit-cost ratio) their primary objectives have, in fact, been multifaceted. The degree of distress or poverty of a particular area, the economic development of a particular area, and sheer political maneuvering are all shown to have played some role in the allocation of appropriations in the past. Finally, a brief review of a set of suggestions presented by other observers concerning the refinement of these criteria for the future allocation of water resource funds is presented. It will be noted that these suggestions provide for recognition of both economic efficiency and income redistribution in choosing between future alternatives. The point made in this section will be a key one: The criteria used in the past included in some vague way both income redistribution and economic efficiency, and moreover, contemporary observers quite legitimately view them both as acceptable goals for social policy and urge their refinement and use in the future allocation of resource development funds.

In the third chapter, the concepts of economic efficiency and regional income redistribution through water resource appropriations are further analyzed. Specifically, three questions are treated. First, is there evidence that, in fact, economic efficiency has been an effective Congressional criterion for choice? Second, can it be inferred from the data on appropriations that Congress has appropriated a relatively greater share of funds to low per capita income states, and moreover, does this imply some desire to make use of such a program in aiding low income or distressed areas? Third, does the evidence imply that such a redistribution has led to a reduced disparity in regional per capita incomes?

The fourth chapter builds on the concept of income redistribution through Federal fiscal transactions and analyzes such redistribution in a particular region for a specific period of time. The yearly water resource appropriations are presented for ten individual southern states on both an absolute and per capita basis. Through this analysis, the South is compared with the non-South and each southern state, with its neighbors. The choice of the southern states, which constitute the nation's lowest income region, is natural in dealing with the regional income redistribution aspects of a Federal expenditure program. The main part of this chapter, indeed, one of the important interlocking segments of the entire study, is a detailed empirical analysis of the income redistribution toward the ten southern states since 1946 caused by the Corps program.

In the fifth chapter, the second interlocking segment, empirical tests are used to determine the economic efficiency (or lack of efficiency) of the 163 southern postwar projects at the time of their construction. The tests used in this analysis include the Eckstein test,[42] its alternative of a higher single interest rate,[43] and the McKean test which is based on the marginal internal rate of return [44] as well as a dual rate of interest test developed in an appendix to Chapter Five. For those projects that pass the tests, the presumption is that national resources have been allocated efficiently and the increase in national income is the greatest possible per dollar investment in water resource projects. For those projects that do not pass the tests, the presumption is that resources have not been efficiently allocated and that the projects should not have been undertaken. The projects are separated into two distinct groups by the application of these investment criteria, and a monetary estimate of national resource misallocation in these southern rivers and harbors projects is presented.

The sixth chapter is an attempt to demonstrate the effect of the application of the pure economic efficiency criteria on regional income distribution. By elimination of those inefficient projects

42. Otto Eckstein, *Water-Resource Development: The Economics of Project Evaluation.*
43. John V. Krutilla and Otto Eckstein, *Multiple Purpose River Development: Studies in Applied Economic Analysis.*
44. Roland McKean, *Efficiency in Government Through Systems Analysis: with Emphasis on Water Resources Development.*

dictated by Chapter Five from the analysis of southern income redistribution presented in Chapter Four, a new figure for net benefit is obtained for each of the ten southern states, that is, the net benefit or net income redistribution which would have occurred if, in fact, Congress had acted with economic efficiency as its sole criterion. The main point of this final chapter is an empirical demonstration that, given the goal of maximizing the size of the national income, the construction of such projects is an inefficient means of securing a redistribution of income to favored groups. Clearly, this conclusion has definite implications for the proposed use of either or both of the goals as criteria for future project choice.

In the final section, the Epilogue, a rather unorthodox attempt is made to combine both of these primary determinants of changes in economic welfare into a single multidimensional approach. By positing a socially determined marginal utility of income function, estimation of the welfare impact of the economic changes described in the earlier sections of the study is attempted.

2

The Congressional Bases for Project Choice: Efficiency, Regional Aid, and Political Manipulation

WHEN THE processes of a Federal expenditure program such as the Corps program are studied, any attempt to isolate the criteria which determine the allocation of appropriations appears to border on the impossible. Because of the tortuous maze of bureaucratic procedures through which a prospective project must pass (stated often and proudly by Congressmen to be seventeen separate and independent stages), there often seems to be no coherent set of criteria. However, because such final allocation does appear to follow a pattern and because recent attempts have been made to clarify the goals of governmental activity, this chapter investigates the nature of the formal process of project approval and attempts to isolate those factors to which the decision-making unit of the Federal government reacts in choosing between alternative investments.

The Formal Process of Project Approval

The path which an individual project must travel to secure construction appropriations is indeed treacherous. In fact, without the continual prodding of *ad hoc* interested groups as well as organized lobbies, the chances that an individual project could complete the trek on its own merits are very small. Official literature specifies a minimum of 17 major stages[1] but outside observers see at least 32 stages during which some sort of decision-making

1. U.S. Corps of Engineers, Department of the Army, *Survey Investigations and Reports; General Procedures,* EM 1120-2-101, 1958 (mimeographed instructions in district offices of Corps of Engineers), pp. 7-11.

13

behavior can take place.[2] In this section, the process of decision-making is described and the key decision-making unit in this process is defined.[3]

The initial step in this formal process of project approval begins with local interests. Suffering flood damage or desiring additional navigation improvements, a local interest group will normally contact its Congressman or Senator and request the Federal government to investigate the feasibility of providing the desired services. Federal concern must be initiated in this way because Congressional authorization is required before any investigation of a project's feasibility. To secure the necessary authorization for such investigation, the Senator or Representative presents the local request to the Committee on Public Works of the appropriate Congressional body. This request for investigation then becomes, as a matter of routine, incorporated into the succeeding omnibus rivers and harbors or flood control bill.[4] It appears that up to this point in the process no decision to eliminate or exclude any project is made: each request is carried at least this far.[5]

This automatic authorization process, however, does not imply that the project will be examined immediately.[6] Because examination appropriations are made in lump sums and are insufficient to

2. Arthur Maass, *Muddy Waters*, p. 37.

3. Lest any misunderstanding of the nature of this analysis arise, the object of this description and definition is only the formal process of project approval. Any decision-making that may occur outside of this framework, such as informal understandings between Congressmen, between a Congressman and the Corps, between the Corps and local interests, or between any other combination of these loci of interests will be largely ignored in this description and only cursorily treated later in the chapter. A rather complete documentation and analysis of this political phenomenon exists elsewhere. See *ibid.*, Robert de Roos and Arthur Maass, "The Lobby That Can't Be Licked," *Harpers*, August, 1949, pp. 21 ff., Ben Moreell, *Our Nation's Water Resources—Policies and Politics*, and Arthur Maass, Maynard Hufschmidt, et al., *Design of Water Resource Systems*, Ch. 15.

4. This procedure is described by Representative Mansfield of Texas, the chairman of the Rivers and Harbors Committee of the House in 1945. See U.S., *Congressional Record*, 79th Congress, 1st Session, 1945, p. 1374.

5. In 1947, the House Committee on Public Works attempted to limit in some way this procedure by requiring projects to display initial need or feasibility, but this action was nullified by the failure of the Senate Committee to follow suit.

6. Note that the term authorization here refers to approval of preliminary examination and not to the authorization for construction.

cover all of the investigation authorizations, the initiation of such investigation remains in the hands of the Chief of Engineers. Although this may mean substantial delay for a project, in time, all projects receive such preliminary examination.[7]

At the conclusion of this preliminary examination, the first weeding out occurs. After holding hearings ". . . to ascertain the views and desires of local people"[8] and engaging in a field reconnaissance of the area, the District Engineer submits the results of the preliminary examination to the Chief of Engineers. If this preliminary report is favorable, i.e., if it appears likely that such a project will be economically justified, a full-scale survey is undertaken.[9] If not, the project is effectively eliminated, and notice of such conclusion is sent to interested parties.

This, then, is the first decision, and it is made by the District Engineer and assented to by both the Division Engineer and the Chief of Engineers. This decision, it should be noted, is formed on economic grounds and is based on a most imprecise set of information—some vague indication that the project's expected benefits are or are not greater than its expected costs.

The project becomes eligible for a complete survey and economic base study if it passes this preliminary examination stage in the process. The survey stage, although following much the same general procedure, is substantially more complete than the preliminary investigation. Hearings are again held, extensive field surveys are undertaken, and, in this stage, a detailed plan of improvement is developed which is "best suited for [the] problems under consideration and the area in question."[10] If, and only if, the benefit-cost ratio is favorable, the District Engineer will recommend the project for construction. This survey report is then reviewed by the Division Engineer, the Chief of Engineers, the

7. Maass, *op. cit.*, p. 24.
8. U.S. Corps of Engineers, Department of the Army, *op. cit.*, p. 8.
9. Maass, *op. cit.*, p. 29. "A favorable preliminary examination—one which indicates that there is a reasonable possibility that an improvement may be economically justified—constitutes an automatic authorization for a survey." Even if this first report is unfavorable, the project is not necessarily dead. After submission to Congress and a delay of three years, a new investigation can be authorized and undertaken.
10. U.S. Corps of Engineers, Department of the Army, *loc. cit.*

Board of Engineers for Rivers and Harbors, other interested Federal agencies, and the states involved. After being evaluated by the executive office of the President (Bureau of the Budget) as to the conformance of the project to the program of the President, the report is submitted to Congress. This step completes the action required by the Chief of Engineers according to the Congressional investigation authorization. Favorable or unfavorable, action on the report is now left to the discretion of the Congress. Up to this point in the process, however, the major decisions concerning project recommendation have been made by the Corps of Engineers and have been based entirely on the benefit-cost ratio, i.e., only those projects with a ratio less than one are not recommended: the rest continue the journey.[11]

After the Chief of Engineers forwards the report to Congress and, more specifically, to the Committees on Public Works of the Senate and the House, hearings are held on the nature of the project and other information contained in the survey report. The survey report is then published, usually by the House Committee, and is then known as the project document. Upon completion of the hearings, the committees draw up a bill known as an omnibus authorization bill. In this bill, the projects which the Congress considers eligible for construction are described and portions of the project document are quoted. From the House Committee on Public Works, the bill goes to the floor where some projects are deleted and additional projects are added. When the House passes it, the bill moves to the Senate committee, which usually increases the amount of the House authorization. The bill now passes to the Senate floor where the same procedure occurs as in the House. Amendments are proposed adding and deleting projects, and a bill is also passed here. The differences between the House and Senate versions of the bill are ironed out in a conference committee appointed by both houses for such a purpose.

Although the authorization stage is an important hurdle for a given project, it does not appear to be the core of the decision-

11. U.S. Corps of Engineers, Department of the Army, *loc. cit.* "A favorable recommendation by the District Engineer will depend on whether the benefits to be derived . . . exceed the costs to be incurred."

making machinery. While failure to secure authorization effectively assures the demise of a project, any project which does possess a favorable benefit-cost ratio will in all likelihood eventually secure authorization. Sentiment concerning the relation of the authorization stage to the actual construction of the project is typified by the extended remarks of Representative Smith of Mississippi to the House, "A project authorization is not even an empty promise to build." [12] A similar statement which bears substantially the same implication was presented by Senator Russell of Georgia, a member of the Senate Appropriations Committee:

> . . . I have been hearing this question discussed ever since I have been here, for 13 years, as to just what the responsibility was on the Appropriations Committee to conform to authorization. I have about come to the conclusion that the Appropriations Committee feels its responsibility very keenly where it wants to make the appropriation, and where it does not, it recalls the fact that it was argued "This is merely an authorization, and it will come before the Appropriations Committee." [13]

Since 1942, a substantial amount of activity has been permitted to occur after the project was authorized but before it received construction appropriations. In each annual appropriations bill, substantial amounts have been allocated to detailed planning and to the formation of the "definite project report." Until recently, the allocation of these planning funds has been left to the discretion of the Chief of Engineers. Since 1958, however, Congress has stipulated in the appropriations bill the amount of planning funds allocated to each project.

The content of the definite project report is similar to that of the survey document. The data on local conditions, estimates of cost, estimates of projected benefits, and financial considerations are, however, endowed with an accuracy not present in previous reports. The engineering proposals are also those that will be followed in the event of construction. This report is prepared by the District Engineer, often with the assistance of the Board of

12. U.S. *Congressional Record,* 83rd Congress, 1st Session, 1953, p. A431. Statement quoted from the *Memphis Commercial Appeal* (Tennessee).
13. U.S. Congress, Senate Committee on Appropriations, *Hearings, First Deficiency Appropriations Bill, 1946,* p. 473.

Engineers for Rivers and Harbors, and sent by him to the Chief of Engineers for approval.

Again in this phase some decision-making occurs. The project which does not receive planning funds is dealt a severe blow, and the project which does receive such funds has its chances for construction substantially raised. However, there are exceptions to both cases; that is, projects with no definite project report often find a place in the appropriations bill while those possessing such a report are often left to dry on the vine.

Such a Civil Functions Appropriations Bill providing funds for the construction of individual projects is passed each year by the Congress. As pointed out, some of these projects possess a definite project report while others of them are drawn from the backlog of authorized projects not possessing such a report. In composing such an annual bill, the Congress relies on a tedious and somewhat nebulous procedure.

Each year, the Bureau of the Budget presents the Corps of Engineers with a total construction appropriation figure which is felt to be consistent with the President's program. The Corps then fills out this proposed budget by allocating a part of it to projects which are under construction and the remainder to so-called new starts. In Corps terminology, this list of projects is called the annual budget request. This budget request is then reviewed by the Bureau of the Budget which evaluates each requested project according to its criteria[14] and formulates a new and, usually, smaller list of its own.

Because of inevitable differences between the two lists, the Appropriations Committees of both the Senate and the House hold hearings to aid in the formation of a final, single list to present to the Congress. Through this process some of the projects in the budget request are deleted and others, not in the request, are added.

14. The criteria applied by the Executive Office at the present time are those stipulated in a policy statement accepted in 1962: The President's Water Resources Council, *Policies, Standards, and Procedures in the Formulation, Evaluation, and Review of Plans for Use and Development of Water and Related Land Resources.* This document replaced the Bureau's much disputed *Circular A-47* which had been in effect since 1952. See U.S. Bureau of the Budget, *Circular A-47.*

The bill, as it is presented to the floor of the House, usually contains a smaller total appropriation than the budget request. On the floor of the House, amendments are presented which again juggle the list of projects to be included and the appropriation associated with each project. Upon passage by the House, the bill goes to the Senate. The Senate, with advice from its Appropriations Committee, further modifies the list of projects, adding some and omitting others. The bill as it passes the Senate has inevitably been larger than its counterpart in the House in both total appropriations and number of projects. The discrepancies in the two bills are then eliminated through negotiation between the two Houses, and the final list is submitted for final passage in the form of a Conference Report.

It is in this stage, then, that the final and binding decision appears to be made. Not only does the Congress, operating mainly through the Appropriations Committees, possess the power to modify, destroy, or ignore the proposals presented by the Corps and the Bureau of the Budget, but it often takes great delight in doing so. As Representative Aspinall of Colorado remarked on the floor of the House: "[T]heir [the Bureau of the Budget] holdings under A-47 are not binding and should not be held to be binding upon the Congress of the United States." [15] Senator McClellan of Arkansas sums up the attitude of the members of Congress in the following statement and thus, with a degree of finality, defines the role of the decision-making unit:

[T]he responsibility for finally selecting the projects rests with the Congress of the United States, primarily with the Committee on Appropriations, which has the initial responsibility for making recommendations to this body.[16]

Thus, the appropriation process is the heart of the binding decision, and the Congress, in the passage of the appropriations bill, acts as the final arbiter, the key decision-making unit in the entire process.

Two additional comments, however, should give an insight into

15. U.S. *Congressional Record*, 84th Congress, 1st Session, 1955, p. 4743. For a similar statement see U.S. *Congressional Record*, 85th Congress, 2nd Session, 1958, pp. 3794–3803.

16. U.S. *Congressional Record*, 80th Congress, 2nd Session, 1948, p. 6060.

this process of appropriation. First, even though it is the Congress which makes the final and binding decision, the final appropriation is influenced substantially by the budget approvals submitted by the Bureau of the Budget. Although substantial modifications of these lists do occur, the basic list exists as the core of the final appropriation.[17] Moreover, a substantial degree of rapport appears to exist between the Congress and the executive agencies. As Eckstein states:

In the long run, however, Congress influences the choice of projects more subtly, through the anticipation of Congressional wishes on the part of the agencies in drawing up their budget requests.[18]

In fact, Senator Douglas of Illinois stated at one time a desire to place an even greater degree of responsibility for the decision-making function upon the Bureau of the Budget. His proposal, made on the floor of Congress, suggested that the Congress eliminate from the appropriations bill all those ". . . projects that have been previously disapproved by the Bureau of the Budget."[19]

Second, it should be noted that the appropriations bills as reported from the Appropriations Committees appear incapable of being cut on the floor of either the House or the Senate—they can only grow. Because of the pressure to please constituents and the fear that attempted project cuts will bring retaliation, Senator Douglas states that ". . . the whole operation of present-day popular government makes it impossible now for the Members of the Senate to cut the bill on the floor or even in Committee."[20]

With the final passage, the appropriations bill is sent to the President. Upon receiving his signature (if he doesn't veto) the bill becomes law and the funds become available for the letting of construction contracts. With the completion of final plans and assurances of local co-operation, ". . . the successful bidder," in

---

17. As Maass states, "[I]t may be said that Congress has, in part, transferred the responsibility . . . from its own body to the executive agency. The Engineer Department has recognized the nature of this transfer and has developed its planning procedure in response thereto." Maass, *op. cit.,* p. 38.

18. Eckstein, *Water Resource Development,* pp. 5–6.

19. U.S. *Congressional Record,* 81st Congress, 2nd Session, 1950, p. 11178.

20. U.S. *Congressional Record,* 85th Congress, 1st Session, 1957, p. 4612.

bureaucratic terminology, "will mobilize his plant, equipment, and personnel, and start construction." [21]

Criteria in the Allocation of Construction Appropriations

The formal and prescribed process of project approval having been described, and the Congress identified as the chief decision-making unit, an attempt is now made to describe the criteria or goals which this unit both explicitly and implicitly applies in allocating such appropriations among individual projects. That is, Congressional sentiment toward the allocation of appropriations is shown to be diverse and multifaceted, not uniform and unique. Any attempt to impose a set of rational criteria where, in fact, such a set may well not exist, is clearly fraught with pitfalls; nevertheless, it is hypothesized that Congressional statements and actions do seem to point rather systematically to the interaction of three broad forces which affect such allocation: (1) economic efficiency, (2) regional economic aid or income redistribution, and (3) political manipulation.

EFFICIENCY. Evidence of the existence of a goal which could be called economic efficiency seems to appear in two separate and distinct forms. First of all, some vague concept of efficiency is built into the very system of project planning and approval, and second, the expressed sentiments of members of the decision-making unit toward both the benefit-cost technique and other efficiency considerations together with their actions appear to point to the effective existence of such an objective in the final allocation of appropriations.

From the very inception of Corps activity in both the development of navigation facilities and flood control measures, some emphasis has been placed on the degree of economic efficiency of the projects to be constructed. The first tangible evidence of such concern is presented in the act which created the Board of Engineers for Rivers and Harbors in 1902. This act stipulated that, in reviewing the economic merits of a proposed navigation project,

[the board] . . . shall have in view the amount and character of commerce existing or reasonably prospective which will be benefited by the

21. U.S. Corps of Engineers, Department of the Army, *op. cit.*, p. 10.

improvements . . . [and] the relation of the ultimate cost of such work, both as to cost of construction and maintenance, to the public commercial interests involved. . . ."[22]

In 1925, this attitude was consolidated when Congress directed the Corps to prepare estimate-of-cost reports on national rivers and tributaries to ensure their ". . . most effective improvement. . . ."[23] With the adoption of the responsibility for flood control activity in 1936, the Congress further reaffirmed and clarified this position by requiring that, for such projects to be authorized, benefits must exceed costs, "to whomsoever they may accrue."[24] Since that time then, all water resource projects have been evaluated by a method of economic analysis called benefit-cost analysis. As the Hoover Commission stated in 1955:

Each report . . . contains a statement of benefits and costs. . . . It is general Corps practice not to recommend, and that of Congressional committees not to authorize, projects in which estimated benefits do not exceed estimated costs.[25]

Moreover, since the inception of benefit-cost computations, the techniques applied have been continually modified and refined to more accurately identify and measure both benefits and costs. Genuine progress toward this goal of increasing the accuracy of such computation can be seen in the manuals on the preparation of survey reports issued by the Corps,[26] the standards and procedures

22. Act of June 13, 1902, sec. 3, 32 Stat. 372, quoted in U.S. Commission on Organization of the Executive Branch of the Government, *Report on Water Resources and Power*, pp. 869–870.

23. U.S. Commission on Organization of the Executive Branch of the Government, *op. cit.*, p. 856.

24. Ben Moreell, *Our Nation's Water Resources*, p. 133.

25. U.S. Commission on Organization of the Executive Branch of the Government, *op. cit.*, p. 47.

26. U.S. Corps of Engineers, Department of the Army, *op. cit.*; U.S. Corps of Engineers, Department of the Army, *Examinations and Surveys: Secondary Benefits in Flood Control Evaluation*, EM 1120-2-112, September, 1957; U.S. Corps of Engineers, Department of the Army, *Examinations and Surveys: Relation of Flood Damages and Flood Control Benefits to Market Value of Land*, EM 1120-2-111, June, 1957; U.S. Corps of Engineers, Department of the Army, *Survey Investigations and Reports: Economic Base Studies*, EM 1120-2-118, November, 1959; U.S. Corps of Engineers, Department of the Army, *Survey Investigations and Reports: General Procedures*, EM 1120-2-101, Change 12, May, 1961.

used in evaluation by the Bureau of the Budget,[27] and the intermittent reports of other Federal agencies and study commissions.[28] Through these studies, relevant concepts such as secondary benefits, associated costs, price levels, interest rates, periods of analysis, and cost allocation to multiple-purpose projects have become more clearly defined, and problems of empirical measurement have been pointed out and solved. Without doubt, there exists some concept of efficiency which is embodied in the very procedures of water resource development. The very methods used in project planning and approval apply the goal of economic efficiency as a criterion in making a choice between alternative water resource investments.[29]

The concept of economic efficiency also manifests itself both in statements of the members of the key decision-making unit—the Congress—and in the behavior of the unit itself. In an attempt to correctly grasp the attitude of Congress toward this criterion, two approaches appear feasible. First, the attitudes of individual Congressmen toward the concept of efficiency as expressed by their own statements can be examined, and second, the projects which do receive construction appropriations can be evaluated according to a pure efficiency criterion. That is, the attitude of Congress toward efficiency as a criterion can be evaluated by examining what Congressmen claim their attitude to be and also by inferring their attitude from their actions.[30]

The statements by Congressmen concerning the use of benefit-cost calculations in the justification of water resource investment

27. U.S. Bureau of the Budget, *Circular A-47*, December, 1952; U.S. Bureau of the Budget, *Circular A-47*, Revised, 1957; and The President's Water Resources Council, *op. cit.*

28. Federal Inter-Agency River Basin Committee, Subcommittee on Benefits and Costs, *Qualitative Aspects of Benefit-Cost Practice*, April, 1947; Federal Inter-Agency River Basin Committee, Subcommittee on Benefits and Costs, *Measurement Aspects of Benefit-Cost Analysis*, November, 1948; Federal Inter-Agency River Basin Committee, Subcommittee on Benefits and Costs, *Proposed Practices for Economic Analysis of River Basin Projects*, May, 1950; Federal Inter-Agency Committee on Water Resources, Subcommittee on Evaluation Standards, *Proposed Practices for Economic Analysis of River Basin Projects*, May, 1958.

29. See footnote 13, Chapter Three.

30. In this chapter only the former of these approaches is utilized. The latter approach is the subject of a substantial portion of the remainder of the volume.

appear to run the gamut from complete disdain of the benefit-cost technique to a sincere desire to increase the accuracy of the computations and to adopt the technique as sole criterion. A typical position is cogently expressed by Representative Abernethy of Mississippi in the following statement:

Sound government principles demand that no appropriation should be made for a flood control project when it is candidly admitted by the War Department Engineers that the project is economically unsound. I believe in a fair, adequate, and economically sound flood control program. But to be such, the benefits from construction of the works should far exceed the [costs].[31]

The following two statements, the first by Representative Keating of New York and the second by Senator Douglas of Illinois, also illustrate this position of respect for benefit-cost analysis and a desire for its use as a criterion:

Mr. Chairman, the form of the bill before us troubles me deeply. Sound and approved projects are mingled with projects which have no sound reason for being there. It should be altered by an amendment to eliminate projects . . . [which are not economically justified].[32]

.   .   .   .

We should eliminate doubtful and deferable projects on which the benefit-cost ratio is less than one to one.[33]

A substantial portion of Congressional opinion not only favors the use of the benefit-cost ratio as a criterion but also desires to increase the stringency of such a criterion through the use of higher cut-off levels and other techniques. Representative Smith of Mississippi agrees as he again quotes from the *Memphis Commercial Appeal:*

We think, too, that economic justification . . . should be proved beyond all possibility of successful challenge and that there should be stricter proof requirements.[34]

31. U.S. *Congressional Record,* 79th Congress, 1st Session, 1945, p. 11215.
32. U.S. *Congressional Record,* 85th Congress, 2nd Session, 1958, p. 3997.
33. U.S. *Congressional Record,* 81st Congress, 2nd Session, 1950, p. 11178. For additional statements which bear the same sentiment see U.S. *Congressional Record,* 83rd Congress, 1st Session, 1953, p. 5712; *ibid.,* p. 7421; *ibid.,* 84th Congress, 1st Session, 1955, p. 8519; *ibid.,* 85th Congress, 1st Session, 1957, p. 14558; *ibid.,* 85th Congress, 2nd Session, 1958, p. 13216; *ibid.,* 86th Congress, 1st Session, 1959, p. 10039; *ibid.,* 86th Congress, 2nd Session, 1960, p. 16142.
34. U.S. *Congressional Record,* 83rd Congress, 1st Session, 1953, p. A431. Statement quoted from the *Memphis Commercial Appeal* (Tennessee).

One of the most documented statements to this effect was presented on the floor of the Senate by Senator Proxmire of Wisconsin in 1962. In a detailed case study of the Glen Elder project in Kansas which occupied over 70 pages in the *Congressional Record,* Mr. Proxmire effectively pointed out serious problems in the present application of the benefit-cost technique, problems stemming from the use of an inappropriately low rate of interest as well as other problems resulting in a consistent overestimation of future project benefits and a consistent underestimation of project costs.

Unfortunately, there has been a tendency on the part of Members of Congress to ignore interest cost or to fail to compute in terms of its real meaning. The fact is, . . . we have been able to exaggerate the benefits by accepting a discount rate which has no relationship whatsoever to the best and best known measurement of future value, that is, the going interest rate. As a result of these assumptions, the benefits of Federal projects are grossly overstated. If meaningful assumptions were used, the cost of many multi-million dollar projects would vastly exceed all alleged benefits.[35]

Representative Taber of New York, after presenting a table illustrating the effect on a few projects of the use of a 4 percent interest rate (instead of the 2.5 percent rate used by the Corps), expresses this same sentiment:

If they are figured on the basis of the present money market, there is hardly a project in the whole bill that would qualify.[36]

At the opposite extreme, there occasionally appears a Congressional opinion which not only is critical of individual benefit-cost computations or the benefit-cost concept itself but also is disdainful of the entire concept of an efficiency criterion. This attitude runs from the inability of Representative Rayburn of Texas to understand how the period of amortization could have any effect on the size of a project's benefit-cost ratio [37] to the attack by Representative

35. U.S. *Congressional Record,* 87th Congress, 2nd Session, 1962, pp. 21325 and 21371.

36. U.S. *Congressional Record,* 86th Congress, 2nd Session, 1960, p. 10975. For additional statements which bear the same sentiment see U.S. *Congressional Record,* 84th Congress, 2nd Session, 1956, p. 8744; *ibid.,* 85th Congress, 1st Session, 1957, p. 13992; *ibid.,* p. 9676; *ibid.,* p. 9686; *ibid.,* p. 4618; *ibid.,* 86th Congress, 1st Session, 1959, p. 19149.

37. U.S. *Congressional Record,* 83rd Congress, 1st Session, 1953, p. 5716.

Trimble on the Bureau of the Budget's attempt to formulate more appropriate standards of project evaluation.[38]

However, in addition to these comments which make overt reference to the rather rigid efficiency criterion embodied in benefit-cost computations, there is another somewhat more subtle set of attitudes which display real concern for the efficiency or national income maximization consequences of Federal investment. These sentiments are based on the anticipation that the construction of projects in certain areas will yield a social product which exceeds the benefit estimate calculated by the Corps. That is, project construction in regions which are well endowed with resources but whose resources are in a low state of development (i.e., regions with high resource to capital and population ratios) may well be expected to yield a stream of external economies which, while not appearing as primary project outputs, nevertheless accrue as economic benefit to the community at large. Because these economic gains which accrue in such a developmental context may well bulk large in comparison with calculated benefit estimates, they are quite consistent with the concept of economic efficiency even in its narrowest sense.[39] Because this realization is often both present and expressed in Congressional chambers, it should be considered as a legitimate declaration of concern for the economic efficiency of Federal expenditures.

To substantiate the existence of a desire to take advantage of these economies present in the high-potential areas, the following statements are presented: Senator Knowland of California has stated:

I have tried in my service in the Senate, not to be sectional in any degree. I have supported the development of the great Tennessee Valley

38. U.S. *Congressional Record,* 84th Congress, 1st Session, 1955, p. 4742. For additional statements which bear the same sentiment see U.S. *Congressional Record,* 84th Congress, 1st Session, 1955, p. 8536; *ibid.,* 85th Congress, 1st Session, 1957, p. 9711.

39. The economic theory of this position has been analyzed and well defended by Julius Margolis. See Julius Margolis, "Secondary Benefits, External Economies, and the Justification of Public Investment," *Review of Economics and Statistics,* XXXIX (August, 1957), 284–91. For a quite different point of view see Jack Hirshleifer, James C. De Haven, and Jerome W. Milliman, *Water Supply: Economics, Technology and Policy,* pp. 133–137.

area under the TVA . . . [and] the flood control projects in the Mississippi Valley because I believed they were necessary for the economic development of that region.[40]

Much the same sentiment and concern is present in the statements of Representative Lanham of Georgia and Representative Donohue of Massachusetts.

[T]here are many appropriations, large sums appropriated for the Northwest, and they are absolutely necessary because it is that section of our country that offers the greatest opportunities for the development of our natural resources.[41]

. . . .

[T]he Congress has repeatedly demonstrated their belief that in any regional water control problem the Federal Government should assume a major share of responsibility when Federal participation is necessary . . . to accomplish broad regional objectives.[42]

Thus, not only is the concept of efficiency built into the very system of project approval but also there exists substantial sentiment among individual Congressmen in support of such a criterion. This position is tenable in spite of some Congressional opinion implying a failure to understand—or, if understanding, opposition to— the application of the benefit-cost ratio. It should also be stated that, in Congressional debates and hearings, the cry for a more adequate application of an efficiency criterion has been heard louder and more often in recent years—most notably, in the years after 1957.

REGIONAL AID. In asserting and defending the claim that economic aid is an effective force in determining the Federal government's allocation of water resource investment, the meaning of the term economic aid is first determined. The term economic aid will possess a twofold meaning. The first meaning embodies the concept of immediate need, and the hypothesis which it yields is that Congress tends to favor those areas which have recently experienced large floods, those rivers and harbors which require immediate dredging,

40. U.S. *Congressionl Record,* 80th Congress, 2nd Session, 1948, p. 5960.
41. U.S. *Congressional Record,* 81st Congress, 1st Session, 1949, p. 11942.
42. U.S. *Congressional Record,* 84th Congress, 2nd Session, 1956, p. 2257. For additional statements which bear this same sentiment see U.S. *Congressional Record,* 83rd Congress, 1st Session, 1953, p. 5700; *ibid.,* 84th Congress, 2nd Session, 1956, p. 2276; *ibid.,* 85th Congress, 1st Session, 1957, p. 4618.

and other areas which possess water problems requiring immediate action.

To state that immediate need is a criterion used by Congress should in no way imply that all or even most of the projects constructed can demonstrate the existence of disaster conditions. It does mean, however, that if a given project is located in a region which does possess such conditions, the chances for its receiving appropriations are greatly enhanced. In discussing the basic nature of the Corps program, Senator Ives of New York put it this way:

I maintain that, in these days of everincreasing Federal expenditures only those new public works projects should be undertaken which are necessitated by the most critical circumstances.[43]

This is an echo of the plea made by Representative Johnson of Texas a few years earlier:

[W]e need the money to get started to save human lives. On the basis of the humanitarian plea, if there is nothing else that can be used as an argument justifying this appropriation, I ask you to give us this appropriation.[44]

and a precursor of a similar plea by Representative Short of Missouri a few years later:

Bear in mind that [this area] has been declared a . . . hardship area. That alone, I think, would almost justify the construction of this dam. . . .[45]

Both Representatives Johnson and Short used the term *justify(ing)*. By outright statement, it is clear that these two individuals wish "immediate need" to serve as a criterion in the justification of Federal expenditure.

As evidence that Congress does indeed act upon this criterion, it should be pointed out that after every major flood disaster Federal allocations flow to the affected area. It was in 1928 that the Mis-

43. U.S. *Congressional Record,* 81st Congress, 2nd Session, 1950, p. 5158.

44. U.S. *Congressional Record,* 79th Congress, 2nd Session, 1946, p. 1096.

45. U.S. *Congressional Record,* 83rd Congress, 1st Session, 1953, p. 5611. For additional statements which bear the same sentiment see U.S. *Congressional Record,* 80th Congress, 2nd Session, 1948, p. 1779; *ibid.,* 83rd Congress, 2nd Session, 1954, p. 3265; *ibid.,* 84th Congress, 1st Session, p. 8512; *ibid.,* 85th Congress, 2nd Session, 1958, p. 18752; *ibid.,* 86th Congress, 1st Session, 1959, pp. 11647–11648; *ibid.,* p. 13093; *ibid.,* p. 18927; *ibid.,* 86th Congress, 2nd Session, 1960, p. 10979.

sissippi River project was adopted by Congress, one year after the great Mississippi flood which took some 250 lives and yielded an estimated 365 million dollars in property damages.[46] In more recent times, the haste to build flood control reservoirs in New England came directly on the heels of the disastrous flood conditions of 1955.

The second meaning of economic aid is somewhat broader and could reasonably be considered synonymous with the concept of aid to depressed or low income areas; that is, it is hypothesized that Congress tends to favor low income and depressed areas in the allocation of construction appropriations. This second concept of aid could also be interpreted as the desire for regional income redistribution. Thus, in much the same way that immediate need appears to be a relevant consideration in investment allocation, it appears that some regions tend to be favored because of their low stage of development, i.e., because of either their low per capita income or their long-run depressed state.

In terms of total governmental activity, this trend has already been noticed. As Seymour Harris states:

As federal activities have extended and spending grown, cash transfers from one region to another have tended to rise. Since the early thirties, these activities have resulted in a flow of funds from industrial to agricultural areas; from the Northeast to the South and West; from the rich to the poor.[47]

. . . .
[W]hy, when the federal government pumps cash into the Southeast for hydroelectric power, thus reducing costs for an area that is growing in part at New England's expense, should New England refuse such aid? [48]

This Federal activity aimed at income redistribution to poorer areas has been strongly defended by several Congressmen and Senators. Senator Fulbright of Arkansas is one of the most articulate spokesmen for this policy. In the hearings on the Reconstruction Finance Corporation, he stated:

New England has been exploiting the Southwest of this country for 150 years. They have practically drawn all the capital from these areas into

46. A. D. Frank, *The Development of the Federal Program of Flood Control in the Mississippi River*, pp. 193 ff.
47. *The Economics of New England*, p. 104.
48. *Ibid.*, p. 105.

Boston. I see no public interest to help pouring it all back [in the form of RFC loans to New England firms], if we are going to be frank about it. It is not a distressed area compared to Arkansas and Alabama and Mississippi today.[49]

Elsewhere, he has substantiated his position as follows:

We have been accustomed to handicaps since the Civil War but we now feel that the other areas have . . . been given a sufficient head start.[50]

The same type of sentiment prevails with respect to the particular program of water resource development. Not only do Congressmen from low income and depressed regions possess additional arguments to support projects in their districts but Congressmen of developed and high per capita income regions often acquiesce and support their arguments. A reading of the hearings and floor debate should suffice to demonstrate the validity of this position. As Harris puts it: "Continued [Federal] help is offered to the low-income and debtor areas, but is not usually available to older regions . . . ."[51]

The following statements by Representatives and Senators serve to illustrate the use of such arguments. Using the lower per capita income of the district which he represents as an argument in justification of a project for this region, Senator Fulbright states:

An appropriation to this project now . . . would mean economic encouragement to an area with the lowest per capita income of any in the whole United States. It would give aid to a part of the country which because of its economic conditions has been losing population at a time when all other areas have recorded population gains.[52]

Senator Ellender of Louisiana followed this plea by stating that the Committee on Appropriations has, in fact, considered this low per capita income problem in recommending project appropriations. A less refined but nevertheless succinct statement of such an argument is presented by Representative Davis of Tennessee:

49. U.S. Congress, Senate Subcommittee of the Committee on Banking and Currency, Hearings, *Study of the Reconstruction Finance Corporation*, 81st Congress, 2nd Session, 1950 (Washington, D.C.: Government Printing Office, 1950), p. 321.
50. U.S. *Congressional Record*, 81st Congress, 2nd Session, 1950, p. 11191.
51. Seymour Harris, *op. cit.*, p. 92.
52. U.S. *Congressional Record*, 84th Congress, 1st Session, 1955, p. 9877.

Somewhere in Holy Writ it is written, "when you glean the corners of thy fields, thou shalt leave the corners to the poor and needy." With all deference and reverence I gather the lesson from this passage and believe that the committee should have left a little more in the corners for the lower Mississippi. . . ."[53]

Indeed, recently, this identical sentiment has, to some extent, been incorporated with Congressional blessing into the standards which the Bureau of the Budget applies to proposed projects in such regions. In distinction from the previous set of standards as stipulated in *Circular A-47*, the present policy provides for the inclusion as benefits, project labor costs

. . . and other resources required for project construction, . . . operation, . . . maintenance, and added area employment, . . . to the extent that such labor and other resources would—in the absence of the project— be unutilized or underutilized [in those designated areas of] . . . chronic and persistent unemployment or underemployment.[54]

Thus, it is clear that within Congress the needs of individual regions have been given at least verbal recognition, and the concept of regional aid is present as one phase of the multifaceted goal of water resource policy. Insofar as it is true both that representatives from low income and depressed regions possess additional arguments in support of their projects and that Congressmen from other areas recognize these regional needs, the existence of this objective cannot be easily denied. In Chapter Three the regional flow of Federal appropriations since 1946 will be analyzed in an attempt to empirically verify the application of this objective, i.e., to verify whether or not the low income and depressed regions have, in fact, attracted a disproportionate share of Federal appropriations. POLITICAL MANIPULATION. In much the same manner that immediate need and regional economic aid are themselves made up of various components, so too, political manipulation is evidenced

53. U.S. *Congressional Record,* 83rd Congress, 2nd Session, 1954, p. 3360. For additional statements which bear the same sentiment see U.S. *Congressional Record,* 79th Congress, 2nd Session, 1946, pp. 1099 and 6299; *ibid.,* 80th Congress, 2nd Session, 1948, pp. 7096 and 5911; *ibid.,* 81st Congress, 1st Session, 1949, pp. 3138 and 11953; *ibid.,* 83rd Congress, 1st Session, 1953, pp. 5611, 5614, 5699, and 5700; *ibid.,* 84th Congress, 2nd Session, 1956, p. 11080; *ibid.,* 86th Congress, 1st Session, 1959, pp. 3995, 4015, 4026, 11636, 11639, 11625, and 13089; *ibid.,* 86th Congress, 2nd Session, 1960, p. 16155.
54. The President's Water Resources Council, *op. cit.,* p. 5.

in a wide variety of forms: the application of blind and blunt power in securing projects for one's own narrow constituency, regional coalitions of Congressmen in direct support of private lobbies, the age-old practice of political backscratching, the unofficial understandings of Congressmen with the Corps and local interest groups and lobbies. In the words of Senator Proxmire:

Certainly anyone who has served in Washington a few months, let alone 4 or 5 years, recognizes that political pressure is very potent on the executive branch, as well as on Congress. It is such pressure which at the present time determines where the money will be spent. . . . Such pressure . . . governs that determination because Congress does not have any clear objective criteria to be applied. . . .[55]

In an attempt to present a brief (and consequently incomplete) description of the workings of such a force, two of the more blatant and overt of its manifestations will be presented and supported by Congressional statements. These two forms of such manipulation will be called, for lack of better terms, sectionalism and logrolling.

Securing water resource projects on a sectional basis guided by the motive of sheer political success is difficult to distinguish from the allocation of such appropriations to certain regions because of the goal of economic efficiency or regional aid as discussed in the preceding sections. Although at times they may coincide, a careful search of Congressional statements, accusations, and attitudes has demonstrated that both forces are, in fact, present.

Arthur Maass and Robert de Roos first pointed out this sectional coalition between Congressmen and private interest groups. It was the southern Congressmen, they felt, who had banded together with southern rivers and harbors lobbies in an attempt to secure

---

55. U.S. *Congressional Record*, 87th Congress, 2nd Session, 1962, p. 21338. See also Irving K. Fox and Orris C. Herfindahl, "Attainment of Efficiency in Satisfying Demands for Water Resources," *American Economic Review*, LIV (May, 1964), 198–206. They state: "The structure of interest group relationships which generates decisions on water investments by Federal agencies is an elaborate one. . . . Perhaps the most important is that the beneficiaries of a federal water investment project commonly bear only a small portion of the costs of a project. . . . The quite natural result is that the [Federal] agency allies itself with local and regional organizations representing those who will benefit. . . . [This] generates a powerful joint effort to secure favorable Congressional action on the projects decided upon."

appropriations for their constituency through pressure on the Corps, individual Congressmen, and Congressional Committees.

The Corps has the whole-hearted support of the so-called "Rivers and Harbors Bloc," led largely by men from the lower Mississippi area. These men, given permanent seating by our Democracy, have high seniority on the committees dealing with navigation and flood control. . . . One of them, Senator John J. McClellan, was a member of the Hoover Commission and entered an impassioned minority defense of the Corps.

Staunchly behind the Rivers and Harbors Bloc is the National Rivers and Harbors Congress—an organization dedicated to the principle that no stream is too small for a federal handout, no levee tall enough, no channel deep enough, no harbor improved enough. . . . The president today is Senator John J. McClellan.[56]

In the words of the Rivers and Harbors Congress itself:

[T]he National Rivers and Harbors Congress has been perhaps a more controlling force on legislation approved than that of any other organization.[57]

This coalition and the results of its activities was in much the same manner deplored by Representative Sabath of Illinois on the floor of the House in the following manner:

For the information of the House, of the $119,000,000 in the rivers and harbors section of this bill, $93,000,000 goes to 11 Southern States. Perhaps they need it. Perhaps they do not. Of the $995,000,000 for flood control provided for in the bill, nearly one-half is of direct benefit to those same Southern States. The remaining 37 States share in the balance.[58]

. . . .

Many of these projects in the South, as proposed by the Corps of

56. Robert de Roos and Arthur Maass, *op. cit.*, p. 25. In addition to Senator McClellan's presence in the Rivers and Harbors Congress, one also finds Representative Short of Missouri as chairman of the board and Representative Brooks of Louisiana as vice-president. Representative Passman of Louisiana at the same time served as president of the Mississippi Valley Flood Control Association, an organization with the same set of goals as the National Rivers and Harbors Congress.

57. National Rivers and Harbors Congress, *National Rivers and Harbors Congress and Its Work* (Washington, D.C., 1940), quoted in Maass, *op. cit.*, p. 50.

58. U.S. *Congressional Record*, 81st Congress, 1st Session, 1949, p. 11939. By 1951, Senator Warren Magnuson of Washington felt that the West had joined the South in the formation of a unified coalition as he read and supported an editorial from the *Wenatchee Daily World* (Washington) entitled "The South

Engineers, show a genuine need for deepening some of the creeks that a man with a good chew of tobacco could spit over.[59]

The end result of such power politics has been noted numerous times in both houses of the Congress in statements similar to the following by Representative Eberharter of Pennsylvania:

Mr. Chairman, I am afraid that the Corps of Engineers has gotten into the habit of turning down any requests for worthwhile projects . . . in the East, and giving everything to states in the South and West.[60]

In addition to this complex system of organized pressure politics of a sectional nature based on the coalescing of multiple interests and powers, there exists the simple, polite, and socially acceptable practice of logrolling. Being ubiquitous in nature, this practice will tend to have less of a sectional influence on the flow of funds but, insofar as its prevalence causes it to substantially affect the allocation of appropriations, logrolling must be both noted and described. Senator Paul Douglas has most succinctly described the practice both in his book concerning governmental economy and on the floor of the Senate.

The only way a congressman can get his own project included in the final bill is to make an open or tacit agreement that he will support similar, if less meritorious, projects advanced by his colleagues.[61]

. . . .

This bill is built up out of a whole system of mutual accommodations, in which the favors are widely distributed, with the implicit promise that no one will kick over the applecart; that if Senators do not object to the bill as a whole, they will "get theirs." It is a process, if I may use an inelegant expression, of mutual backscratching and mutual logrolling.[62]

and the West." "As they [the North and East] gain an appreciation of the great national wealth potential in water use, more and more supporters will be found. . . . But for the present, it's still largely a South-and-West team that's carrying the ball." See U.S. *Congressional Record,* 82nd Congress, 1st Session, 1951, p. 11031.

59. U.S. *Congressional Record,* 81st Congress, 1st Session, 1949, p. 11940.

60. U.S. *Congressional Record,* 83rd Congress, 1st Session, 1953, p. 5701. For additional statements which bear the same sentiment see U.S. *Congressional Record,* 79th Congress, 1st Session, 1945, p. 11204; *ibid.,* 79th Congress, 2nd Session, 1946, pp. 1096 and 1099; *ibid.,* 80th Congress, 2nd Session, 1948, pp. 1795 and 1798; *ibid.,* 81st Congress, 1st Session, 1949, pp. 3126 and 3138; *ibid.,* 81st Congress, 2nd Session, 1950, pp. 5158, 5196, 5273, and 5278; *ibid.,* 83rd Congress, 1st Session, 1953, pp. 5598 and 7423; *ibid.,* 84th Congress, 1st Session, 1955, p. 10317; *ibid.,* 84th Congress, 2nd Session, 1956, p. 8707.

61. Paul H. Douglas, *Economy in the National Government,* pp. 101–102.

62. U.S. *Congressional Record,* 84th Congress, 2nd Session, 1956, p. 10191. For

This assertion and others of a similar nature are endowed with a substantial degree of credibility when Congressmen such as Representative Rogers of Florida publicly describe their own behavior in angry statements such as the following concerning an "understanding" that failed:

> Nevertheless, the gentleman from Georgia obtained an appropriation in a deficiency appropriation bill upon the theory that he would help us to get out a project if we voted for his project down there in Georgia. So I voted for the project.[63]

This sort of conduct, somewhat inadequately described by the term political manipulation, has led editorial writers, academic observers, and Congressmen themselves to echo the claim of Representative Rees of Kansas when he declared, "[This measure] can be classed as a pork barrel measure. [T]here is something in it for . . . everybody." [64]

In conclusion then, the position that the criteria used by Congress are both multifaceted and nebulous but that, in some vague way, they include both efficiency and regional income distribution appears to be both reasonable and defensible. To deny the influence of either of these goals or the influence of blunt political manipulation would present a rather incomplete and distorted image of the reality to be described. From this basis some suggestions concerning future criteria which have been presented by recent observers of water resource policy are investigated.

---

additional statements which bear the same sentiment see U.S. *Congressional Record,* 79th Congress, 1st Session, 1945, pp. 11205, 11206, and 11215; *ibid.,* 80th Congress, 2nd Session, 1948, p. 5925; *ibid.,* 81st Congress, 2nd Session, 1950, p. 5198; *ibid.,* 84th Congress, 1st Session, 1955, p. 8539. Also, see *Wall Street Journal,* April 5, 1950.

63. U.S. *Congressional Record,* 79th Congress, 2nd Session, 1946, p. 1091.

64. U.S. *Congressional Record,* 85th Congress, 2nd Session, 1958, p. 11624. This statement is given support in the following colloquy between Senator Ellender and General Cassidy of the Corps of Engineers before the Senate Committee on Appropriations:

Senator Ellender: "That is, is each section of the country well taken care of or is the distribution according to your way of thinking?"

General Cassidy: "As well as possible within the authorized projects. One of our criteria is good distribution around the country . . . [that is,] . . . good geographical distribution."—U.S. Congress, Senate Committee on Appropriations, *Hearings, Civil Functions Appropriation Bill, 1962,* 87th Congress, 1st Session, 1962, p. 3.

*Suggestions Concerning the Future Application of Criteria in
Allocating Water Resource Investment*

Now that the existence of some nebulous combination of the
concepts of economic efficiency and regional aid or income redistribution as criteria determining past decisions has been verified,
the role which present-day observers foresee these concepts playing
in the formation of acceptable criteria for future social policy will
be investigated. Out of the voluminous material which has come
forth in recent years concerning water resource policy, only a few
statements, namely the positions of Otto Eckstein, Roland McKean,
and John Krutilla, are selected for brief treatment as a sample of
private observations. Otto Eckstein's study *Water-Resource Development* appeared in 1958. In this work, Eckstein analyzes both
the economic theory behind benefit-cost analysis and the application of the benefit-cost concept by the Bureau of Reclamation and
the Corps of Engineers. All factors other than economic efficiency
are assumed to be beyond his purposes, and his entire study pro-
ceeds to analyze and prescribe changes in the present system of
economic evaluation. In Eckstein's own words, his analysis,

. . . treats benefit-cost analysis as a means of . . . selecting the most
desirable projects from the point of view of economic efficiency.[65]

Although his study focuses only upon the criterion of efficiency and
deals only with its application and improvement, Eckstein realizes
and points out the role which other, nonefficiency criteria may and
will play:

[O]ne of the criteria on which a project must be judged, and which
benefit-cost analysis disregards altogether, is the redistribution of income
which a project brings about.[66]

Rather contemporaneous with the work of Eckstein there appeared two other contributions; in one of them Eckstein himself
participated. Both of these studies had more to say than did Eckstein
on the multifaceted nature of criteria to be applied in choosing
between alternative water resource projects. The position taken by
Roland McKean in a study which also appeared in 1958 is, in princi-

65. Eckstein, *op. cit.*, p. vii.
66. *Ibid.*, p. 17.

ple, similar to that of Eckstein. Because the government intervenes in the development of water resources, largely to effect the outputs of goods and services which would not be produced appropriately or not be produced at all by private enterprise (even though the value of the outputs can be measured), and because the nation desires to maximize the size of the national income, McKean observes that ". . . it does make sense to look at cost-benefit estimates . . . ." [67] On this basis, he develops an efficiency criterion which, he suggests, evaluates the relationship between a project's benefits and costs more appropriately than does the traditional benefit-cost ratio. Having developed this criterion, however, he states clearly that it can serve only as a partial criterion.

[O]ur partial criterion can only tell which projects are "efficient." By itself, this test cannot tell us which position is best in any ultimate sense . . . . Hence, it is deemed appropriate here to have the cost-benefit measurements shed light on efficiency in this limited sense, and to have further exhibits shed light on redistributional effects. [68]

With an explicit denial that he is recommending the use of regional income distribution as a criterion, McKean does recognize the importance of such impact and accordingly provides data concerning regional income effects in his exhibit of the proper and appropriate information to be included in a project report.

It is not argued here that the effects on regional wealth distribution *ought* to be an important consideration, but it is believed that those effects will nonetheless be given a great deal of attention. If so, indicators of those effects should be explicitly stated. [69]

The second of the studies contemporary with the Eckstein work was a joint effort by Eckstein and John Krutilla. This study also recognizes the effect of regional income distribution as well as economic efficiency to be a salient factor in project choice. Stating that their main purpose is to fill the "need to spell out . . . the efficiency considerations involved in the development of river basins," [70] they nevertheless recognize the need to describe the "differences in the pattern of income distribution which attend

67. McKean, *Efficiency in Government*, p. 107. See also pp. 131 and 150.
68. *Ibid.*, pp. 132-133.
69. *Ibid.*, p. 242. See also pp. 201 and 208.
70. Krutilla and Eckstein, *Multiple Purpose River Development*, p. 4.

different water resources policies." [71] Because it is felt that regional wealth distribution will be used as a criterion in choosing between alternative investment opportunities, they strongly posit the need of precisely describing the expected redistributional outcome of each alternative so that the decision-maker, in applying his own value judgments, will at least anticipate the expected results of his decision.

The most recent contribution to this study on the objectives of water resource development comes, it seems, as a response to the previous studies. Whereas these studies recognize the importance of both efficiency and income distribution in the decision-maker's portfolio, Stephen Marglin attempts to define an objective ranking function given the goals of maximizing both efficiency and desired income redistribution. By beginning his argument with the statement that the maximization of national welfare is the prime objective of water resource development, he goes on to say:

In view of the three dimensional nature of national welfare—the size of the economic pie, its division, and the method of slicing—we believe it unwise to attempt to define a single index [criterion] for this broad objective; instead we shall develop alternative objectives for the most important ways in which water-resource development can contribute to national welfare: . . . efficiency . . . and income redistribution. [72]

From this sampling of the major nonpublic contributions to water resource planning, it appears true that both the concept of economic efficiency and the concept of income redistribution to particular groups are recognized as proper criteria for future investment decisions. In three of the four works, this recognition is supported either by suggestions concerning the design of such a multifaceted criterion or by suggestions concerning inclusion of the proper information on the expected redistributional effects to allow the decision-maker to attach importance weights to each of the criteria consistent with his judgment on the nature of the marginal utility of income function. Clear indication is thus given that future decisions will in all probability be based on the goal of

71. *Ibid.*, p. 265. Chapters 7 and 8 of their study are devoted to an analysis of regional income redistribution caused by the construction of a hypothetical Federal electric power installation.

72. Maass, Hufschmidt, *et al.*, *op. cit.*, p. 18.

regional and group income redistribution as well as on efficiency.

With much the same approach as outside observers, official and semiofficial public statements also deal with multifaceted criteria for the forming of investment decisions. Again equitable income distribution, regional development, and other social goals have been mentioned as legitimate objectives for water resource development. A very clear expression of this approach has been presented in a recent publication by the Bureau of the Budget.

This statement of proposed policy begins with the judgment that "The community . . . obviously rejects the ultimate pattern of income distribution . . . ," [73] and from this premise concludes that ". . . since considerations of equitable distribution of productivity gains may enter into the deliberations of the Government, they should become one of the criteria of choice for water resources development." [74] In proposing a process to set standards and criteria, this panel suggests the following:

The broad objectives to be attained through water resources development would be laid out by Congress and the President. These objectives should be framed in terms of gains in national income, of progress toward a more equitable distribution of income by increasing the income of disadvantaged groups, and of other economic and social objectives . . . . [75]

Although this statement is not an official government position, the government has recognized both efficiency and regional income redistribution goals in official publications before the statement was made and has largely accepted it in official statements afterwards. Brief reference will here be made to but a few of these statements. In an early statement, the Bureau of the Budget *Circular A-47*, discussing the criteria to be applied by the executive office in the review of project reports, placed great emphasis upon economic efficiency in defining concepts to be included as benefits and costs. Also, however, "the efficiency of the program or project in meeting regional . . . needs" [76] is stated as a further criterion. The "Green

73. U.S. Bureau of the Budget, *Standards and Criteria for Formulating and Evaluating Federal Water Resources Development*, p. 6.
74. *Ibid.*, p. 8.
75. *Ibid.*, p. 60.
76. U.S. Bureau of the Budget, *Circular A-47*, p. 5.

Book," while again heavily emphasizing the necessity of total annual benefits exceeding estimated annual costs and while refusing to include secondary benefits in the form of purely regional gains in the computation of total benefits, states the following in referring to criteria:

The public policies governing the development of the Nation's water and related land resources are not necessarily determined solely on the basis of economic considerations. Thus, for example, regional development and national defense have been objectives of various resource development programs.[77]

Most recently, in the statement establishing a new executive policy to supercede *Circular A-47,* a concrete and rather complete official acceptance of this position was declared.

All viewpoints—national, regional, State, and local—shall be fully considered and taken into account in planning resource use and development. Regional, State, and local objectives shall be considered and evaluated within a framework of national public objectives . . . . Significant departures from a national viewpoint required to accomplish regional, State, or local objectives shall be set forth in planning reports . . . . Hardship and basic needs of particular groups within the general public shall be of concern . . . .[78]

Thus, here also, there appears to be a growing recognition of the multidimensionality of the social welfare function. Again the proposals suggest a growing need for including the income redistributional impact of Federal expenditures in the criteria for project choice. As an extension of this recognition and need, these forces are analyzed both in their *ex ante* roles as criteria for choice and in their *ex post* roles as actual determinants of changes in welfare.

77. Federal Inter-Agency Committee on Water Resources, *op. cit.,* p. 3.
78. The President's Water Resources Council, *op. cit.,* p. 2.

3

The Criteria for Project Choice:
Application and Efficacy

SINCE WORLD WAR II then, Congressional choice in the allocation of water resource investment appropriations has been determined by a rather nebulous and multifaceted set of forces. As the evidence in Chapter Two suggested, these forces can be broadly labeled as economic efficiency, regional aid or regional income redistribution, and political manipulation. With the general nature of Congressional sentiment toward these goals of water resource investment in mind, an attempt is made to empirically evaluate the application and efficacy of these criteria in the actual allocation of past appropriations and, in particular, to analyze the results of the interplay of the first two of the three criteria, that is, those criteria which, in principle at least, should be measurable.

Economic Efficiency as Applied by Congress

Is there sufficient evidence to justify calling economic efficiency a criterion for project choice? In the preceding analysis of the determinants of Congressional choice, the force labeled economic efficiency was seen to be rather clearly manifest in three distinct forms. Not only was it built into the very system and process of project approval but it was also present in a multitude of Congressional statements referring to both the nature and application of a strict efficiency criterion and to broader efficiency concepts, notably, the desire to exploit the development potential in regions possessing the opportunity for such returns. In this section, only the efficiency criterion as a strict economic efficiency test will be applied; its other prime manifestation will be treated later.

To broach such an analysis, it is clear that the concept of

economic efficiency must first be defined, as it obviously means different things to different observers. The budget analyst, the businessman, the economist, the Congressman—to each of these people the word *efficient* carries a different meaning and therefore elicits widely divergent sets of standards.[1] Consequently, that which may appear as economically efficient to a Congressman may, to an economist, resurrect gross images of the waste of national resources.

What then does the economist's strict efficiency standard require for a proper allocation of resources? Cut to its barest essentials, it says this: if it is income which one desires to maximize with a given expenditure, the allocation of this expenditure must be guided into those uses which will return the greatest amount of income for each dollar spent. In the case of Federal government expenditures, if the goal is that of maximizing national income, the problem becomes one of allocating the expenditure of dollars raised in taxes to return the greatest amount of national income for each tax dollar committed (either immediately or in the future). If the return in the form of additions to national income is denoted by B, in which B is the present value of the annual stream of benefits, and the volume of the resources to be committed by taxpayers is denoted by K + O, in which K is the dollar volume of immediate investment and O is the present value of future operation, maintenance, and repair cost committed by the expenditure, then a given volume of K + O is allocated in the most efficient manner only if B is at a maximum. To put this in another way, each additional dollar of expenditure is allocated most efficiently if it is devoted to that use which possesses the highest ratio of B to K + O.[2] Only then, by ranking the projects by benefit-cost ratio and allocating funds to projects with the highest ratios first and moving to projects with successively lower ratios until the budget is exhausted, can the efficiency criterion be fulfilled.

1. For outstanding evidence of this fact see U.S. Congress, Joint Economic Committee, *Federal Expenditure Policy for Economic Growth and Stability,* Joint Committee Print, 85th Congress, 1st Session, November 5, 1957, especially the papers in Section IV, pp. 221–265.

2. Eckstein, *Water Resource Development,* pp. 39 and 53–65. It should be noted that not all economists accept this precise definition of efficiency. For modifications of this criterion and a discussion of their significance, see Chapter Five.

Judged by this efficiency optimum, how has Congressional performance fared? To make an empirical evaluation of Congressional performance, three things are essential: (1) each stated benefit-cost ratio must accurately depict the expected relative performance of the project; e.g., a project bearing a ratio of 1.6 must bear substantial evidence that it will increase national income per tax dollar committed more than a project bearing a ratio of 1.5, (2) the complete range of available projects together with their benefit-cost ratios must be present to allow for their ranking, and (3) the list of projects actually chosen and their ultimate cost and benefit-cost ratios must be present so that the actual allocation of a given budget may be compared with the ideal allocation. For this analysis, it will be assumed that the first of the requirements is indeed present; that is, it will be assumed that the benefit-cost ratios presented by the Corps are accurate portrayals of the economic reality.[3] The second requirement is somewhat more difficult. Although in principle it appears to be a feasible task, in practice securing the complete range of available alternatives becomes nearly impossible. Consequently, it will be assumed that the projects from a single omnibus authorization bill are representative of the entire backlog of authorized projects. The authorization bill which will be used as the representative sample is the bill passed in 1960.[4] In fulfillment of the third requirement, the efficiency of the new construction starts chosen for inclusion in a single appropriation bill will be evaluated in the light of the representative sample of the alternatives open to Congress, that is, in light of the projects included in the authorization bill which just preceded the appropriation bill. The new construction starts to be evaluated are those included in the Public Works Appropriation Bill of 1962 [5] which was passed in the summer of 1961, the year following the passage of the authorization bill.

Late in the 1960 session of Congress, an omnibus authorization bill containing 550 million dollars' worth of new water resource

3. This assumption will be relaxed in drawing conclusions concerning the operation of the efficiency criterion.
4. U.S. Congress, *H. R. 7634,* 86th Congress, 2nd Session.
5. U.S. Congress, *H. R. 9076,* 87th Congress, 1st Session.

projects and about 900 million dollars' worth of additional authorizations for large river basin projects was signed by the President. The bill in its final form was, in dollars of ultimate cost, nearly four times larger than when it passed the House in the 1959 session. Whereas the bill contained 56 projects as it passed the House, it contained 154 after it passed the Senate. Although it was declared ". . . clean as a hound's tooth" [6] as it passed the House, Senator Dirksen felt that, as it passed the Senate, ". . . the bill would permit currently uneconomical projects to be justified for authorization." [7] The composition of the bill as modified in conference and as finally passed is summarized in Table 2.

As the bill became law then, nearly 550 million dollars' worth

TABLE 2

Benefit-Cost Ratios of Projects in the Omnibus Authorization Bill of 1960 [a]

Benefit-Cost Ratio	Number of Projects	Ultimate Federal Cost, Thousands of Dollars	Percent of Total Ultimate Federal Cost
not available [b]	7	40,141	7.2
less than 1	1	560	.1
1.0–1.19	10	41,955	7.6
1.2–1.39	33	215,148	39.1
1.4–1.59	22	104,751	19.0
1.6–1.79	9	7,520	1.4
1.8–1.99	12	18,726	3.4
2.0–2.49	15	37,919	6.9
2.5–2.99	10	29,800	5.4
3.0–3.99	8	10,794	2.0
4.0–5.99	11	20,097	3.7
6.0–or more	12	22,494	4.1
Total	150	549,905	100.0

a. Compiled from U.S. Congress, House, *House Report 541*, 86th Congress, 1st Session; U.S. Congress, Senate, *Senate Report 1524*, 86th Congress, 2nd Session; and U.S. Congress, House, *House Report 2064*, 86th Congress, 2nd Session.

b. Two of the projects in this category do not require benefit-cost analysis as they are justified on the basis of national defense.

6. U.S. *Congressional Record*, 86th Congress, 1st Session, 1959, p. 13596. Statement by Mr. Davis of Tennessee.

7. U.S. *Congressional Record*, 86th Congress, 2nd Session, 1960, p. 13053.

of brand new projects became added to the existing backlog of projects eligible to receive construction appropriations. A few aspects of these new eligible projects warrant special attention. First, the range of benefit-cost ratios in the bill is particularly striking. From an unjustified project with a ratio of less than 1, the ratios ranged upward to 27 and 68, that is, projects whose estimated first year benefits will completely cover and even double the entire investment cost—surely a wide range from which to choose new construction starts. Also of significance is the tendency for projects to cluster at the lower end of the distribution. Almost one half of the projects are in that range which most observers would designate as doubtful or marginal [8] and only 21 percent of the ultimate dollar cost of the bill is represented by projects with benefit-cost ratios greater than 2.00. In attempting to grasp in a single number the quality of the bill, it is legitimate to claim that the projects in the bill possess a weighted average benefit-cost ratio of 1.80.[9] Finally, an aspect not visible in the table but which should nevertheless be mentioned is the substantial disparity between the efficiency of the projects in the original House bill and those added by the Senate. Whereas the House bill had a weighted average benefit-cost ratio of 2.52, the weighted mean of the projects added by the Senate was a meager 1.40.[10] In the House bill, 20 percent of the projects had ratios of more than 6.00, and over 50 percent possessed ratios of more than 2.00. Of the projects which were added by the Senate, only 1 percent had ratios of more than 6.00, and less than 30 percent had ratios of more than 2.00.

Those new construction starts which were included in the 1962 Public Works Appropriation Bill will now be isolated from this representative sample of eligible projects. Through this process

8. For reasons discussed later, most economists who have analyzed the problem consider a project with a Corps benefit-cost ratio below 1.4 or so to be a marginal project.

9. The formula used to compute the average is as follows:
$$\overline{X}_w = \Sigma (X \cdot W) / \Sigma W$$
in which $\overline{X}_w$ is the weighted mean, X is the benefit-cost ratio, and w is the estimated total Federal cost of a given project. It could be stated that the typical dollar spent on the bill's contents would be invested in a project with a benefit-cost ratio of $\overline{X}_w$.

10. This computation for the Senate projects excludes one sizable project which was deleted from the final form of the bill.

not only will the absolute benefit-cost ratio of the chosen projects be secured but also, and more importantly, the level of efficiency of these projects will be compared with the level of efficiency of those projects eligible for choice.

The Appropriation Bill of 1962 was a rather typical one with regard to its travels through the legislative machinery. As usual, both the number of new construction starts and the total appropriation grew continually as it passed both houses of Congress and became law. From the Corps budget request to the final form of the bill, the number of new construction starts rose from 50 to 78, and the total Federal cost represented by the new starts grew from 507 million to 749 million dollars, an increase of nearly 50 percent. Table 3 is a tabulation of the new starts included in the final form of the 1962 bill as well as in its pre-passage stages.

TABLE 3

*Benefit-Cost Ratios of New Construction Starts
in the 1962 Public Works Appropriation Bill* [a]

Benefit-Cost Ratio	Number of Projects				Ultimate Federal Cost, Thousands of Dollars	Percent of Total Ultimate Federal Cost
	Budget Request	House Bill	Senate Bill	Final Bill		
not available	2	5	12	11	12,650	1.7
less than 1	0	0	0	0	—	—
1.0–1.19	2	4	7	6	68,262	9.1
1.2–1.39	11	12	17	17	249,588	33.3
1.4–1.59	5	6	10	10	50,160	6.7
1.6–1.79	6	6	6	6	78,068	10.4
1.8–1.99	0	0	0	0	—	—
2.0–2.49	7	7	9	8	77,345	10.3
2.5–2.99	6	7	7	7	91,077	12.2
3.0–3.99	2	3	4	4	81,889	10.9
4.0–5.99	6	6	6	6	34,290	4.6
6.0–or more	3	3	3	3	5,903	.8
Total	50	59	81	78	749,232	100.0

a. Compiled from U.S. Congress, House, *House Report 1634*, 87th Congress, 1st Session; U.S. Congress, Senate, *Senate Report 1768*, 87th Congress, 1st Session; U.S. Congress, House, *House Report 2181*, 87th Congress, 1st Session; U.S. Congress, Senate, Subcommittee of the Committee on Appropriations, *Hearings on Public Works Appropriations, 1962*, H. R. 9076, Vols. I and II; and U.S. Congress, House, Subcommittee of the Committee on Appropriations, *Hearings on Public Works Appropriations, 1962*, H. R. 9076, Vols. I and II.

As with the omnibus legislation, the tracing of this bill through its pre-passage stages makes it clear that no real improvement in the efficiency of the bill is added by Congress to the budget request of the Corps. The weighted average benefit-cost ratio of the projects included in the request was 2.17. The projects added and deleted by the House did little to change the over-all ratio, but the bill as it passed the House did possess a slightly higher ratio of 2.20. The Senate, however, in the addition of 125 million dollars' worth of projects substantially lowered the over-all ratio. By the addition of these projects which possessed an average ratio of only 1.17, the weighted average for the entire bill was decreased to 2.04. In conference this situation was somewhat adjusted by the deletion of nearly 50 million dollars' worth of projects with the extremely low average ratio of 1.05. The bill in its final form possessed an average benefit-cost ratio of 2.10—lower than both the budget request and the House bill.

If the 150 projects in the omnibus authorization bill are treated as representative of the entire backlog of available projects, a comparison can be made of the general structure of the group of new starts and the group of projects authorized and eligible for construction appropriations. A comparison of Tables 2 and 3 illustrates, first of all, that the 78 new starts possess a higher percentage of ultimate cost in the higher class intervals than do the projects in the omnibus bill. Conversely, the projects in the omnibus bill tend to have the higher percentages in the lower class intervals. For example, whereas 73 percent of the total ultimate cost of the omnibus bill is represented by projects with benefit-cost ratios below 1.60, only about 50 percent of the total ultimate cost of the group of new construction starts is represented by such marginal projects. While but 22 percent of the ultimate cost of the omnibus bill is represented by projects having ratios greater than 2.00, 29 percent of the ultimate cost of the new starts is so represented. This condition is reflected in the average benefit-cost ratio of the two distributions. The average ratio of 2.10 carried by the group of new starts is substantially higher than the 1.80 average ratio of the projects in the authorization bill. This comparison, however, is far from ideal. Because of the basic non-homogeneity in the two distributions, there is but little basis here upon which to reach a conclusion on the efficacy of the efficiency criterion. A more apt test appears possible by isolating those projects among the new construction starts in the 1962 bill which were drawn from the 1960 omnibus bill and comparing these projects with the entire set of projects in that bill.

Of the 150 projects authorized in the 1960 omnibus legislation, 29 were included among the 78 new construction starts in the succeeding appropriation bill. Table 4 presents the breakdown of these 29 projects.

TABLE 4

Breakdown of the 1962 New Construction Starts Authorized in the 1960 Omnibus Bill by Benefit-Cost Ratio [a]

Benefit-Cost Ratio	Number of Projects	Ultimate Federal Cost, Thousands of Dollars	Percent of Total Ultimate Federal Cost	Percent of Ultimate Federal Cost in each Class Interval of Omnibus Bill
not available	—	—	—	—
less than 1	—	—	—	—
1.0–1.19	2	15,399	11.5	36.7
1.2–1.39	5	22,326	16.7	10.4
1.4–1.59	3	31,472	23.6	30.0
1.6–1.79	1	97	.1	12.9
1.8–1.99	—	—	—	—
2.0–2.49	3	3,730	2.8	9.8
2.5–2.99	6	25,481	19.1	85.5
3.0–3.99	2	8,811	6.6	81.6
4.0–5.99	4	17,485	13.1	87.0
6.0–or more	3	8,578	6.4	38.1
Total	29	133,379	100.0	24.3

a. See footnote to Table 3.

A few aspects of this group of 29 projects should be noted. First of all, nearly 50 percent of the dollar value of the projects display benefit-cost ratios above 2.00—a comparatively large percentage. More significantly, the proportion of the authorized projects with high benefit-cost ratios chosen for inclusion as new starts is significantly greater than the proportion of authorized projects with low ratios. This can be seen by comparing the 29 projects with the entire omnibus bill. Stated in a somewhat different way, while less than 25 percent of the projects in the omnibus bill (measured in terms of ultimate cost) were chosen to receive construction appropriations, over 80 percent of the projects in the omnibus bill with benefit-cost ratios greater than 2.50 were chosen as new construction starts. This effect is likewise registered in the weighted average benefit-cost ratio of these new construction starts. Whereas the entire omnibus bill carried an average of 1.80, the 29 new starts picked from the bill possessed a ratio of 2.84, more than a full unit greater than the over-all average.

What conclusions then can be drawn from the results of such a choice among alternatives? Perhaps this question can best be answered by dealing with the opposite question; i.e., what conclusions cannot be drawn from the above evidence? Primarily, it is obvious that Congress is not motivated solely by a desire to maximize efficiency. The inclusion of 10 projects with ratios below 1.60 immediately negates such a supposition. If, in fact, efficiency had been the sole criterion, even the weighted average ratio of 2.84 would appear rather low. By arranging the eligible projects of the authorization bill in order of their benefit-cost ratios from highest to lowest and moving down the list until the budget was exhausted, a substantially modified result would have occurred. If the budget of 133 million dollars which was committed to the 29 projects drawn from the 1960 legislation was allocated most efficiently among projects in that bill, no project having a ratio of less than 1.80 would be chosen, and the weighted average would be 3.39 as opposed to the present 2.84. Furthermore, not only can we not claim that Congress is solely motivated by a desire to maximize efficiency, but from this evidence we cannot even conclude that Congress always chooses with at least one ear cocked to an efficiency goal. To so reason would be to infer a general tendency from the facts of a particular case.

What then does this evidence tell us? First, if it can be assumed that the 150 projects in the omnibus bill are a representative sample of the entire backlog (a seemingly plausible assumption) then it can be concluded that in choosing new starts, Congress pays at least some degree of attention to a project's benefit-cost ratio. This is supported by the rather significantly larger average benefit-cost ratio of the 78 new construction starts as opposed to the average benefit-cost ratio of the omnibus bill. Second, with no necessary assumptions, it can be concluded that in choosing new starts in 1962 from the 1960 omnibus bill, efficiency was, in fact, a criterion. The significant difference in average ratios (2.84 as opposed to 1.80) would deny that the 29 new starts from the bill were merely a simple random sample. This evidence then, in conjunction with Congressional sentiments implying favor shown to projects with high benefit-cost ratios,[11] would lead an observer to conclude that some (as opposed to no) general regard is paid to the level of a project's benefit-cost ratio and, consequently, to a criterion called economic efficiency.[12]

From this evidence then, it is obvious that Congressional behavior deviates rather far from the economist's ideal. The big hurdle for any individual project is the ratio of 1 to 1, and, having attained this goal, each project stands on relatively equal ground in terms of conformity to regulations. Moreover, Congress has a serious lack of interest in improving the accuracy of the present benefit-cost technique. Marginal or doubtful projects continue to receive Federal appropriations in spite of recent Congressional claims concerning the exclusion of marginal projects from the list of new construction starts. The ideal still lies far from attainment,

---

11. See footnotes 31 to 36, Chapter Two.

12. The evidence presented (and consequently the conclusion based upon the evidence) rests on the assumption made previously concerning the accuracy of the benefit-cost computations. If this assumption cannot be maintained, the conclusion must be modified. Based on a substantial contribution by Otto Eckstein, it appears that the assumption cannot, in fact, be maintained. Because of the excessive inclusion of secondary benefits, the use of rail rates which exaggerate real costs in the computation of navigation benefits, and the use of an interest rate substantially below the real cost of funds, the stated benefit-cost ratios tend to be greater than the real ratios. Consequently, when any project with a ratio of 1.40 or less is considered to be a marginal or doubtful project, it can be seen by an examination of Tables 2 and 3 that a significant portion of dollar expenditure in the present program is not justifiable on economic grounds. That is, it is not likely that those projects with benefit-cost ratios below 1.40 will have a positive effect on the level of national income. See Eckstein, *op. cit., passim* and U.S. Congress, Joint Economic Committee, *op. cit.,* article by Otto Eckstein, "Evaluation of Federal Expenditures for Water Resource Projects," pp. 657–667.

but evidence supports the claim that efficiency, in some vague way, does take its place among the nebulous set of criteria for choice among alternatives. At the very minimum it manifests itself as a distinct, yet undefined, preference for those projects bearing high rather than low benefit-cost ratios, a preference based upon a gauge of efficiency secured through substantial analysis of economic repercussions. This, then, is a claim which can be made for no other sizable Federal government spending program.[13]

Regional Income Redistribution as a Congressional Criterion

Has there been a tendency for either low income and depressed or high development-potential regions to be favored in the postwar Corps of Engineers program? In Chapter 2, it was demonstrated that, in addition to and largely contradictory with the strict efficiency criterion, the criterion of regional aid to low income or depressed areas has also possessed substantial Congressional support. Moreover, substantial sentiment, not inconsistent with the strict efficiency criterion, was displayed favoring projects in regions possessing sizable and recognized development potential. Because each of these asserted forces are rather distinctively regional in character, empirical verification of their efficacy appears to be a feasible task. In response to the obvious need for such verification, the remainder of this chapter will attempt to (1) isolate the areas receiving substantial appropriations, (2) test the hypothesis that Congress has appropriated a relatively greater share of funds to both low per capita income states and particular regions of high development potential, and (3) ascertain the degree to which the Corps program has reduced the disparity in state per capita incomes.

A flow-of-funds type analysis covering the 17-year period since

13. This general conclusion has been posited elsewhere recently. See Fox and Herfindahl, *American Economic Review*, p. 199. They state: "The attention which has been given to the economics of water use has resulted in the application of reasonably sophisticated techniques of economic analysis in the design of water resources projects, and there can be little doubt that the standards and procedures now in use are effective in preventing the construction of many uneconomic projects."

World War II, 1946 to 1962, will be used to isolate the areas receiving substantial appropriations. Because the primary objective of this study is to substantiate (or negate) Congressional claims with evidence, no assumption concerning the actual benefit of a given appropriation to a state's residents will be made. It is sufficient in this context simply to claim that the absolute amount of appropriations to the projects in a given state is a gauge of Congressional intent concerning that state. That is, if the Far West received a disproportionate share of appropriations, it will be claimed that Congress for some reason desired to support projects in the Far West more than projects in the rest of the country. Likewise, if Michigan received more than Maryland, Congress, it will be claimed, desired, for some reason, to benefit Michigan more than Maryland.[14]

Because benefit to a particular geographical region, in fact, means benefit to the residents of that region, the analysis will be performed on a per capita basis. Table 5 presents data on total appropriations, per capita appropriations, per capita income, rank by per capita appropriations, and rank by per capita income for each of the 50 states.

Several aspects of this data are of substantial importance both in understanding Congressional behavior and in appraising the impact of the Corps program on various areas of the country. A particularly striking aspect concerns the great disparity in both total and per capita appropriations among the states. Over the 17-year period, total appropriations range from a high of 615 million dollars spent on projects in the state of Washington to slightly over 2 million dollars spent on projects in Nevada. Although some of this disparity can be attributed to the greater potential for navigation and flood control expenditure in those states normally known as wet as opposed to those normally known as dry, it is obvious that not all or even a major part can be so attributed.[15] States such as Wis-

14. Note that *desire* here is a key word. It is irrelevant in this context whether or not Michigan actually benefited more than Maryland. The greater per capita appropriation to Michigan projects will be taken as evidence of Congressional intent to benefit Michigan more than Maryland.

15. Because the appropriations considered here are for the development of rivers and harbors as well as flood control, *wetness* should not be restricted

TABLE 5

Total Appropriations, Per Capita Appropriations,
Per Capita Income, Rank in Per Capita Appropriations,
and Rank in Per Capita Income, by State, 1946 to 1962

State	Total Construction Appropriation,[a] Thousands of Dollars	Per Capita Appropriation,[b] Dollars	Annual Per Capita Income,[c] Dollars	Rank in Per Capita Appropriation[d]	Rank in Per Capita Income
North Dakota	433,719	693	1496	1	35
South Dakota	427,033	640	1431	2	38.5
Oregon	603,971	367	1810	3	18
Washington	615,073	235	1922	4	12
Arkansas	404,232	219	1003	5	49
Oklahoma	326,471	143	1431	6	38.5
Louisiana	398,829	134	1313	7	42
Kentucky	372,802	125	1207	8	46
Kansas	251,562	123	1679	9	26
Vermont	40,744	106	1428	10	40
Alaska	17,693	99	2366	11	2
Nebraska	122,143	89	1724	12	23
Idaho	49,974	80	1501	13	33
Tennessee	271,363	79	1218	14	44
West Virginia	150,380	78	1336	15	41
Mississippi	161,065	74	900	16	50
Montana	36,373	57	1815	17	17
Missouri	229,214	55	1732	18	21
New Mexico	42,482	52	1456	19	36
New Hampshire	28,855	51	1600	20	28
Florida	187,141	49	1585	21	31
Georgia	178,380	48	1244	22	43
Iowa	128,896	48	1683	23	25
California	604,035	46	2171	24	7
Texas	395,360	46	1594	25	30
South Carolina	87,011	39	1064	26	48
Alabama	113,787	36	1111	27	47
Virginia	90,571	25	1485	28	34
Ohio	213,502	24	1910	29	13
Michigan	171,577	24	1925	30	11
Hawaii	12,863	23	1691	31	24
Arizona	22,759	22	1595	32	29
Illinois	198,027	21	2164	33	8
Pennsylvania	229,335	21	1854	34	15
Delaware	7,457	20	2505	35	1
Indiana	78,632	18	1764	36	19
Connecticut	40,380	17	2312	37	3
Massachusetts	79,798	16	1999	38	10
Minnesota	45,152	14	1670	39	27

TABLE 5 (Continued)

State	Total Construction Appropriation,[a] Thousands of Dollars	Per Capita Appropriation,[b] Dollars	Annual Per Capita Income,[c] Dollars	Rank in Per Capita Appropriation[d]	Rank in Per Capita Income
North Carolina	58,465	14	1208	40	45
Rhode Island	10,313	12	1845	41	16
Colorado	19,100	12	1740	42	20
New Jersey	66,194	12	2144	43	9
Maryland (including Washington, D.C.)	33,906	10	2221	44	6
Nevada	2,146	10	2257	45	4
New York	144,012	9	2235	46	5
Maine	6,122	7	1448	47	37
Utah	2,497	3	1525	48	32
Wyoming	3,380	1	1858	49	14
Wisconsin	3,106	1	1730	50	22
United States	8,217,971	50			

a. The data on total appropriations were computed from information in the House Reports on the Senate-House Conference on each of the annual Civil Functions Appropriation Bills as follows: 1946, *Congressional Record*, 79th Congress, 1st Session, p. 11049; 1947, *Congressional Record*, 79th Congress, 2nd Session, p. 3989; 1948, *Congressional Record*, 80th Congress, 1st Session, p. 10391; 1949, *Congressional Record*, 80th Congress, 2nd Session, p. 7897; 1950, *Congressional Record*, 81st Congress, 1st Session, p. 14051; 1951, *House Report 1797*, 81st Congress, 2nd Session; 1952, *House Report 1197*, 82nd Congress, 1st Session; 1953, *House Report 2497*, 82nd Congress, 2nd Session; 1954, *House Report 889*, 83rd Congress, 1st Session; 1955, *House Report 1892*, 83rd Congress, 2nd Session; 1956, *House Report 1085*, 84th Congress, 1st Session; 1957, *House Report 2413*, 84th Congress, 2nd Session; 1958, *House Report 1049*, 85th Congress, 1st Session; 1959, *House Report 2670*, 85th Congress, 2nd Session; 1960, *House Report 1152*, 86th Congress, 1st Session; 1961, *House Report 2181*, 86th Congress, 2nd Session; 1962, *House Report 1268*, 87th Congress, 1st Session; and from Conference Reports of the miscellaneous Supplemental or Deficiency Appropriation bills which contained Civil Functions appropriations. In each case the appropriation was allotted to the state in which the specific project was located. In the cases in which a project was physically in two or more states, the appropriation was divided equally among the states involved. In the cases in which the project was a comprehensive river basin project flowing through two or more states, the appropriation was allocated to the state in which the actual expenditure took place as determined from Chief of Engineers, U.S. Army, *Annual Report*. The Arkansas River project and the Mississippi River project are cases in which such an adjustment took place. Those items in the Mississippi River project, such as dredging and revetments whose location could not be so determined, were allocated to the states concerned in the proportion of their river bank mileage to total river bank mileage. The figures are adjusted slightly to eliminate some small transfers to other departments and some small allowance for slippages.

b. The state population figures used for per capita appropriation estimates are averages of the 1950 and 1960 census figures for each state. They were secured from the *Statistical Abstract of the United States, 1961*, p. 10.

c. The state per capita income figures are likewise averages of the 1950 and 1960 census figures for each state. They were secured from the *Statistical Abstract of the United States, 1962*, p. 319.

d. The states are ranked from highest to lowest. The ranks are based on calculations to the nearest cent whereas the per capita data in the table is in terms of the nearest dollar. This allows states which have the same per capita appropriation in the table to possess different ranks.

consin, Maine, and Maryland—all of which have substantial sea-coasts and/or river flows—rank among the very lowest in terms of both per capita and total appropriations. On the other hand, states such as North and South Dakota and Montana, typically known as rather dry states, are found toward the top of the list. Other phenomena must be sought in explanation of such results.

When the geographic regions that have received the highest level of appropriations are compared with the regions that have received the lowest level of appropriations, a certain rather clear pattern becomes manifest. This pattern, although imperfect, tends to substantiate the two regional hypotheses presented previously. First of all, it is clear that, of those states which are distinctly favored, all are clustered into three particular regions: the Far West, North and South Dakota, and the South-Southwest. Of the ten states which have received appropriations of 300 million dollars or more, three are located on the West Coast, two are represented by North and South Dakota, and the remaining five are clustered in the South and eastern part of the Southwest.[16] This same general pattern appears in per capita appropriations. Of the top eight states in per capita appropriations, two are in the Far West, two are represented by North and South Dakota, and four are in the South. However, those states which received the lowest appropriations appear to be largely from another, quite different, geographic region. Of the ten states with the lowest per capita appropriation, six of them are located in the North and North-Central regions, and all possess substantial coast lines and harbor facilities. In contrast to the top ten states, each of which received over $100 per capita in project appropriations, each of the lowest ten received less than $12 in per capita appropriations. Further analysis of the table reveals much the same pattern. For example, of the top 50 percent of the states ranked by per capita appropriations, only two states

---

to states possessing flood problems as the term implies. Those states with substantial ocean coastal regions are also *wet* in this context insofar as the development of ocean harbors exists as a potential for Federal Corps expenditures.

16. These ten states are (in order of their total appropriations from highest to lowest): Washington, California, Oregon, North Dakota, South Dakota, Arkansas, Louisiana, Texas, Kentucky, and Oklahoma.

from the area east of the Mississippi River and north of the Mason-Dixon line are found: New Hampshire and Vermont. Stated alternatively, the area containing more than 50 percent of the total United States population received less than 20 percent of the total appropriation. Of significance in this pattern is the fact that two of the three favored regions (the South and the Far West) are rather generally considered to be either low income and hardship areas or areas of rather substantial productive resource investment opportunities, whereas the states in the region receiving the lowest appropriations (the North-North Central region) possess neither of these characteristics.

Just as a great disparity exists between the appropriations received by individual states and geographical areas, so another phenomenon also is present. This phenomenon, seen by relating the annual per capita income of the 50 states to the level of their per capita appropriation, also substantiates the hypothesis that Congress has favored low income and hardship areas. In Table 6 it is shown that the richer a state, the less it tends to receive in per capita appropriations.

TABLE 6

Comparison of Median Rank in Per Capita Appropriation and Per Capita Income [a]

Groups of Ten States From Highest to Lowest Per Capita Appropriation	Median Rank by Per Capita Appropriation	Median Rank by Per Capita Income
Top ten states	5.5	38.5
Next ten states	15.5	30.5
Next ten states	25.5	30.5
Next ten states	35.5	17
Bottom ten states	45.5	15

a. Computed from Table 5.

As the rank in per capita appropriation increases (as one moves down the list of states from highest to lowest per capita appropriation) the rank in per capita income tends to decrease (one moves to states with progressively higher per capita income). This tendency can be measured more accurately by the use of Spearman's Coefficient of Rank Correlation.[17] By applying this measurement, a negative correlation coefficient of −.426 was found, a significant coefficient assuring the existence of an inverse relationship between these two variables.[18] Figure 1 displays the extent of this relationship.

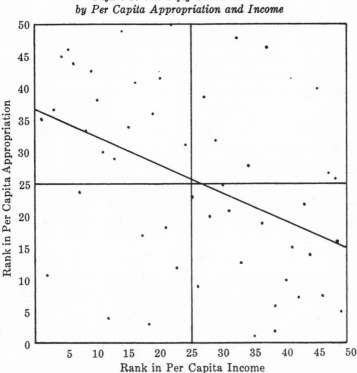

*Figure 1. The Fifty States Ranked
by Per Capita Appropriation and Income*

By combining this evidence with the previous analysis of Congressional sentiment which depicted a desire to favor particular regions both on grounds of welfare (income redistribution) and on grounds of exploiting the external growth economies latent in high potential areas, what conclusion can we reach? First, with respect to

17. The formula for Spearman's Coefficient is as follows:
$$R_s = 1 - [(6 \Sigma D^2)/(N^3 - N)]$$
in which D is the deviation in rank of the two variables of a given state and N is the total number of observations.

18. The coefficient of rank correlation between per capita income and total appropriation (instead of per capita appropriation) is −.262.

the low income and depressed areas, the evidence is fairly substantial. Not only were the ten states receiving the largest appropriations found to cluster largely in the lowest income region of the country, the South, but a fairly close inverse relationship between per capita income and per capita appropriations was found when all 50 states were considered. Moreover, with respect to depressed and hardship areas, the case of West Virginia stands out. Not only were the projects in this state pleaded on the grounds of easing the tremendous soft coal unemployment situation but also from the data it appears that these pleas did not fall on closed ears. West Virginia is fifteenth in the nation as far as per capita appropriations are concerned which places it substantially above its neighbors—Maryland, Pennsylvania, Ohio, and Virginia.

When the Congressional sentiment concerning the desire to exploit productive resources in high potential regions is compared to the evidence, less substantial conclusions can be made. Nevertheless, the evidence which does exist seems to substantiate the claim. Surely by most standards, areas in the Far West, especially the Columbia River and Central Valley regions, exist as prime examples of largely unexploited, high resource to capital areas. Consequently, it is not surprising to find these regions to be ranked rather high in both the volume of absolute appropriations and in per capita appropriations. From this evidence it appears reasonable to accept the hypothesis that the stated Congressional desire to exploit the potential productivity of these regions also functions as an effective determinant of the allocation of Corps appropriations.

Thus, both the desire to aid low income regions and the desire to exploit regional development potential give evidence of being reasonably well-defined aspects of the multifaceted criterion applied by Congress in the allocation of water resource investment funds. Because in both of these cases the evidence appears to coincide with the expression of Congressional opinion cited previously, it seems to be a valid conclusion that Congress has, in fact, acted in conformance with its stated intent. That is, because of this agreement, the evidence does appear to demonstrate causality as well as the simple existence of significant covariation.

The Redistributive Effects of the Federal Program

Has the Corps program led to an equalization of state per capita incomes, and if so, to what extent? Critics of Federal expenditure programs have often raised the charge that such spending must of necessity redistribute income among the states, which redistribution would be absent if the program was performed on a regional, state, or local level. With respect to Federal public works investment in water resources, the charge is well founded. As shown in the previous section, through this program rich states tend to receive relatively small disbursements and poor states relatively large ones. However, because the appropriation has its source in general tax revenues, the actual expenditure is only one of the two halves of the process of interstate income redistribution. By assuming that the incidence or burden of the money spent on the program is

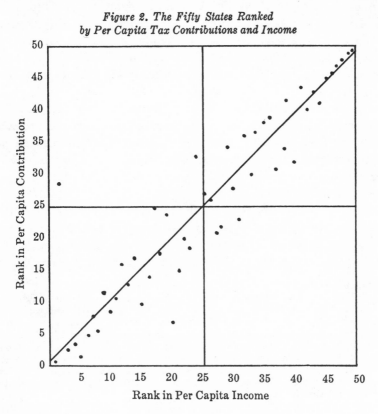

Figure 2. The Fifty States Ranked
by Per Capita Tax Contributions and Income

identical to the incidence of the total Federal tax bill, the other half of the process can be estimated. Table 7 presents an estimate of the tax contribution made by each state's residents in support of the total Corps appropriation on both a relative and a per capita basis. The method used in making this estimate is one suggested by Harold M. Groves and is described briefly in Appendix A. Figure 2 points out the close positive relationship between the per capita tax contribution and per capita income.

The incidence of per capita Federal taxes used in support of the 17-year Corps program ranges from a high of $124 in Delaware to a low of $15 in Mississippi. By definition, the mean per capita contribution is equal to the mean per capita appropriation of $50. Although the means are equal, it should be noted that the distribution of states according to per capita appropriation has a much larger variance than the distribution of states by per capita tax incidence.[19] Moreover, as Figure 2 shows, the relationship between per capita tax incidence and per capita income is positive and very close. The application of Spearman's Coefficient of Rank Correlation to this data gives the extremely high value of +.920.[20]

Consequently, not only do the rich states tend to receive relatively less per capita than do poor states but they also tend to contribute relatively more, in the form of taxes, to the program. These two factors give strong implication that the income redistribution which has occurred under the program has been both substantial and in the direction of minimizing the differences in state per capita incomes.

In attempting to both verify the existence of such an equalizing effect and to appraise its magnitude, some necessary assumptions and definitions must be presented. To determine the sheer existence of such an equalization, the following general approach will be

19. See column 3 of Table 5.
20. In an article presented before the Joint Economic Committee, Professor James A. Maxwell ran the same sort of rank test between per capita tax incidence and per capita income for the year 1953. The correlation coefficient which he obtained was +.934—extremely close to the one obtained here. A rank correlation test between the state per capita tax incidence data which Maxwell used and the per capita tax incidence data used in this study yielded a coefficient of +.966. See U.S. Congress, Joint Economic Committee, *op. cit.*, article by James A. Maxwell, "Adjustment of Governmental Responsibilities Via Grants," pp. 200–212.

TABLE 7

Relative Tax Incidence, Per Capita Contribution to Corps Appropriations, Rank in Per Capita Contribution and Per Capita Income, by State, 1946 to 1962

State	Percent of Total Federal Tax Revenue Contributed [a]	Per Capita Contribution for Corps Program,[b] Dollars	Rank in Per Capita Contribution [c]	Rank in Per Capita Income
Delaware	.58	124	1	1
New York	15.53	80	2	5
Connecticut	1.97	71	3	3
Nevada	.19	69	4	4
Maryland (including Washington, D.C.)	2.87	66	5	6
Illinois	7.49	65	6	8
Colorado	1.19	62	7	20
California	9.70	61	8	7
Massachusetts	3.50	59	9	10
Pennsylvania	7.18	54	10	15
Michigan	4.64	54	11	11
New Jersey	3.54	53	12	9
Ohio	5.72	53	13	13
Rhode Island	.53	53	14	16
Missouri	2.46	49	15	21
Washington	1.80	49	16	12
Wyoming	.18	48	17	14
Oregon	.97	47	18	18
Nebraska	.77	46	19	23
Wisconsin	2.07	46	20	22
Minnesota	1.75	44	21	27
New Hampshire	.30	43	22	28
Florida	2.11	43	23	31
Indiana	2.18	42	24	19
Montana	.32	41	25	17
Kansas	1.00	40	26	26
Iowa	1.32	40	27	25
Texas	4.29	40	28	30
Alaska	.08	38	29	2
Idaho	.29	37	30	33
Maine	.42	36	31	37
Vermont	.17	36	32	40
Hawaii	.24	35	33	24
Arizona	.43	35	34.5	29
Oklahoma	.97	35	34.5	38.5
Utah	.32	34	36	32
Virginia	1.42	32	37	34

TABLE 7 (Continued)

State	Percent of Total Federal Tax Revenue Contributed [a]	Per Capita Contribution for Corps Program,[b] Dollars	Rank in Per Capita Contribution [c]	Rank in Per Capita Income
North Dakota	.24	32	38	35
New Mexico	.32	32	39	36
Louisiana	1.12	31	40	42
Tennessee	1.16	28	41	44
South Dakota	.22	27	42	38.5
Georgia	1.23	27	43	43
West Virginia	.66	27	44	41
North Carolina	1.40	27	45	45
Kentucky	.97	27	46	46
Alabama	.85	22	47	47
South Carolina	.63	22	48	48
Arkansas	.45	20	49	49
Mississippi	.40	15	50	50

a. The percentage share of total expenditure borne by each state was determined by a method suggested by Harold M. Groves. The details of its application are presented in Appendix A.

b. The per capita contribution was secured by summing a state's total incidence for the periods 1946 to 1954 and 1955 to 1962 and dividing this by the average population in the state during the entire period. See footnote 2 in Appendix A and the second footnote of Table 5.

c. Ranked from highest per capita contribution to lowest.

taken: For each of the 50 states, the difference between per capita receipts and contributions will be determined for the 17-year period from 1946 to 1962. This difference can be expressed more precisely as follows:

$$D = \left(\frac{g}{P}\right) - \left(\frac{\frac{t}{T} \cdot G}{P}\right)$$

in which g is the dollar amount of Corps construction appropriations received by a given state during the time period under consideration, P is the population of the state during the period, t is the amount of Federal tax borne by the state during the period, T is the total tax revenue of the Federal government during the period, and G is the total Corps construction appropriation during the period. If the difference for a given state is negative, the state's residents will have contributed more toward the Corps construction program in the form of taxes [(t/T) G] than they received from the program in appropriations (g). The states will then be ranked by the value of D, the net per capita gain (or loss) in the flow-of-funds attributable to the Corps program, and their per capita income over the time period considered. When the Spearman test is applied to these two variables and a negative correlation exists, it will be concluded that the Corps program has tended to equalize the distribution of state per capita incomes with the size of the co-efficient, roughly indicating the degree of equalization.[21]

To appraise the magnitude of such a redistribution, both the benefits and the costs which accrue to a state must be more precisely defined.[22] In the following analysis, therefore, it will be assumed that the construction appropriation equals the present value of the benefits of the Corps program to the state. Also, it will be assumed that the state's share of the Federal tax burden to meet construction costs is equal to the present value of total program costs to the state.[23] The net flow-of-funds effect is presented

21. In the application of this type of statistical test, complete equality between the appropriations received by a given state and the benefits which accrue to that state is not necessary. What is essential is that there be a close positive relationship between the construction cost of a project and the real value of the project to the beneficiaries at a point in time. It is assumed, therefore, that the residents of a state which receives more appropriations than another state are benefited more than the residents of the state receiving a smaller volume of appropriations.

22. See the detailed discussion of the problems involved in such measurement found in Chapter Four, pp. 84 ff.

23. Because, as will be shown later, the present value of gross benefits of Corps projects exceeds the value of the project construction appropriation and because the total cost of participation to a state's residents is greater than simply the tax burden for construction costs, both the figures for total benefits and for total costs are understated by the appropriation and tax burden figures. The effect, therefore, on the difference between these two variables, i.e., the difference in which we are interested, will remain relatively unaffected. If the benefit-cost ratio is stated as:

$$Z = \Sigma[B/(1+i)^t]/\Sigma[O/(1+i)^t] + K$$

where B is the estimated annual benefit, K is the construction cost, and t is the estimated life of the project, O is the annual operating, maintenance, and repair cost, and if:

1. $O = 0$ for all projects
2. i is the social rate of time preference
3. $Z = 1$
4. all benefits accrue locally, and
5. there are no local costs,

construction appropriation would equal the present value of benefits, and the tax burden for construction costs would equal total state costs.

for each of the states over the 17-year period in Table 8 and Figure 3.

TABLE 8

Total Tax Incidence for Corps Construction, Net Flow-of-Funds Effect, Net Per Capita Flow-of-Funds Effect, and Rank in Net Per Capita Effect, by State, 1946 to 1962

State	Total Tax Burden For Corps Appropriation,[a] Thousands of Dollars	Net Aggregate Flow-of-Funds Effect,[b] Thousands of Dollars	Net Per Capita Flow-of-Funds Effect,[c] Dollars	Rank in Net Per Capita Flow-of-Funds Effect
North Dakota	19,926	413,793	661	1
South Dakota	18,187	408,846	613	2
Oregon	77,144	526,827	320	3
Arkansas	36,974	367,258	199	4
Washington	126,934	488,139	187	5
Oklahoma	79,327	247,144	108	6
Louisiana	92,007	306,822	103	7
Kentucky	79,609	293,191	98	8
Kansas	82,503	169,059	83	9
Vermont	13,890	26,854	70	10
Alaska	6,778	10,915	61	11
Mississippi	32,894	128,171	59	12
Tennessee	95,266	176,097	51	13
West Virginia	52,059	98,321	51	14
Nebraska	63,463	58,680	43	15
Idaho	23,475	26,599	43	16
Georgia	100,082	78,298	21	17
New Mexico	25,902	16,580	20	18
South Carolina	48,730	38,281	17	19
Montana	26,176	10,197	16	20
Alabama	69,768	44,019	14	21
New Hampshire	24,521	4,334	8	22
Iowa	108,540	20,365	8	23
Missouri	202,196	27,018	7	24
Florida	164,718	22,423	6	25
Texas	348,205	47,155	5	26
Virginia	116,203	−25,632	−7	27
Hawaii	19,783	−6,920	−12	28
Arizona	35,683	−12,924	−13	29
North Carolina	114,112	−56,647	−13	30
California	796,627	−192,592	−15	31
Indiana	179,096	−100,464	−23	32
Ohio	469,533	−256,031	−29	33
Michigan	380,810	−209,233	−29	34

TABLE 8 (Continued)

State	Total Tax Burden For Corps Appropriation,[a] Thousands of Dollars	Net Aggregate Flow-of-Funds Effect,[b] Thousands of Dollars	Net Per Capita Flow-of-Funds Effect,[c] Dollars	Rank in Net Per Capita Flow-of-Funds Effect
Minnesota	139,863	−94,711	−30	35
Maine	34,281	−28,158	−30	36
Utah	26,571	−24,074	−30	37
Pennsylvania	589,353	−360,018	−33	38
Rhode Island	43,759	−33,446	−40	39
New Jersey	290,600	−224,406	−41	40
Massachusetts	289,706	−209,908	−43	41
Illinois	614,827	−416,800	−44	42
Wisconsin	170,195	−167,089	−45	43
Wyoming	14,976	−11,676	−47	44
Colorado	96,210	−77,110	−50	45
Connecticut	161,696	−121,316	−54	46
Maryland (including Washington, D.C.)	231,295	−201,318	−56	47
Nevada	15,454	−13,308	−60	48
New York	1,267,141	−1,123,129	−71	49
Delaware	47,444	−39,987	−105	50

a. See the first footnote of Table 7.
b. Column 2, Table 5 minus Column 2, Table 8.
c. Column 3, Table 5 minus Column 3, Table 7.

From this evidence, several conclusions can be drawn. Primarily, it is clear that a substantial redistribution has taken place among the states. Because of the pattern of the two flows which compose the monetary exchange, certain types of regions have gained at the expense of others. First of all, the poor states have gained at the expense of the rich. The coefficient of correlation existing between states ranked by per capita income and by per capita net gain (or loss) in the flow-of-funds is a rather large —.626. Of the richest ten states in terms of per capita income, only one (Alaska) shows a net gain, and of the twenty richest states, only four show a net gain. Of the ten poorest states, only one (North Carolina) shows a net loss, and of the twenty poorest states, only four show a net loss (a symmetrical relationship).

Viewed from a geographical perspective, this redistribution is also very clear. Of the area east of the Mississippi and north of the Mason-Dixon line, only two small states (Vermont and New Hampshire) show a net gain, while the rest of the area demonstrates varying degrees of net loss. Of the ten southern states, all except

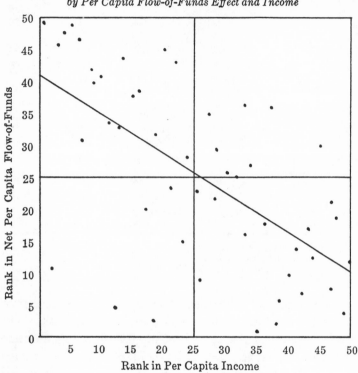

Figure 3. The Fifty States Ranked by Per Capita Flow-of-Funds Effect and Income

one (North Carolina) show a net gain. In the Far West, only California displays a net loss. Redistribution of wealth among states has occurred, and the direction of the redistribution is clear —from rich to poor and from North-Northeast to other areas. From a net per capita gain of $661 to North Dakota residents to a net per capita loss of $105 to Delaware residents, it becomes apparent that the Corps program has shifted substantial amounts of wealth from some population groups to others. Moreover, the shift has unquestionably tended to equalize state per capita incomes.

Conclusion

What, then, can be concluded from the evidence of this chapter? Primarily, it appears rather clear that Congressional motives have, in fact, been nebulous and multifaceted. Of the various motives, strict economic efficiency appears to be the least outstanding and most uncertain. A fair appraisal would seem to take the following approach: Although projects with high benefit-cost ratios tend to be chosen before projects with low ratios, no consistent or persistent pattern is manifest. In fact, substantial amounts continue to be spent on projects with very low or marginal ratios when, in fact, projects with higher ratios are available.

Second, a somewhat stronger and more consistent motive seems to be present in both the force of aid to low income and depressed areas and the drive to exploit development potential in areas of substantial opportunities for productive resource investment. As the evidence has shown not only have Congressmen often spoken of such goals but also their actions have to a large extent been consistent with their utterances. Income has, in fact, been redistributed. Certain geographic regions have been aided to the relative neglect of others, and a significant favoring of both low income and high potential regions and states has been noted. Finally, evidence of a strong tendency toward the equalization of state per capita incomes has been presented.

4

An Analysis of Regional Income Redistribution

THE FIRST three chapters have analyzed the meaning, nature, and significance of the existing goals of Federal water resource investment expenditures. A substantially more pervasive analysis of the Corps General Construction program is now undertaken in separate empirical investigations of the allocative efficiency and redistributional impact of the program.[1] These two effects, it should be noted, are the principal determinants of the welfare impact of the Corps program. In these investigations, first the impact of both of these effects in a particular section of the country during a particular period of time is evaluated, and then these analyses are combined in an attempt to demonstrate the inter-relationship of these two effects. Chapter Four will deal with the income redistributional effect of the program, Chapter Five, the analysis of economic efficiency, and Chapter Six, the discussion of the inter-relationship of the two effects. In each of these analyses the section of the country which will be treated consists of ten southern states,[2] and

1. The General Construction budget is by far the most substantial of the Corps budgets, comprising well over 90 percent of the total budget.
2. The ten states included in the study are Alabama, Arkansas, Florida, Georgia, Kentucky, Louisiana, Mississippi, North Carolina, South Carolina, and Tennessee. This particular grouping of states was chosen because of existing river basin topology and the resulting interdependence of projects constructed in a single river basin. The inclusion of Virginia, for example, would have introduced a completely separate river basin (the Chesapeake Bay Basin) into the analysis even though Virginia composes but a relatively small portion of the entire basin. In dealing with problems of regional income redistribution, this grouping is a most appropriate choice; it constitutes the lowest income region of the country. In per capita income terms these states ranked, respectively, 47, 49, 30, 42, 46, 43, 50, 44, 48, and 45. With the exception of Florida, they are the lowest 9 out of 50 states. Robert E. Graham, Jr. and Edwin J. Coleman, "Consumer Incomes Up in All Regions in 1960," *Survey of Current Business*, XLI (August, 1961), 13.

the period of time is the seventeen years after World War II, i.e., 1946 to 1962.

From the previous discussion of both the nebulous set of goals of the Congressional decision-making process and the regional allocation of postwar Corps appropriations, it appears certain that the South has, in some way, been affected by the resulting income redistribution. For an insight into the trend of such a regional impact, the construction appropriations received by individual southern states and by the region as a whole since 1946 are presented.[3] Through this preliminary and rather general analysis, the South is compared to the non-South and each southern state is compared with its neighbors, its region, and with the nation as to its success in attracting construction appropriations. In the second section of this chapter, a more technical analysis of the net income redistribution impact on each southern state by year is presented, and there both the costs to a state of participating in the Corps program as well as the benefits which are expected to accrue from it are taken into account.

The Flow of Construction Appropriations Since 1946

Federal government appropriation through the Corps of Engineers for the construction of rivers and harbors and flood control projects occurs under two distinct headings, which means two separate sets of Congressional hearings, two separate investment decisions, and two separate budget accounts. These two categories are known as "Construction, General" and "Construction, Mississippi River and Tributaries." In the case of the Mississippi River program, Congress makes lump sum appropriations with no specific breakdown for individual projects. However, Congress allocates funds project by project in the General Construction program. The ten southern states studied here receive appropriations from both of these budgets. Individual projects in

3. It is in its role as an index of future benefits to state residents that the appropriation figure is of interest. The construction expenditure itself has little value to the residents of a given state; the stream of benefits that accrue to the state's residents from the use of this appropriation is the really significant variable. However, a portion of the appropriation expenditure may also accrue as income payments to the state's residents.

these states receive funds from the General Construction budget and, because of the location of the Mississippi Valley, the entire appropriation for flood protection along the Mississippi River is spent in the South. Table 9 depicts the trend of these relevant budgets and the trend of the total Corps construction budget in the seventeen years after World War II.

From Table 9 it is clear that the size of the total Corps program

TABLE 9

Rivers and Harbors Construction Appropriations to the
U. S. Army Corps of Engineers by Fiscal Year, 1946 to 1962

Fiscal Year	Budget, Thousands of Dollars		
	Construction General Appropriation [a]	Mississippi River Expenditures [b]	Total
1946	126,154	17,661	143,815
1947	169,419	27,464	196,883
1948	268,978	30,012	298,990
1949	437,396	43,411	480,807
1950	469,235	54,204	523,439
1951	483,323	48,484	531,807
1952	431,377	42,390	473,767
1953	402,308	58,207	460,515
1954	287,945	38,138	326,083
1955	306,250	30,929	337,179
1956	426,815	35,904	462,719
1957	450,758	40,880	491,598
1958	459,720	42,041	501,761
1959	621,320	53,153	674,473
1960	686,649	53,631	740,280
1961	733,934	54,531	788,465
1962	756,977	54,845	811,822

a. The data in this column are taken from House-Senate Conference Reports for each of the seventeen years for all the bills involved including the annual Public Works Appropriation Bills and Supplemental and Deficiency Appropriation Bills in particular years. Because Corps budget requests are made on each project only one year in advance, the amount of the appropriation corresponds very closely to the amount of the expenditure. Any difference between expenditures and appropriations in any given year will occur when the Corps was not able to utilize all of its appropriations for a given project in a given year. The figures are adjusted slightly to eliminate some small transfers to other departments and some allowance for anticipated slippages. See the first footnote of Table 5.

b. The data in this column represent construction expenditures rather than appropriations. The reason for this is twofold: (1) appropriation data are not broken down between construction and maintenance, and consequently, it is impossible to separate them, and (2) appropriation data are not broken down by specific project and hence could not be allocated to specific states. The expenditure data are secured from Chief of Engineers, U.S. Army, *Annual Report*, 1946 to 1962.

has grown rapidly in the postwar period. The annual appropriation for 1962 was substantially larger than at any time since the war and substantially larger than at any time since the program's inception. Indeed, the 1962 appropriation was nearly six times as large as the 1946 appropriation.[4]

Most of this postwar growth occurred in two distinct periods—the years directly after the war and the years just before 1962. In the six years after the war, the General Construction program grew substantially each year. Indeed, by 1951, the annual appropriation was approximately 500 million dollars, a figure nearly four times that of the appropriation in 1946. Most of this early growth occurred as an attempt to return Corps domestic activity to its prewar basis and, in fact, to make up for lost time in fulfilling the mandate of the Flood Control Act of 1936. Moreover, there existed a strong need to provide employment for returning servicemen during this early postwar period. During the following four fiscal years, however, the early trend of appropriations reversed its direction. Three of these four years showed absolute decreases from the previous year's appropriation. With the advent of the Korean War in 1951, all projects except those essential for national defense were either curtailed or delayed. Furthermore, beginning in 1953, the administration changed from Democratic leadership favoring a large public works program to Republican leadership which had different thoughts on the issue. From the very beginning of his term, President Eisenhower declared a "no new starts" policy which maintained its effectiveness for some three years.

In 1956, however, this situation underwent another, rather complete reversal. Unhappy with the declining level of Corps activity, Congressmen reacted violently to the President's budget, which included dwindling appropriations on nearly completed projects. In retaliation, they added some 47 million dollars of unbudgeted appropriations to be applied to 107 unbudgeted new projects. The level of total appropriations consequently jumped in that year by nearly 40 percent. Since 1956, the growth in total

4. The data in Tables 9 to 12 are computed from appropriation data expressed in current dollars. All of the figures would be somewhat lower if expressed in constant dollars.

appropriations has continued unabated until 1962 when the funds set aside for new construction work alone surpassed 800 million dollars and the entire Corps program including operation, maintenance, and repair costs as well as administrative costs nearly equaled the one-billion-dollar figure.

The significance of the study of the appropriation data for individual states and regions is twofold. First, this is the value in which Congress appears to be most vitally interested as the size of the appropriation is equated with the value of the subsidy to any particular region. It is the appropriation itself by which a Congressman gauges his success in securing Federal funds for his constituents and not the real economic value which stands behind such an appropriation. Second, although it is only the appropriation which seems to interest the individual Congressman, there is a relationship between the size of the appropriation and the gross benefit which accrues to the residents of an area. In fact, this relationship could under certain circumstances be an equivalent one, in which case a dollar of appropriations would be worth a dollar of benefits to the residents of a state.[5] Thus, because the appropriation figure serves as both a gauge of Congressional success and a crude index of gross benefits to a state or region, the data on the flow of appropriations to the South is analyzed both by state and over time.

The cross-sectional data is studied first and then the relationship of southern appropriations to total appropriations over time. In Table 10, the data on total water resource appropriations to the Corps of Engineers is presented for both the nation and for the ten southern states. This data includes appropriations to both the General Construction program and the Mississippi River project. Of the total program construction appropriations of some 8.25 billion dollars, about 2.25 billion dollars or 27 percent was allocated to projects in the ten southern states. This represents an average appropriation of over 72 dollars per person in these states, whereas the per capita appropriation of the average United States resident was less than $50. On a per capita basis then, the South appears to have received nearly one and one-half times the appropriation

5. An example of such an equivalent relationship was presented in footnote 23, Chapter Three.

of the country taken as a whole and nearly one and two-thirds times the per person appropriation of the other 40 states. With 18.6 percent of the population and 27 percent of the total appropriation, it is clear that the Corps program has been relatively concentrated in the southern region of the country.

More striking than this general concentration of the program in the southern states is its concentration in specific states of the South. Of the ten southern states, three of them (Arkansas, Louisiana, and Kentucky) received 53 percent of total appropriations to the South. On the other hand, the lowest three (Alabama, North and South Carolina) received only 11 percent. In per capita terms, this disparity is seen still more clearly. The three top states received a per capita appropriation of $150, with Arkansas, the top state in both absolute and per capita appropriations, receiving $219 per person. The three lowest states, on the other hand, re-

TABLE 10

Total Appropriations to Corps of Engineers Projects in Ten Southern States in Absolute, Percentage, and Per Capita Terms, 1946 to 1962

State or Region	Total,[a] Thousands of Dollars	Construction Appropriations				
		State Total as Percent of		Dollars[b]	Per Capita as Percent of	
		Total U.S.	Ten-State Total		U.S.	Ten-State Region
Alabama	113,787	1.38	5.10	35.93	72	49
Arkansas	404,232	4.90	18.10	218.86	440	302
Florida	187,141	2.27	8.38	47.85	96	66
Georgia	178,380	2.16	7.99	48.21	97	67
Kentucky	372,800	4.52	16.69	124.18	250	172
Louisiana	398,829	4.84	17.86	133.57	269	184
Mississippi	161,065	1.95	7.21	74.05	149	102
North Carolina	58,465	.71	2.62	13.56	27	19
South Carolina	87,011	1.06	3.90	38.57	78	53
Tennessee	271,363	3.29	12.15	78.91	158	109
Ten-State Region	2,233,073	27.09	100.00	72.51	146	100
Rest of U.S.	6,011,605	72.91		44.49	90	
United States	8,244,678	100.00		49.69	100	

a. See the first footnote of Table 5.
b. The state population data used for per capita estimates are averages of the 1950 and 1960 census figures for each state. They were secured from the *Statistical Abstract of the United States, 1961*, p. 10.

ceived but $26 per capita with North Carolina, the lowest in both absolute and per capita appropriations, receiving less than $14 per person. To state this in still another way, a person in Arkansas has received nearly 4.5 times the appropriation of an average United States citizen, nearly 5 times as much as an average non-South resident, and over 3 times the appropriation of the typical southerner. With 1.1 percent of the population, Arkansas has received 4.9 percent of total Federal Corps appropriations.

The conclusion to be gained from these figures is inescapable. In the struggle to secure Federal appropriations, the South has fared well with respect to investment in water resource development. Moreover, not only the South as a whole, but even more strikingly, specific states in the South appear to have been especially favored. As a gauge of Congressional success, these data are forceful evidence that southern Congressmen and Senators have been more successful than most, with those from some states, notably Arkansas, performing with outstanding success.

Because the remainder of this study deals specifically with the General Construction phase of the total Corps program, the South's position is investigated in this phase alone. One would expect the South's share of appropriations in this phase of the program to be substantially below the average for the entire United States and more particularly below the average for the non-South because the development of the largest river basin in the South, the Mississippi, and a second very important river valley, the Tennessee, are covered by appropriations to completely separate budgets. Table 11 presents data similar to that presented in Table 10 but with the construction appropriations to the Mississippi River budget, all of which financed projects in the South, removed.

From the evidence in Table 11, somewhat similar conclusions can be drawn to those posited earlier. Even with the funds allocated to the Mississippi River project removed from the flow-of-funds to the South, the residents of southern states have fared better than non-South residents. With 18.6 percent of the total United States population, the ten southern states received 20 percent of the appropriations allocated to the General Construction budget. The per capita appropriation to the ten southern states was nearly $49

as compared to $45 per capita for the entire nation and less than
$45 for non-South residents. Even without the Mississippi River
appropriation, the claim that the southern states have been favored

TABLE 11

*Construction, General Appropriations to Corps of Engineers
Projects in Ten Southern States, in Absolute, Percentage,
and Per Capita Terms, 1946 to 1962*

State or Region	Total,[a] Thousands of Dollars	Construction, General Appropriations				
		State Total		Per Capita [b]		
		as Percent of		Dollars [c]	as Percent of	
		Total U.S.	Ten-State Total		U.S.	Ten-State Region
Alabama	113,787	1.51	7.55	35.93 (100)	79	73
Arkansas	273,717	3.64	18.16	148.20 (67.7)	327	303
Florida	187,141	2.49	12.42	47.85 (100)	106	98
Georgia	178,380	2.37	11.84	48.21 (100)	106	99
Kentucky	327,278	4.35	21.72	109.02 (87.8)	241	223
Louisiana	113,415	1.51	7.53	37.98 (28.4)	84	78
Mississippi	6,580	.09	.44	3.03 (4.10)	7	6
North Carolina	58,465	.78	3.88	13.56 (100)	30	28
South Carolina	87,011	1.16	5.77	38.57 (100)	85	79
Tennessee	161,179	2.14	10.70	46.87 (59.4)	103	96
Ten-State Region	1,506,953	20.04	100.00	48.93 (67.5)	108	100
Rest of United States	6,011,605	79.96		44.49 (100)	98	
United States	7,518,558	100.00		45.31 (91.2)	100	

a. See the first footnote of Table 5.
b. See the second footnote of Table 10.
c. The figures in parentheses are the percentages of the total per capita appropriations (Table 10) which are accounted for by appropriations to the General Construction
program (Table 11).

in the flow of Federal water resource investment has support as does the claim that southern Congressmen have funneled public works appropriations into their districts with substantial success.

The disparity among individual states which was noted in data on total appropriations is also evident when only the General Construction phase of the program is observed. In this phase of the total program, projects in Arkansas received nearly 275 million dollars, while projects in Mississippi received but 6.5 million. In per capita terms, Arkansas received $148 per person, while Mississippi projects received a per capita appropriation of $3 per person. The top two southern states (Arkansas and Kentucky) with 3 percent of the nation's population received 8 percent of the total General Construction appropriation and 40 percent of southern appropriations; the bottom pair (Mississippi and North Carolina) possessed nearly 4 percent of the nation's population but received less than 1 percent of the nation's appropriations and but slightly more than 4 percent of southern appropriations.

The trend in the flow of Federal appropriations to the South during the postwar years is as important a concept as the absolute level of these appropriations. The difference between being a declining portion of a growing pie or a growing portion of a growing pie is surely one which warrants investigation.

During the time period covered by this study (1946 to 1962), not only has the Corps program in its entirety grown rapidly but each of its component parts has also shown an upward trend. As Table 12 demonstrates, the change in total Corps appropriations has been positive in 5 of the 6 sub-periods considered, and over the entire period the appropriations have shown an average annual increase of nearly 42 million dollars. Only the period from 1951 to 1954 yielded an average annual decrease in appropriations which, as explained above, resulted from the Korean War and the Eisenhower policy of "no new starts."

Even though the average annual change in appropriations was both positive and rather large, the size of the absolute increments tended to decline somewhat over the period. The results of this phenomenon are clearly seen in the trend of the average annual rate of growth. From the high of 44.2 percent per year in 1946 to

TABLE 12

Growth of Total Corps Construction Appropriations and of Corps Appropriations Allocated to the South, by Time Period, 1946 to 1962

	1946–1948	1948–1951	1951–1954	1954–1957	1957–1960	1960–1962	1946–1962
Average Annual Increase (Decrease) in Total Corps Construction Appropriations, ($000,000)	77.6	77.6	-68.6	55.2	82.9	35.8	41.8
Average Annual Increase (Decrease) in Construction Appropriations Allocated to the South ($000,000)	21.1	21.9	-19.9	9.9	24.4	15.1	11.3
Average Annual Percent Rate of Change of Total Corps Construction Appropriations	44.2	21.2	-17.7	14.8	14.7	4.7	11.4
Average Annual Percent Rate of Change of Total Corps Appropriations to the South	40.6	20.9	-18.3	9.6	19.5	4.5	10.9
Average Annual Percent Rate of Change of Construction General Appropriations to the South	47.2	22.7	-24.5	14.1	24.0	6.0	12.6
Average Annual Percent Rate of Change of Mississippi River and Tributaries Appropriations	50.3	6.7	-8.3	2.4	9.5	1.1	7.3
Percent of Total Corps Appropriations Allocated to the South[a]	31.8	28.4	28.0	24.5	25.0	27.7	27.1

a. The headings for interpreting the final row are: 1946–1948, 1949–1951, etc.

1948, the growth rate declined steadily until it reached a low of 4.7 percent at the end of the period. Although the level of absolute appropriations grew rapidly, the rate of this growth continually fell.

Table 12 also presents the average annual changes in the Corps appropriation allocated to projects in the ten southern states, the rate of change of this appropriation, and the proportion which this appropriation is of the total. Three particular phenomena should be noted. First, it should be observed that the average percentage rate of growth of southern construction appropriations is lower than the rate of growth of the entire program and, consequently, lower still than the phase of the program not located in the South. Therefore, even though the southern phase of the program grew significantly, its rate of growth lagged behind that of the total Corps program. Second, except for the abnormal period 1951 to 1954 and the period 1957 to 1960, the rate of growth of the southern program has been declining. From a high annual rate of growth in the first time period of 40.6 percent, it dropped to 4.5 percent in the last two years.

Finally, look at the trend of the proportion of the Corps program allocated to the South over time. Although projects in the South received over 27 percent of the total Corps appropriations during the 17-year period, this proportion steadily declined throughout the period. From a high of nearly 32 percent of total appropriations attained in the 1946 to 1948 period, this proportion declined to less than 25 percent from 1954 to 1957. Only in the last period did the South demonstrate any sign of regaining its former high proportion.

The explanation of these phenomena is found in the relationship of the two component parts of the Corps program. The Mississippi River program, located entirely in the South, is the key to explaining the South's declining relative position. The level of appropriations to this program has been remarkably stable, and consequently, its rate of growth has been comparatively low. It has grown at an average annual rate of 7.3 percent in comparison to the rate of growth of the total Corps program of 11.4 percent. In every period except the first it displayed a lower rate of growth than the total program. Thus, because the Mississippi River program, with its low rate of growth, is located entirely in the South, the over-all rate of growth of southern appropriations was smaller than the national rate, and the share of the South became a declining portion of a growing pie. This is true even though the rate of growth of General Construction appropriations allocated to the South was 1.2 percent higher than the rate of growth of the total Corps program.

In conclusion then, the South has been favored in the receipt of rivers and harbors and flood control funds. Even more striking has been the success of individual states in the attraction of such funds. Notwithstanding its generally favorable position over the entire period, the South's relative share of appropriations has tended to decline over the period, and the annual percentage rate of growth of appropriations to the South has been lower than that for the country as a whole.

Income Redistribution Impact in the South— An Empirical Study

From the preliminary results presented in the previous sections, it appears certain that a substantial redistribution of income has taken place among the various regions of the country because of the Corps program. Moreover, the evidence suggested that the sectional impact of such federalism has clearly favored the southern states. To extend this finding, in the remainder of this chapter an attempt is made to verify whether, in fact, such a redistribution has taken place and, if it has, to isolate its magnitude by state and by time period through a more refined approach.

Because use of regional income differentials as a criterion for the allocation of Federal appropriation is becoming increasingly important, those factors which determine the regional impact of any Federal expenditure program must be well defined and clearly understood. In the literature, three alternative approaches have been suggested and applied in evaluating the regional impact of development programs. They are: (1) use of an aggregate economic indicator, such as personal income, to compare relative changes in a region with a development program with relative changes for other regions, (2) detailed case-by-case analyses of the effects of an expenditure "on the parameters of the region's production and consumption functions over time and the trend in the structure of markets" [6] and (3) use of regional inter-industry models in tracing the impact of a government expenditure program on the various output sectors of a region.[7] Each of these suggestions, although helpful under certain circumstances, embodies rather serious problems, both conceptual and empirical, and has consequently met with varying degrees of success. From the existence of wide error margins resulting from inappropriate aggregate measuring devices or inadequate regional input-output coefficients to the problem of excess subjectivity which is introduced by rather informal assessment procedures, it is clear that the evaluation of regional impact through any one of these approaches leaves much to be desired. In hope of securing a more satisfactory regional impact evaluation, in this section a rather different technique is adopted.

In this study, the concept of an income redistribution function as suggested by Stephen Marglin[8] is combined with direct estimates of regional costs and expected returns (in terms of real income produced) as proposed by H. G. Schaller[9] in an attempt to determine the net regional impact of the Corps program. However, two adjustments are made in Schaller's method, both of which increase the accuracy of the regional impact estimate. The first adjustment deals with the procedure used in estimating the benefits

6. John V. Krutilla, "Criteria for Evaluating Regional Development Programs," *American Economic Review,* XLV (May, 1955), 132.

7. For examples of these three approaches see, respectively, B. U. Ratchford, "Government Action or Private Enterprise in River Valley Development: An Economist's View," *American Economic Review,* XLI (May, 1951), 299–307, Krutilla, *op. cit.,* 120–132, and R. A. Kavesh and J. B. Jones, "Differential Regional Impacts of Federal Expenditures: An Application of the Input-Output Matrix to Federal Fiscal Policy," *Regional Science Association Proceedings,* II (1956), 152–167.

8. Maass, Hufschmidt, *et al., Design of Water Resource Systems,* pp. 62 ff. The function was suggested by Marglin for use as a criterion in evaluating water resource projects. In this study, it is used empirically to estimate historical redistribution.

9. Howard G. Schaller, "Veterans Transfer Payments and State Per Capita Incomes, 1929, 1939, and 1949," *Review of Economics and Statistics,* XXXV (November, 1953), 325–332; "Social Security Transfer Payments and Differences in State Per Capita Incomes, 1929, 1939, and 1949," *ibid.,* XXXVII (February, 1955), 83–89; and "Federal Grants-in-Aid and Differences in State Per Capita Incomes, 1929, 1939, and 1949," *National Tax Journal,* VIII (September, 1955), 287–299.

of an appropriation to a state's residents and the second, with the estimation of the cost to a state's residents of a Federal expenditure program.

In the estimation of program benefits in his article on Federal grants-in-aid, Schaller appears to ignore the fact that the programs with which he is dealing have a double-barreled income effect.[10] That is, such programs affect regional incomes both through the initial expenditure and also through the benefits yielded by the projects over a long period of time. It is the latter of these two effects that Schaller neglects.[11] He consequently assumes that the entire Federal expenditure accrues as income payments to residents of the state to which the appropriation was made and that this is the total effect of the expenditure on the state's per capita income. Such a position only describes the real benefit of such an expenditure to a state's residents if (1) the expenditure accrues as income only to the residents of the state which receives the appropriation, that is, if there are no expenditure leakages, (2) the factors of production receiving the payment are drawn from the ranks of the unemployed and would have remained there if it were not for the expenditure, (3) there are no multiplier effects attributable to the spending of the increased incomes, and (4) the benefits from the outputs of the project are either nil or accrue entirely to non-state residents.[12]

10. The programs referred to are, for example, the Federal highway program, hospital construction, veterans housing, homes for disabled veterans, agriculture experiment stations, A and M colleges, marine schools, and the Federal airport program.

11. It is a possible alternative that Schaller was thinking of the initial investment cost of the projects as measuring the flow of benefits of the projects to the state's residents. This approach then implicitly assumes that the initial expenditure merely diverts resources (yielding an initial effect of zero) and that the initial investment cost of the projects equals the present value of the stream of expected benefits. Insofar as it is this sort of framework under which Schaller is operating, it would appear more appropriate to use the benefit estimates themselves (if available) rather than using a dummy variable in which all deviations from the simplified conditions required to make the conclusion true must be assumed away.

12. The type of expenditure program treated both in this study and in Schaller's, with its reliance on heavy construction equipment and materials such as steel and cement, imply substantial non-state expenditures or leakages negating the reality of condition (1). Insofar as this is true, Schaller's estimate overstates the direct income effect on a state. Because the postwar

Inasmuch as none of these conditions appears realistic, the approach in this study is substantially different. With the assumption that the initial income effect is zero, the long-run benefits produced by the project are accepted as an estimate of the value of the appropriation to a state. The conditions upon which this is based are similar in nature to those necessary for Schaller's method, but they appear to be a great deal more appropriate in forming an estimate for projects possessing such a dual impact. These conditions are: (1) the project benefits accrue only to the residents of the state; that is, there is no leakage of benefits; (2) the additional expected benefit resulting from a project creates no additional multiplier effects; and (3) the income effects from the initial expenditure, inasmuch as they do more than merely divert resources, accrue entirely to non-state residents.

Because the benefits of a rivers and harbors or flood control project appear to be more regionally oriented than the expenditure, condition (1) as used in this study appears more realistic than Schaller's condition (1). Inasmuch as there are such benefit leakages, the error will be offset by ignoring the direct income effects emphasized and, in all likelihood, overstated by Schaller. That is, the overestimation of one of the income effects will be compensated for by the underestimation of the other. Also, because the estimates of project benefits used in this study are based on the concepts of alternative cost and imputed market value limited

---

period has been one of relatively full employment, condition (2) also appears weak. An estimate of direct benefit in the case that factors were merely diverted would necessitate an estimation of the differences in the rates of remuneration of productive factors caused by the Federal expenditure combined with the variation in the pattern of resource allocation in the state caused by the same expenditure. Inasmuch as there was mere diversion, Schaller's estimate again overstates the direct income effect. The inevitable existence of multiplier effects and the consequent negation of condition (3) causes Schaller's estimate to be an understatement of the direct income effect. However, because of both first and second round income leakages and the existence of the mere diversion of factors, these multiplier effects are not likely to be substantial. Consequently, the use of the expenditure figure as an estimate of direct income effects in all probability substantially overstates the real value of this effect. This in combination with the complete failure to include the longer-run outputs yielded by the projects (which appear to be larger than the original appropriation and far less geographically disperse) implies that Schaller's method probably understates the combined, double-barreled effect of the expenditure.

by the recipients' willingness to pay,[13] there is no need of a condition corresponding to Schaller's condition (2). Finally, because present consumption expenditures are not affected to any great extent by the receipt of future expected benefits, the multiplier effects will tend to be rather small, implying a small departure from reality of this study's condition (2).[14]

Consequently, the use of project benefits as an estimate of the value of Federal expenditure appears justified in that the overstatement which results from the leakages of benefits to non-state residents is offset by the omission of Schaller's direct income effect. If the amount of benefit leakages were equal to the direct income effects (which as noted previously are probably overstated by the appropriation figure), the estimate of project benefits as used in this study would, in fact, be correct.

The second modification of Schaller's approach is a great deal more basic. In both the article on veterans' transfer payments and the article on Social Security transfer payments, Schaller speaks of income redistribution without reference to the source of the Federal out-payment, that is, without reference to the costs which must be borne by a state's residents in support of the Federal program.[15] For example, if he found that New York received $8 per capita from a given Federal expenditure program and Georgia received $4 per capita, he would conclude that the program had led to an increased disparity in state per capita incomes. If, in fact, New York had contributed $10 per capita to the program in the form of taxes and Georgia had contributed but $2, Schaller's method would still lead him to claim an increased disparity of state per

13. Eckstein, *Water Resource Development*, p. 52.

14. This implicitly assumes the acceptance of the standard Keynesian consumption function in which marginal consumption expenditures are regarded as a function of additional current income. For a different and somewhat longer-run view see William Hamburger, "The Determinants of Aggregate Consumption," *Review of Economic Studies*, XXII (No. 1, 1954), 23–34.

15. Schaller, "Veterans Transfer Payments and State Per Capita Incomes, 1929, 1939, and 1949," *op. cit.*, p. 327. "This method assumes that the gross amounts of the veterans payments contribute to differences in state per capita incomes. Thus, the effects of the transfers are the result of state differences in the number of transfer recipients per capita and/or in the size of the payment per recipient." See also Schaller, "Social Security Transfer Payments and Differences in State Per Capita Incomes, 1929, 1939, and 1949," *op. cit.*, p. 84.

capita incomes when, in fact, the disparity has been reduced. This conclusion results from considering only the Federal outlays and ignoring the sources of the outlays.

To correct this defect, the present study will consider both the benefits to a state's residents resulting from the Federal outlay and the costs (in the form of taxes) borne by the state's residents in support of the program. Through this approach, the error of considering only the gross effects of the program is eliminated, and thereby the net benefit of the program to the state is isolated.

This method, then, combines the concept of an income redistribution function with direct estimates of the returns and costs to a state's residents attributable to the Corps General Construction program.[16] By first presenting a general income redistribution function and then refining it to fit the situation at hand, an estimate of the real exchange of income can be made. Such a function for any given region, x, would be:

$$I_x = R_x - C_x \qquad (1)$$

in which I_x is the net income redistribution to region x from a given Federal program, R_x is the gross return derived by the residents of this region from the program, and C_x is the actual cost levied upon this group to obtain the return. This concept of income redistribution deviates somewhat from the commonly accepted concept. Whereas the common meaning connotes the existence of a fixed stock of whatever is being redistributed (so that a loss to one group necessitates an equivalent gain to another), the present concept does not. Moreover, the concept as used here deals with only one of the two or more groups involved. That is, if a group enters a transaction and if, from the transaction, it receives in value more than it is forced to give up, this method would lead to the conclusion that income is redistributed toward that group.

If it is tentatively assumed that both the returns from and charges for the program occur during a period of time in which the group involved is indifferent to the time pattern of returns and charges, say a single moment of time, the determination of the

16. It should be noted that the analysis presented in this section excludes activity under the Mississippi River budget.

variables in the function would be greatly facilitated. In such a case, the returns would be equal to the maximum amount which the recipients of the outputs would be willing to pay in order to receive them (i.e., the area under the aggregate demand curve for the outputs) and the charges would be equal to the out-of-pocket costs to the group in that moment of time.

In the absence of such an abstraction, the simplified world of purity vanishes and the world of the best estimate comes to take its place. Presuming then that such indifference to time patterns does not exist, it is essential that the earlier function (1) be modified to incorporate an allowance for time preference. One such feasible modification would be to measure both the group's willingness to pay for program outputs and the necessary charges required from the group to secure these returns as the group would view them at a given moment in time. In this case, the function would become

$$I_{xt} = P(R_x)_t - P(C_x)_t \qquad (2)$$

Thus, the net redistribution of income to group x attributable to a given program as evaluated at time t (I_{xt}) equals the present value of the stream of gross benefits to the group evaluated at time t $[P(R_x)_t]$ less the present value of the stream of costs borne by the group also evaluated at time t $[P(C_x)_t]$

If this general approach to the empirical estimation of regional impact is accepted, both the several measurement problems encountered and the approximations used in the remainder of the study must be explicitly stated and analyzed. First, consider the income supplementing term of the equation $[P(R_x)_t]$. For an empirical purist, such a measurement of present real value poses an impossible task for the discipline in its present state of development because the concept of real value can only be approached through an evaluation of the willingness to pay of the recipients of the outputs, including the empirically unmeasurable concept of consumers' surplus. Moreover, as soon as the concept value is mentioned, the existence of a price is implied. If this price is to be a meaningful concept in the analysis, it must be a perfectly competitive price determined in the market by producers who maximize nothing but profit and by consumers who maximize only utility and which price equals the marginal cost of production. Also, the measurement of psychic gain through the tool of an aggregate demand curve necessitates constancy in the marginal utility of income to consumers. Still further, because the estimate is to be made at a given point in time, an appropriate interest rate must be used to discount the expected future stream of benefits. To accurately estimate the real effect, this rate must reflect the social rate of time preference of the beneficiaries of the project. Finally, the effects of the program outputs, both direct and indirect, must be confined to the region within which the project is located.

The extreme problems which these conditions pose for a single project—to say nothing of an entire program—call for several reasonable approximations to be made to ensure practical measurability. First, it is assumed that the present value of the expected stream of outputs at the time of project construction approximates the willingness to pay for these outputs by the recipients of them. This present value figure is computed from the estimate of annual project benefits as used by the Corps in their benefit-cost analyses and was secured from the eleven southern district Corps offices for each of the 163 projects used in the study.[17] This estimate is then allocated to the state in which the project is located during the period of project construction. The proportion of total present value allocated in any given year is determined by the fraction of the total Federal construction cost of the project which was appropriated in that year. The pitfalls which accompany the use of this data are well known and recognized, but, because no other more accurate yet feasible alternative is in sight, this Corps data is accepted as an adequate approximation of the real value of project outputs.[18] Second, because of the need to discount an estimated stream of expected future project outputs to secure an approximation of real present value, an appropriate rate of time preference must be obtained. Because of the impossibility of obtaining the time preference pattern of the beneficiary group of every project, this

17. A list of these projects together with some relevant information on each is presented as Appendix C.

18. For a discussion of estimation techniques and their limitations, see Eckstein, *op. cit.*, pp. 110–258.

must also be a reasonable surrogate. Consequently, a rate of 4.5 percent is accepted as an estimate of the national rate of time preference and is used to approximate the regional rate of time preference.[19] Finally, it must be assumed that the economy is operating at full employment so that the initial expenditure merely diverts resources and that the benefits yielded by the projects are confined to the residents of the region within which the project is located, which expected benefits yield no secondary multiplier effects.[20]

In evaluating the necessary charges to the region, that is, the income depleting term of the function $[P(C_x)_t]$, the method of estimation and the assumptions upon which it is based must again be made explicit. The necessary charges which are borne by southern states attributable to the postwar Corps program appear to fall into two mutually exclusive categories: those charges borne directly and those borne indirectly. Of those charges borne directly, two types can be distinguished: (1) the initial out-of-pocket charges borne locally and (2) those future operation costs for which local interests assume responsibility. Two types of indirect charges can also be distinguished: (1) those Federal taxes borne

19. William L. Miller, "The Magnitude of the Discount Rate for Government Projects," *Southern Economic Journal*, XXVIII (April, 1962), 348–356. Miller's study is a modification of a study by Otto Eckstein in which he estimated the proper rate to be 5.5 percent for the year 1955. See Krutilla and Eckstein, *Multiple Purpose River Development*, pp. 78–133.

20. In performing the actual calculation, a minimum and maximum estimate were made for the present value of estimated project benefits to make some allowance for price level changes during the period of construction. The higher of the two estimates is based on the assumption that the relationship between inputs and outputs is a physical relationship correctly estimated by the Corps and expressed in monetary terms. Any deviation of actual from estimated construction cost is therefore assumed to be a simple price level change affecting both inputs and outputs uniformly. The Corps claims that, during a postwar period which they analyzed, 57.8 percent of such cost differences were attributable to such price level changes. See U.S. Army Corps of Engineers, *Report on the Federal Civil Works Program as Administered by the Corps of Engineers*, 1952, pp. 93–102. The lower of the two estimates is based on the assumption that all deviations of the actual construction cost from the expected construction cost were a result of only construction material price changes. Inasmuch as actual deviations are caused by a combination of both of these factors, the correct estimate must lie within the range dictated by this maximum and minimum. Thus, in the statistical results presented later in the study, the benefit estimates are medians of the maximum and minimum estimates.

by each state in support of total Corps General Construction appropriations and (2) the state's share of future estimated operation costs on all Corps projects for which the Federal government assumes responsibility.[21] As with the income supplementing term of the equation, the empirical estimation of these variables is most problematical. Questions of real value, interest rates, and allocation of burden again pose insurmountable problems to the empirical purist. Again, reliance must be placed on manageable, yet reasonably accurate, approximations.

The method used in the study to estimate the direct costs to a state's residents is fairly straightforward. For both the initial out-of-pocket costs and the locally borne, future operation costs, the Corps of Engineers estimates at the time of project construction are used. The present value figure for the future charges is again obtained by using the 4.5 percent rate of interest. As with the regional benefit estimate, the proportion of the total present value of a project's direct costs which are allocated to the region in any given year is determined by the fraction of the total Federal construction cost which was appropriated to the project in that year.

Estimation of the indirect regional charges requires a rather more complicated technique. To estimate those Federal taxes borne by the residents of any given state in support of each year's Federal appropriation to the Corps General Construction program, the modification of the Groves's technique used earlier is again ac-

21. There is one additional cost which falls into neither of these categories, namely those costs which are payments for project benefits. Of the total annual benefits which resulted from the construction of the 163 southern projects, about 20 percent were of this reimbursable nature. However, because the reimbursements accrue to the general fund of the treasury, they cannot be allocated to any one function or group but rather belong to the entire body of taxpayers. Because the national expected gain from these payments equals the national expected loss, the net gain (or loss) to any given region within the nation depends upon the relationship of the relative incidence of total expected reimbursable costs to the relative incidence of Federal taxes (assuming that such reimbursable collections will, because they accrue to the general fund of the treasury, reduce Federal taxes in proportion to regional Federal tax incidence). By assuming that the regional incidence of the reimbursable costs of Corps projects is identical to the regional incidence of Federal taxes, such payments were excluded from the study. Consequently, because of the relatively small Federal tax load borne by the South combined with the relative concentration of the Corps program in the southern states, the study in all probability overstates the net impact figures to some, rather small extent.

cepted.[22] Through this approach, the proportion of the total Federal tax burden which is borne by each state for any given year can be estimated. By assuming (1) that a state's residents contribute to any Federal program in proportion to their contribution to the total Federal tax take and (2) that the marginal and average Federal tax burdens on any given state are equal, the necessary charges paid by a state's residents in support of Corps construction in any given year can be estimated.

The concept of the individual state's share of future Federal operation costs arises as the Federal government, when constructing certain projects, commits itself to an annual expenditure of operating charges for the life of these projects. In any given year, therefore, the Federal commitment is increased by the present value of the future operating charges for those projects on which construction was commenced in that year.[23] Thus, for any given state, the burden of this annual commitment is the share of the Federal present value which it must bear. The modification of Groves's technique was again used to estimate this commitment.

The following, slightly simplified example will illustrate specifically the approach used in the study. The question which is posed is the following: in any given year (say 1959) how did a given state (say North Carolina) fare when the value at time t (1959) of what it received from the program is compared to the value at time t (1959) of what it contributed? In 1959, North Carolina received construction appropriations on only one project,

22. See Appendix A.
23. In estimating the present value of the annual Federal commitment, the following approach was used: First, the arithmetic mean of the ratio of annual Federal operating costs to estimated Federal investment cost weighted by Federal construction expenditure was computed from Corps data for the entire body of projects constructed in the South since the war:

$$\bar{X}_w = \Sigma [C_t \cdot (O_t/K_t)]/\Sigma C_t$$

when C_t is the Federal construction expenditure for a given project and (O_t/K_t) is the ratio of Federally borne, annual operating costs to estimated Federal investment costs. This mean ratio was then accepted as the best guess of the ratio for the entire Corps program during this period. From this mean ratio (which was .008 in the study), the present value of the annual Federal commitment of future operating costs was determined for each year's Federal construction appropriation. This present value figure was, finally, taken as an estimate of the expected cost to the body of taxpayers at time t (the time of the construction appropriation) of this additional commitment.

the Manteo Bay project. The total estimated Federal cost of this project was $1,145,000, but $1,339,000 or 117 percent of the estimated cost was actually spent in constructing the project. The benefits to be yielded from this project were estimated by the Corps to be $228,485 annually for a period of 50 years, which when discounted at an annual rate of 4.5 percent yields a present value of $4,515,000. In 1959, $722,000 was appropriated or 54 percent of the total appropriation. From this data then, the present value of benefits in 1959 was estimated to be $2,645,000. This value represents the estimate for the $P(R_x)_{1959}$ term in the redistribution function. For the $P(C_x)_{1959}$ term, the following items make up the total estimate: 54 percent of total local construction costs or $6,000; 54 percent of the present value of local operation, maintenance, and repair costs or $4,000; 1.256 percent (North Carolina's share of the total Federal tax burden) of total Corps General Construction appropriations in 1959 or $7,804,000; and 1.256 percent of the present value of the additional Federal commitment for future operating costs in 1959 or $1,234,000—all of which totals $9,048,000. Thus, it is concluded that, in 1959, North Carolina experienced a net benefit of —$6,403,000 from the program, the amount by which $P(C_x)_t$ exceeds $P(R_x)_t$.

From both the theoretical and illustrative discussion of the net benefit function then, it is clear that a numerous and complex set of forces interact to determine the regional impact of a Federal expenditure program. In attempting to summarize some of the more obvious of these forces, the major determinants of the two elemental terms of the net benefit function are defined. First, consider the gross benefit term of the equation. For any region, this term depends upon two primary variables: (1) the amount of the appropriation received by projects in that region during a period of time and (2) the productivity of those projects. That is, the gross value of the program to a region is a function of both the number and size of the projects constructed in the region and the returns per unit of cost of those projects. Second, the major determinants of the cost term of the equation must react through the four sub-terms of which total regional cost is composed. These sub-terms are: (1) the initial charges borne locally, (2) the present value of future charges borne locally, (3) the region's share of Federal taxes in support of national Corps construction appropriations, and (4) the region's share of the present value of the Federal commitment of future operation costs of all projects constructed under the Corps program. Thus, the major abstract determinants of the size of this composite term are some combination of the size of the total Corps program, the income level of the region in question (upon which the regional Federal tax burden depends), the proportion of both initial and future costs which the region bears for its own projects and, finally, the proportion of future costs which the Federal government bears on all of the projects which it constructs under the program.

The results secured from this approach applied to all of the 163 projects are presented in Tables 13 through 15. With these results, three facets of the program's regional impact are discussed. First, the absolute gross and net benefits and costs of the program to the ten southern states are presented; second, the gross and net per capita benefits and costs to these states are analyzed; and finally, the trend of net benefits over time to the entire region is discussed.

In Table 13, a substantial net redistribution of income in favor of the South is shown to have taken place through the Corps program. As the figures demonstrate, the General Construction appropriation of about 1.5 billion dollars (see Table 15) to the ten states yielded about 2.3 billion dollars in gross benefits or about 150 percent of the value of the appropriation. After the necessary program charges of nearly a billion dollars, which were borne by the states, have been deducted, the net impact of the program on the southern region totals something over 1.3 billion dollars.

As for individual southern states, the results are extremely varied. In both gross and net benefit estimates, Kentucky appears to have been the state most favorably affected, displaying a gross gain of 500 million dollars and a net gain of 400 million dollars. The residents of two lowest states, Mississippi and North Carolina, actually contributed a larger amount to the program than they received from it, experiencing losses of about 24 million and 56 million dollars, respectively. The three states which reaped the highest net benefit (Kentucky, Arkansas, and Louisiana) experi-

TABLE 13

Returns and Costs to Ten Southern States
From the Corps of Engineers General Construction Program, 1946 to 1962

State	Gross Returns [a]	Costs	Net Returns [a]
	Thousands of Dollars		
Alabama	156,253 (7)	76,459	79,794 (7)
Arkansas	337,167 (3)	47,319	289,848 (2)
Florida	341,312 (2)	218,190	123,122 (6)
Georgia	232,799 (5)	107,118	125,681 (5)
Kentucky	494,651 (1)	98,012	396,639 (1)
Louisiana	307,134 (4)	112,692	194,442 (3)
Mississippi	15,160 (10)	39,039	–23,879 (9)
North Carolina	60,610 (9)	116,394	–55,784 (10)
South Carolina	127,070 (8)	48,145	78,925 (8)
Tennessee	229,794 (6)	98,584	131,210 (4)
Ten-State Region	2,301,950	961,952	1,339,998

a. Each state's rank is in parenthesis after the estimate.

enced a total net gain of nearly 900 million dollars or two thirds of the total for the ten-state area. On the other hand, the lowest three states (South and North Carolina and Mississippi) taken together experienced a net loss with only South Carolina receiving a positive impact. Finally, the case of Florida presents an interesting example of the divergence between net and gross impact. Although it ranked second in terms of gross benefits with an estimate of over 340 million dollars, it ranks sixth in terms of net benefits with nearly two thirds of the gross benefit figure absorbed in necessary charges. Because a large proportion of the total state costs are absorbed by Federal tax commitment (which is itself based on state income), Florida ranks relatively low in relation to the rest of the South in net impact; it bears nearly 25 percent of the total southern tax burden.

Whereas Table 13 is a presentation of the distribution of absolute benefits, Table 14 shows the distribution of per capita effects; a similar yet somewhat different picture is seen. Again, it is evident that the southern region experienced a substantial positive impact from the program. If the costs of the program are ignored, the South received nearly $75 per person. After the costs of participating in the program are accounted for, the net per capita effect is greater than $43.

TABLE 14

Per Capita Returns and Costs to Ten Southern States
From the Corps of Engineers General Construction Program, 1946 to 1962

State	Per Capita Gross Returns [a]	Per Capita Costs	Per Capita Net Returns [a]
		Dollars	
Alabama	49.47 (8)	24.27	25.20 (8)
Arkansas	182.55 (1)	25.61	156.94 (1)
Florida	87.27 (4)	55.79	31.48 (7)
Georgia	62.92 (6)	28.95	33.97 (6)
Kentucky	164.77 (2)	32.65	132.12 (2)
Louisiana	102.86 (3)	37.74	65.12 (3)
Mississippi	6.97 (10)	17.95	−10.98 (9)
North Carolina	14.06 (9)	27.00	−12.94 (10)
South Carolina	56.33 (7)	21.35	34.98 (5)
Tennessee	66.82 (5)	28.67	38.15 (4)
Ten-State Region	74.77	31.26	43.51

a. Each state's rank is in parenthesis after the estimate.

In analyzing the per capita impact on individual states, Arkansas is seen to be the top state with gross returns of $182 per person and net gains of $157 per person. The effect of this Federal program actually cost the average resident of North Carolina $13 and the average resident of Mississippi $11. Also, it is seen that on a per capita basis, only the top three states have benefited more than the region as a whole, while the seven lowest states have a net benefit figure below that of the entire region. Finally, the effect of the relatively greater Federal tax burden carried by Floridians is again evident in Table 14, as per capita costs of the program to Florida residents are double the per capita costs to the rest of the region. Whereas Florida ranks fourth in the gross per capita benefit figure, it ranks seventh when allowance is made for necessary charges.

The postwar trend in the level of appropriations and the gross and net impact of the program on the South is shown in Table 15. The effects of the Eisenhower policy of "no new starts" and the curtailment of expenditures during the Korean War are clearly visible. From 1950 to 1959, none of the series display any trend whatsoever. Only in recent years has the program regained the rapid growth which it displayed in the immediate postwar period.

TABLE 15

Annual Appropriations and Returns to Ten Southern States From the Corps of Engineers General Construction Program, 1946 to 1962

Fiscal Year	Appropriations	Gross Returns	Net Returns
	Millions of Dollars		
1946	25.6	32.6	16.8
1947	47.0	66.5	44.0
1948	55.6	82.9	43.8
1949	86.8	126.0	73.3
1950	100.0	150.9	92.3
1951	102.6	154.6	93.2
1952	91.9	146.5	88.0
1953	69.3	99.1	47.9
1954	53.2	71.2	36.8
1955	58.1	88.2	49.6
1956	70.5	11.2	56.1
1957	80.2	131.6	73.5
1958	68.6	106.0	47.4
1959	112.1	163.2	85.9
1960	150.7	229.9	142.9
1961	165.0	268.9	170.3
1962	169.7	272.6	175.3
Total	1506.9	2301.9	1340.0

Thus, the use of this income redistribution function has defined three important phenomena. First, it is clear that the South has experienced a substantial and favorable redistribution of income as evidenced by the positive net benefit figures. Second, this impact has affected individual states in an extremely diverse manner, with some states reaping a large positive impact and some states experiencing losses. Finally, the trend of both appropriations and net benefits to the South has been upward with the decade of the 1950's displaying remarkable stability.

5

An Analysis of Allocative Efficiency

IN RECENT years, the form of the existing investment criterion used by the Federal government has undergone substantial scrutiny in the work of several professional economists.[1] These studies had as their goal a refinement of the objective efficiency criterion used by those Federal agencies concerned with the evaluation of investment opportunities.[2] Consequently, the embryonic form of the existing criterion was extended, modified, and, in one case, completely abandoned by the criteria which they proposed. This study is an application of these indisputably superior criteria to the postwar Corps of Engineers water resource projects in the ten southern states. Through this approach an attempt will be made to estimate the misallocation of Federal funds and national resources in this area caused by the application of the existing agency criterion. The analysis will be presented in the following five stages: (1) a discussion of the existing criterion and the criticisms which surround it, (2) an analysis of the proposals suggested in the studies cited, (3) a discussion of the application of these proposals to the projects and the assumptions upon which such an application rests, (4) the presentation of the evidence concerning the effect of the application of the proposed criteria on the projects, and (5) an estimation

1. Primarily Eckstein, *Water Resource Development;* McKean, *Efficiency in Government;* Krutilla and Eckstein, *Multiple Purpose River Development;* and Hirshleifer, De Haven, and Milliman, *Water Supply,* to mention only the main contributors.
2. Because the U.S. Army Corps of Engineers and the Bureau of Reclamation were the primary agencies concerned with such evaluation, these studies centered about water resource investment decisions. See Federal Inter-Agency Committee on Water Resources, *Proposed Practices,* 1958; U.S. Bureau of the Budget, *Circular A-47;* and President's Water Resources Council, The, *Policies, Standards, and Procedures.*

of the misallocation of national resources resulting from the construction of economically unjustified projects as determined by the proposed criteria.

Present Benefit-Cost Analysis and Its Deficiencies

In the analysis of the worthwhileness of any long-lived capital purchase, an evaluation of the streams of costs and returns is a necessary element. However, there is no universal technique by which these streams can be evaluated and compared. With each interpretation of the investor's stipulated goal and with each definition of his constrained variable, a different and unique criterion emerges. Thus, for example, the corporation decision-maker defines his goal to be (in all likelihood) maximum profits, stipulates his constrained variable to be the capital budget, and then develops a criterion to isolate that set of proposed projects which both maximizes his goal and exhausts his constrained budget.

In general, this sort of process is appropriate for governmental as well as private decision-making. However, because the government is a social institution, both the goal and the constrained variable relevant to the private sector lose their meaning. Consequently, in governmental investment analysis to secure economic efficiency, the goal of the program is taken to be the maximization of total national income and the constrained variable is defined as the social cost devoted to the support of the program and is largely represented by the budget of some governmental unit. Because this study is concerned specifically with economic efficiency, all of the criteria dealt with are designed to point to that set of projects which will maximize the expected increases in national income resulting from any governmental expenditure (national cost).

At present, the criterion applied by the Corps of Engineers in project evaluation is known as the benefit-cost ratio, and it takes the following form:

$$Z = \frac{\sum \frac{B}{(1+i)^t}}{K + \sum \frac{O}{(1+i)^t}} \tag{1}$$

in which B is the expected annual benefit in the form of additions to national income from a project, i is the rate of interest used to discount the future streams of benefits and costs, t is the estimated life of the project, K is the fixed investment cost, and O is the estimated annual operation, maintenance, and repair costs. Since 1946, the expected streams of benefits and costs have been evaluated by an interest rate which has fluctuated between 2.5 and 3 percent. The length of project life used for evaluation during this period has typically been 50 years. If, for any given project, the calculated benefit-cost ratio exceeds unity, the project becomes eligible for Congressional authorization. In the law, no mention is made of the possible existence of a budget which is unable to cover all projects bearing a ratio greater than unity.

For several reasons, economists have found that this approach and its application possess substantial deficiencies. The most serious criticism questions the appropriateness of the criterion itself, i.e., the benefit-cost ratio, whereas other criticisms raise doubts concerning the parameters which the Corps applies in evaluating future benefit and cost streams, namely, the rate of interest and the present treatment of risk and uncertainty.

A judgment on the nature of the correct investment criterion rests upon both the goal which the investment must attempt to maximize and the constrained variable which is used to secure attainment of the goal. The benefit-cost criterion has incurred criticism with respect to the definition of both of these concepts.

The most severe criticism of this criterion has been made by Roland McKean.[3] In a rather succinct and pointed analysis, he has offered strong criticisms of both the relevant budget constraint embodied in the benefit-cost ratio (the total "expenditure of money") and the definition of the goal which the ratio attempts to fulfill (the maximization of the present value of the future income stream created by the expenditure). With respect to the constrained variable, his criticism takes this form:

Should we turn to a total-cost budget embracing operating expenses for future periods? No, the problem, for either a government agency or a businessman, is not really the allocation of such a budget.[4]

3. McKean, *op. cit.*, pp. 74–96 and 103–134.
4. *Ibid.*, p. 114.

And, with rejection of the definition of the constrained variable, he automatically (and of necessity) rejects the definition of the quantity to be maximized, i.e., the program goal.[5]

A somewhat different approach, but one which also criticizes the efficacy of the existing criterion, has been presented more recently by Stephen Marglin.[6] His criticism is based on the proposition that benefit-cost analysis, by attempting to maximize a future income stream, has implicitly posited a social goal that is only partially acceptable. Because the populace is interested not only in the absolute size of the national income but also its division and composition, he feels that a criterion which embodies only the concept of absolute size (even though it may be the most important of the community's desires) will lead to a choice of projects which again is not optimum from the standpoint of national welfare. Consequently, rather than making use of a criterion with but a single objective (such as the maximization of national income), Marglin suggests an approach which makes allowance for dual or multiple objectives.

A second area of criticism leveled against the present benefit-cost technique concerns the rate of interest applied in the discounting of future streams of benefits and costs. Current Corps of Engineers manuals stipulate that "average long-term interest rates that will prevail over the life of a project are considered the proper basis for discounting future benefits and costs." [7] This rate, identified as the long-term government bond rate, is also suggested by the "Green Book," [8] the Bureau of the Budget,[9] the 1955 Presidential Advisory Committee on Water Resources Policy,[10] and

5. *Ibid.*, p. 84.
6. Maass, Hufschmidt, *et al.*, *Design of Water Resource Systems*, pp. 18 ff., and U.S. Bureau of the Budget, *Standards and Criteria for Formulating and Evaluating Federal Water Resources Development*, pp. 62–70. For a similar kind of criticism see the Epilogue to this study.
7. U.S. Army, Corps of Engineers, *Survey Investigations and Reports*, EM 1120-2-118 (mimeographed instructions in the district offices of Corps of Engineers).
8. Federal Inter-Agency Committee on Water Resources, *op. cit.*, p. 23.
9. U.S. Bureau of the Budget, *Circular A-47*, p. 14.
10. President's Advisory Committee on Water Resources Policy, The, *Water Resources Policy*, 1955, p. 27.

most recently, by the President's Water Resources Council.[11]

This rate is rationalized on two grounds. First, it is claimed that the conceptual rate of interest appropriate for use by the Federal government is the social cost of capital, i.e., ". . . the risk-free return expected to be realized on capital invested in alternative uses." [12] Second, because the government can borrow funds at the going long-term government bond rate, it is claimed that this rate is an accurate estimate of the social cost of capital. Eckstein and others have demonstrated that two facets of this line of argument are fallacious. Relying on the oft-stated truth concerning the difference between lender's and borrower's risk, Eckstein has demonstrated the necessary conceptual divergence of the rate on long-term government issues from the social cost of capital.[13] In a separate statistical study, he has demonstrated that the actual bond rate falls far short of the real opportunity cost of capital as determined by its value in an alternative use.[14]

Present Federal interest rate policy has been attacked on other grounds as well. These criticisms, rather than objecting to the numerical value of the existing rate, are based upon the conviction that the conceptual meaning attached to the rate of interest by the Federal government is in error. According to McKean, the proper rate of interest should not necessarily portray the social cost of capital as the government claims, but rather that rate of interest should be chosen which will assure ". . . the maximum yield over the planning period, i.e., maximum growth of asset values through the period." [15] Yet another view of the proper purpose of the interest rate is presented by Eckstein and Bain. Rather than a rate reflecting either the social cost of capital or the rate suggested by McKean, they propose the use of an interest rate which ". . . reflects the relative evaluation by the populace of current or earlier income foregone and future or later income gained," i.e., a social rate of time preference.[16]

11. President's Water Resources Council, The, *op. cit.*, p. 12.
12. Federal Inter-Agency Committee on Water Resources, *op. cit.*, p. 24.
13. Eckstein, *op. cit.*, pp. 94 ff.
14. Krutilla and Eckstein, *op. cit.*, pp. 78–127.
15. McKean, *op. cit.*, p. 84.
16. Joe S. Bain, "Criteria for Undertaking Water-Resource Developments,"

Finally, criticism of present evaluation procedures has also cited the treatment of risk and uncertainty components in future streams of costs and benefits. Critics point out that the existing procedure possesses no rigorous or consistent treatment of either risk or uncertainty but rather applies a variety of techniques such as "conservative estimates of benefits," contingency allowances in the estimation of investment costs, and arbitrary limits on the period of analysis. None of these techniques are specifically capable of isolation and evaluation by the decision-maker.[17]

Because of the built-in tendency to overestimate future benefits,[18] the well-recognized underestimation of construction costs in spite of the contingency allowances,[19] and the general lack of a well-defined approach toward the problem, the adjustment for risk and uncertainty is both ephemeral and inconsistent.

Proposals for Revision of Evaluation Procedures

Concurrent with the above-mentioned criticisms came a spate of proposals intended to correct the inadequacies of the present approach. These proposals ranged over the entire field, modifying

---

American Economic Review, L (May, 1960), 315–316. See also Eckstein, *op. cit.*, pp. 99–101.

17. Eckstein, *op. cit.*, pp. 81–91 and 149–160.

18. One of the most significant sources of bias in the estimation of the expected benefit stream enters because of the excessive inclusion of secondary or indirect benefits. Examples of such benefits include reduction of losses of wage payments because of the control of flooding and the increase of property values because of the increased activity caused by navigation improvements. Bias is also introduced by the use of rail rates instead of out-of-pocket rail costs in the estimation of navigation benefits. Elucidation of these and description of many more, less significant but also important, defects in the measurement procedure can be found in the following sources: Eckstein, *op. cit.*, pp. 110–258; U.S. Congress, Joint Economic Committee, *Federal Expenditure Policy*, article by Otto Eckstein, "Evaluation of Federal Expenditures for Water Resource Projects," pp. 657–667; and U.S. Commission on Organization of the Executive Branch of the Government, *Task Force Report*, pp. 126–145, 294–299, 789–821, 935–953, 1275–1299, and 1317–1395.

19. Vivid evidence is available concerning the deviation of actual construction costs from the estimated construction cost at the time the decision was made to construct the project, i.e., the time that it was included as a new start. See U.S. Congress, House, Committee on Public Works, *The Civil Functions Program of the Corps of Engineers, U.S. Army*, House Comm. Print No. 21, 82nd Congress, 2nd Session, 1952. In recent years, this deviation has been substantially reduced, but even today average actual construction cost exceeds the average estimated construction cost including the contingency allowance.

the form of the decision-making criterion, the parameters included in the criterion (the interest rate and the treatment of risk and uncertainty), and the procedures for forecasting a project's variables (benefits and costs). Because of their conceptual superiority, some of these suggestions are described and analyzed and then applied to actual project data.

THE INTEREST RATE CORRECTION (A). This suggestion accepts the basic benefit-cost ratio as an adequate criterion for choice. Objection is raised, however, to the exceptionally low rate of interest used by the Corps to evaluate future streams of benefits and costs. Rather than the long-term bond rate, this proposal claims that a more appropriate estimate of the social (or opportunity) cost of capital should be used. Because the budget committed to water resource development is raised through the taxation of private citizens and therefore any particular public project is constructed and maintained at the expense of its private alternative, this approach contends that national income can only be maximized if funds committed to public projects earn at least as high a return as their value in the private sector.[20] Consequently, the traditional benefit-cost ratio criterion incorporating an interest rate of 4.5 percent, estimated to be the social cost of capital by William L. Miller,[21] and an estimated length of project life of 50 years forms the essence of this correction.

Where B represents the estimated annual stream of benefits, O the estimated annual stream of operation, maintenance, and repair

20. If this concept is incorporated into the benefit-cost ratio criterion, the rate of return on all of the projects with a benefit-cost ratio greater than 1 will be larger than the measure of the social cost of capital which is used. Moreover, if the budget is sufficiently restricted, the social marginal productivity of water resource investment will be greater than the social cost of capital.

21. The opportunity cost of Federal investment was estimated by Eckstein for the year 1955 to be in the range of 5 or 6 percent. See Krutilla and Eckstein, *op. cit.*, pp. 78-130. Harberger, following a somewhat different method, suggests the use of a rate of interest in this same range. See U.S. Congress, Joint Economic Committee, *op. cit.*, article by Arnold C. Harberger, "The Interest Rate in Cost-Benefit Analysis," pp. 239-241. Miller, using a revision of Eckstein's technique, estimated the social cost of capital to be between 4 and 4.5 percent. This revised estimate is used in this test. See William L. Miller, *Southern Economic Journal*, pp. 348-356.

CARL A. RUDISILL LIBRARY
LENOIR RHYNE COLLEGE

costs, and K the investment cost, the traditional form of the benefit-cost ratio expressed earlier can be redefined as:

$$Z = \frac{B}{O + A_{1t}K} \qquad (2)$$

in which A_{1t} is the annual capital charge of both interest and amortization per dollar of investment costs. Given the rate of interest (i) and the length of project life (t), the numerical value of A_{1t} can be secured from a table, "Annuity whose Present Value is 1." [22]

THE ECKSTEIN-KRUTILLA PROPOSAL (B). Again, the traditional benefit-cost framework is preserved. However, in an attempt both to correct the deficiency of the interest rate concept used by the Corps and to preserve the "long-term perspective" of the resource development program, both the interest rate and the length of project life have been modified. Proposing use of the social cost of capital concept and accepting their estimate of this rate, Eckstein and Krutilla suggest that the expected benefit and cost streams be evaluated with a 5.5-percent rate of interest. To preserve the long-term perspective of the program, they suggest using a length of project life of 100 years instead of 50.[23]

THE ECKSTEIN PROPOSAL (C). Eckstein argues elsewhere that, because the program under consideration will provide its benefits to future generations, it is not at all certain that the cost of capital to the present generation provides the correct evaluation. Assuming that, as a nation, we ". . . prefer rejection of present intertemporal preferences in favor of a redistribution of income towards future generations," he proposes using the social rate of time preference in place of the opportunity cost of capital. He defines the social rate of time preference as that rate which a majority of the populace would choose as a guide to long-term investment projects whose income streams will go to large masses of population at a later

22. The numerical value of A_{1t} used in this test is .05060215.
23. Krutilla and Eckstein, *op. cit.* The numerical value of A_{1t} in this case is .05526132.

date.[24] Rather arbitrarily, Eckstein estimates this rate to be approximately 2.5 percent and proposes that projects be evaluated by a benefit-cost ratio which incorporates this rate.[25] However, to ensure that the entire Corps program earns a rate of return equal to his estimate of the opportunity cost of the funds committed (see footnote 21), he recommends that no project displaying a benefit-cost ratio smaller than 1.4 be accepted. The length of project life in this test is again assumed to be 50 years.

THE MCKEAN PROPOSAL (D). Whereas each of the preceding criteria views the relevant budget constraint to be the total "expenditure of money" and consequently aims at the maximization of the present value of the future income stream created by this expenditure, the McKean proposal has a rather different point of view on both the definition of the constrained variable and the quantity to be maximized. By assuming that the future national water resource construction budget is invariate with regard to the volume of necessary operating expenses arising from already constructed projects, McKean views the relevant constraint to be only the capital budget (K).[26] Moreover, he interprets the concept maximum national present value to mean the maximum growth of asset values throughout the period.[27]

With this definition of both the goal and the relevant budget constraint, McKean argues that the appropriate criterion is the internal rate of return rather than the benefit-cost ratio.[28] By apply-

24. See footnote 16.

25. Realizing the impossibility of empirically evaluating this rate, Bain agrees with Eckstein's choice by suggesting reliance "on the . . . cost of governmental funds as a conservative approximation." See Bain, *op. cit.*, p. 316.

26. It should be noted that McKean's argument for such a constraint is based on the judgment that both marketable (e.g. irrigation and power) and non-marketable (e.g. flood control) project benefits are, in some sense, current receipts available for reinvestment by the government. This judgment has been open to severe criticism. See Julius Margolis, "The Economic Evaluation of Federal Water Resource Development," *American Economic Review*, XLIX (March, 1959), 105 and John V. Krutilla, "Some Recent Developments in River Basin Planning and Evaluation," *Journal of Farm Economics*, XL (December, 1958), 1676.

27. This judgment is likewise doubtful. Is it true that the maximum growth of a water resource program is the desired goal of such a program?

28. The formulation for this test is:
$$A_{it} = (B - O)/K$$
Taking t to be 50 years, the value of the rate of return can be determined

ing the recommendation by Harberger which was cited previously that no project bearing a rate of return below 6 percent should be constructed, the McKean proposal, like the others, separates the projects into two groups: the accepted and the rejected.

A PROPOSED ADJUSTMENT FOR UNCERTAINTY (E). As with proposals concerning the criterion and the interest rate, the diversity of the various approaches to the treatment of risk and uncertainty is great. Broadly speaking, one can distinguish some five different proposals. These are: (1) a limit on the period of analysis suggested by the "Green Book" [29] and *Circular A-47* [30] and disposed of by Eckstein,[31] (2) the inclusion of direct and specific safety allowances proposed by the "Green Book" and concurred in by Eckstein (in the case of risks which are not a function of time), (3) the inclusion of a risk premium in *the* interest rate recommended by Eckstein (to allow for uncertainties related to time),[32] (4) a general case-by-case evaluation involving a description of contingencies, a schedule showing a possible range of outcomes, and an analysis of the public attitude toward the disutility (utility) of uncertainty bearing as recommended by McKean,[33] and (5) an approach which makes allowance for the fundamental differences in the nature of expectations concerning costs and benefits through a *dual* rate of interest.[34]

The final of these proposals, i.e., the dual interest rate proposal, although far from a complete treatment, does focus attention on a phase of the problem which has thus far been neglected, namely, the existence of disparate elements of uncertainty present in project costs and benefits. By assuming (1) that a single-valued criterion

---

from a table, "Annuity whose Present Value is 1." It has been pointed out by Hirshleifer that, under certain conditions, this criterion may not yield an unambiguous or unique solution. See Jack Hirshleifer, "On the Theory of Optimal Investment Decision," *Journal of Political Economy*, LXVI (August, 1958), 329–352, and Hirshleifer, De Haven, and Milliman, *op. cit.*, pp. 149, 154, 167, and 169–172.

29. Federal Inter-Agency Committee on Water Resources, *op. cit.*, pp. 22–25.
30. U.S. Bureau of the Budget, *Circular A-47*, p. 13.
31. Eckstein, *op. cit.*, pp. 81–86.
32. *Ibid.*, pp. 86–90.
33. McKean, *op. cit.*, pp. 58–103.
34. This proposal together with an analysis of the assumptions upon which it is based is presented in detail as Appendix B.

is capable of handling problems of risk and uncertainty, (2) that the concept of certainty equivalent is the correct approach in making an allowance for uncertainty, and (3) that the degree of social disutility is a positive function of the degree of uncertainty, the proposal treats this disparity through the insertion of a dual premium into the proper interest rate in the discounting of future costs and benefits. With the assumption that the benefit-cost ratio is the proper general form of the criterion and that a base interest rate of 4.5 percent equals the social cost of capital, a premium of 1 percent is added to the base rate in the discounting of future benefits and a premium of .5 percent is subtracted from the base in the discounting of future costs. Again, 50 years is taken to be the estimated length of project life.[35]

Application of the Proposed Criteria: Method and Assumptions

The conceptual superiority of these proposed criteria having been recognized, the criteria are now applied to the benefit-cost data of the projects already constructed or under construction in the ten southern states since 1946. All of the data is based upon substantial economic base studies as outlined in the Corps Manuals [36] and was obtained from the eleven district offices of the U.S. Army Corps of Engineers which are concerned with project evaluation in these states. Through these studies, estimates of future annual flows of benefits and operation, maintenance, and repair costs as well as

35. In defense of the size of the premium or discount chosen see Eckstein, *op. cit.*, pp. 86–90 and Miller, *op. cit.*, pp. 354–356. Because of the use of the dual rate of interest, the simpler formulation of the benefit-cost ratio as presented on p. 102 cannot be applied. In this case, the traditional form of the ratio must be used in which B, O, and K are defined in the same way but where i_1 is the rate of interest used to evaluate the stream of costs and i_2 is the rate used to evaluate the stream of benefits, i.e.,
$$Z = \Sigma[B/(1+i_2)^t]/K + \Sigma[O/(1+i_1)^t]$$
Given i_1 and i_2 and the length of project life, the factors by which B and O must be multiplied to yield their present value can be secured from a table, "Present Value of an Annuity." The value of the B factor is 16.931418, and the value of the O factor is 21.4821864. In all of these tests, the interest rate(s) is assumed constant for the entire 17-year period. In defense of this assumption see Krutilla and Eckstein, *op. cit.*, pp. 119–120.

36. U.S. Army, Corps of Engineers, *Survey Investigations and Reports*, EM 1120-2-101 (mimeographed instructions in the district offices of Corps of Engineers).

estimates of total investment cost were secured for each of the projects. This is the raw material to which the proposed efficiency criteria are applied in appraising the Corps program.

To illustrate the application of the tests described above, the Corps data for one of these projects will be presented and evaluated by each of the tests. The data used is that presented by the Corps for the Beaver Reservoir installation located in northwest Arkansas. The project was a new start in 1959, and by 1962 it had received some 14.5 million dollars in appropriations. At the time of the decision to construct the project, the Corps estimated that it would produce an annual stream of benefits (B) of $3,614,000, would require $1,182,000 annually in operation, maintenance, and repair costs (O), and $58,238,000 in original investment cost (K). Given this data, the Corps applied its benefit-cost ratio to the project using an interest rate of 2.5 percent and an estimated length of project life of 50 years. The resulting ratio which was presented to Congress was 1.10, which is quite acceptable under the law. By applying the five proposals to this same data, substantially different results appear. These results are presented in Table 16. In no case

TABLE 16

Results of the Proposals When Applied to the Beaver Reservoir Project

	Criteria	Computed Value
A	The Interest Rate Correction	.98
B	The Eckstein-Krutilla Proposal	.82
C	The Eckstein Proposal	1.12
D	The McKean Proposal	.042
E	The Uncertainty Allowance Proposal	.73

is the project found to be acceptable. Proposals A, B, and E each reject the project because it bears a benefit-cost ratio below 1, proposal C rejects it because it bears a benefit-cost ratio below the cut-off minimum of 1.4, and proposal D rejects it because its internal rate of return is below the cut-off minimum of 6 percent.

In performing such a re-evaluation, several necessary assumptions must be made. Because of the inability of economic science to measure the worth of certain phenomena, it should be noted that these intangibles are not included in the estimates of annual benefits or costs. Lives saved through flood control, the "costs" of increasing the size of the Federal government, and contributions of a project to the national defense effort are examples of such benefits (costs) which cannot be measured in dollar terms. It is, therefore, assumed that these intangibles are nonexistent. It is assumed further than the configuration of benefits and operating costs through time is as posited by the Corps, that the stream of values is constant and continuous and stops abruptly at the end of the estimated project life. Moreover, it is assumed that the projects are mutually exclusive and independent, i.e., that side calculations have already been made to determine the best combination of projects to be included in an entire river basin program.[37] In addition, it is assumed that the Corps estimates of benefits and costs are accurate [38] and that the estimated financial costs are adequate approximations of the opportunity costs to be incurred by society in the construction and maintenance of the projects.[39]

The Results of the Study

During the 17-year period from 1946 to 1962, 163 projects in the ten state area received Federal appropriations.[40] Of these 163 projects, 35 were still under construction at the close of fiscal year 1962. The total amount of Federal funds committed to these projects

37. When a project is started which is but an integral part of an entire river basin program, the data for the entire program at the time the project is started is used to evaluate the project rather than the data of the project alone.

38. The doubtful quality of this assumption is well known and recognized (See footnote 18). To simply assume that these estimates are accurate covers up a host of necessary assumptions made in calculating the estimated values— assumptions concerning price projections, population growth, future land use and value, future river tonnage, and future demand for power, to mention but a few.

39. This assumption may appear to be rather heroic, especially with respect to the labor market. However, because most of the labor employed in project construction is skilled labor drawn from a national labor market, the assumption may well be a realistic one even in the case of projects constructed in low income areas with underemployed human resources.

40. This figure excludes projects under the Mississippi River project which bears responsibility for flood control expenditures along the Mississippi. However, two large river basin complexes were broken down into their component parts, and each part was included as a separate project. The Apalachicola, Flint, and Chattahoochee project was divided into five segments and the Arkansas River project into two.

is approximately $2,687,942,000.[41] For 9 of the 163 projects, no benefit-cost computations were performed by the Corps of Engineers because project justification was based on noneconomic grounds. The committed Federal funds accounted for by these 9 projects are $9,339,000. On 7 additional projects, benefit-cost records were neither available from the Corps offices nor could they be secured from the documents or hearings. The Federal funds committed by these projects total $34,602,000. On the remaining 147 projects, the benefit-cost data was secured; it is this data to which the strict efficiency criteria described and discussed above have been applied. The Federal funds committed by this group of projects total $2,644,001,000 or 98.4 percent of the total. The results of the application of these criteria are summarized, together with the original Corps evaluation, in Tables 17 through 22.

TABLE 17

Original Benefit-Cost Ratios of Projects Constructed in Ten Southern States From 1946 to 1962 [a]

Benefit-Cost Ratio	Number of Projects	Federal Funds Committed, Thousands of Dollars	Percent of Total Federal Funds Committed
.60– .79	0	—	—
.80– .99	3	95,970	3.62
1.00–1.19	36	786,339	29.74
1.20–1.39	26	361,375	13.67
1.40–1.59	24	317,093	11.99
1.60–1.79	16	326,066	12.34
1.80–1.99	7	50,492	1.91
2.00–2.49	16	527,768	19.96
2.50–2.99	5	17,890	.68
3.00–4.99	11	147,885	5.59
5.00– or more	3	13,123	.50
	147	2,644,001	100.0

a. The length of project life is assumed to be 50 years unless specifically stipulated to be less by the Corps.

41. The concept of Federal funds committed is a rather hybrid quantity. It consists of the funds already appropriated to the projects plus the latest estimate of the necessary appropriations needed to complete the projects yet under construction.

Table 17 presents the benefit-cost ratios which faced the Congress at the time that the initial appropriation was made on each of the projects, that is, at the time that each project was a new start. Even under the Corps's own concept of efficiency, 3 projects were constructed in which the national outlay exceeded the expected return. Also, it is significant that by far the largest concentration of projects, both in absolute number and in Federal funds committed, is located at the very bottom end of the distribution—the range of benefit-cost ratios which even most liberal interpreters call marginal. The weighted average benefit-cost ratio of the projects as evaluated by the Corps is 1.67.[42]

Table 18 presents the results secured from the application of the Interest Rate Correction (Proposal A). The effect of this re-evaluation is to shift the entire schedule of benefit-cost ratios downward

TABLE 18

Benefit-Cost Ratios of Projects Constructed in
Ten Southern States from 1946 to 1962 When Future Streams
Are Evaluated by a 4.5-Percent Rate of Interest [a]

Benefit-Cost Ratio	Number of Projects	Federal Funds Committed, Thousands of Dollars	Percent of Total Federal Funds Committed
.60– .79	9	295,527	11.18
.80– .99	38	822,616	31.11
1.00–1.19	33	277,009	10.48
1.20–1.39	23	520,679	19.69
1.40–1.59	9	151,749	5.74
1.60–1.79	10	314,496	11.89
1.80–1.99	2	3,346	.13
2.00–2.49	10	185,271	6.25
2.50–2.99	3	74,216	2.81
3.00–4.99	8	9,644	.36
5.00– or more	2	9,448	.36
	147	2,644,001	100.0

a. See footnote, Table 17.

42. The formula used to compute the average is the following:
$$\overline{X}_w = \Sigma (X \cdot W)/\Sigma W$$
in which $\overline{X}_w$ is the weighted arithmetic mean, X is the benefit-cost ratio, and W is the amount of Federal funds committed by a project.

substantially. Whereas the modal class is 1.00 to 1.19 in the Corps distribution, the modal class in this distribution decreases to the .80 to .99 range. This is also reflected in the weighted average benefit-cost ratio which for this distribution is a meager 1.30. Of the 147 projects, 47 were found unacceptable, representing some 42 percent of the committed Federal funds.

Table 19 presents the distribution of projects when the length of project life is assumed to be 100 years to ensure the long-range perspective of the program and when the social cost of capital raised through taxes is accepted as the appropriate rate of interest and is estimated to be 5.5 percent by Eckstein-Krutilla (Proposal B). The effect of this test is more severe than the previous test. Of the 147 projects accepted for construction, 60 fail to pass the efficiency requirement posited by Eckstein-Krutilla. Nearly 45 percent of the committed Federal funds belong in this category. This severity is also reflected in the weighted average benefit-cost ratio which has declined to 1.20.

TABLE 19

Benefit-Cost Ratios of Projects Constructed in Ten Southern States from 1946 to 1962 When Future Streams Are Evaluated by a 5.5-Percent Rate of Interest [a]

Benefit-Cost Ratio	Number of Projects	Federal Funds Committed, Thousands of Dollars	Percent of Total Federal Funds Committed
.60– .79	18	399,153	15.10
.80– .99	42	761,017	28.77
1.00–1.19	35	642,210	24.29
1.20–1.39	12	179,245	6.78
1.40–1.59	9	110,322	4.17
1.60–1.79	8	293,475	11.10
1.80–1.99	6	93,813	3.55
2.00–2.49	6	143,583	5.43
2.50–2.99	3	7,549	.29
3.00–4.99	6	4,186	.16
5.00– or more	2	9,448	.36
	147	2,644,001	100.0

a. The length of project life is assumed to be 100 years unless specifically stipulated to be less by the Corps.

Table 20 presents the results necessary for the application of the criterion suggested by Eckstein (Proposal C). In applying this test, a low rate of interest (2.5 percent) was used to evaluate future streams of benefits and costs, and a cut-off benefit-cost ratio of 1.4 was applied to assure an adequate rate of return of 6 percent. From the table then, it can be seen that 57 of the 147 projects, representing about 43 percent of total funds committed, fail to satisfy the standard posited by Eckstein.

TABLE 20

Benefit-Cost Ratios of Projects Constructed in Ten Southern States from 1946 to 1962 When Future Streams Are Evaluated by a 2.5-Percent Rate of Interest [a]

Benefit-Cost Ratio	Number of Projects	Federal Funds Committed, Thousands of Dollars	Percent of Total Federal Funds Committed
.60– .79	0	—	—
.80– .99	1	94,600	3.58
1.00–1.19	25	477,694	18.07
1.20–1.39	31	568,757	21.51
1.40–1.59	22	187,082	7.07
1.60–1.79	21	514,953	19.47
1.80–1.99	7	91,123	3.45
2.00–2.49	17	450,032	17.02
2.50–2.99	7	97,866	3.70
3.00–4.99	12	148,751	5.63
5.00– or more	4	13,123	.50
	147	2,644,001	100.0

a. See footnote, Table 17.

Based on the suggestion presented by McKean (Proposal D), Table 21 displays the 147 projects by their average rate of return. Again, the bulk of projects are seen to cluster at the lower end of the scale. The weighted average rate of return for the 147 projects is .0644. Application of the recommendation by Harberger, that no project should be constructed which does not anticipate a return of at least 6 percent, results in the rejection of 84 of the 147 projects; nearly 60 percent of the total committed Federal funds have been allocated to projects failing to pass this test.

TABLE 21

*Average Rate of Return of Projects Constructed
in Ten Southern States from 1946 to 1962* [a]

Rate of Return	Number of Projects	Federal Funds Committed, Thousands of Dollars	Percent of Total Federal Funds Committed
.0200–.0299	8	142,786	5.40
.0300–.0399	24	565,658	21.39
.0400–.0499	27	451,244	17.07
.0500–.0599	25	373,030	14.11
.0600–.0699	14	377,531	14.38
.0700–.0799	7	69,783	2.64
.0800–.0899	8	105,099	3.97
.0900–.0999	4	283,728	10.75
.1000–.1499	18	246,059	9.31
.1500–.1999	3	11,431	.43
.2000–.2999	3	4,371	.17
.3000– or more	6	13,281	.50
	147	2,644,001	100.0

a. See footnote, Table 17.

When uncertainty is treated as disutility to the community and when allowance is made for this disutility in the rate of interest, the resulting benefit-cost configuration is as presented in Table 22 (Proposal E). The effect of the premium (discount) is clearly seen in the resulting distribution. Over one half of both the number of projects and the Federal funds committed are excluded by this test. The weighted average benefit-cost ratio in this case falls to a minute 1.11.

In the re-evaluation process then, each of the alternative efficiency criteria, all of which have as their objective the maximization of national income, rejected a significant proportion of the projects. When measured by Federal funds committed, the proportion varies from 42 percent in the case of the 4.5-percent test to 58 percent in the McKean-Harberger proposal.

For any given project, however, the results may be quite varied; i.e., any given project may be accepted by some of the tests and rejected by the others in any combination. Table 23 portrays in a

TABLE 22

Benefit-Cost Ratios of Projects Constructed in Ten Southern States from 1946 to 1962 When Allowance for Uncertainty Is Made in the Criterion ᵃ

Benefit-Cost Ratio	Number of Projects	Federal Funds Committed, Thousands of Dollars	Percent of Total Federal Funds Committed
.60– .79	33	806,581	30.51
.80– .99	46	631,118	20.09
1.00–1.19	24	577,792	21.85
1.20–1.39	12	160,812	6.08
1.40–1.59	8	305,952	11.57
1.60–1.79	7	96,980	3.67
1.80–1.99	2	18,792	.71
2.00–2.49	6	130,900	4.95
2.50–2.99	4	1,918	.07
3.00–4.99	3	3,708	.14
5.00– or more	2	9,448	.36
	147	2,644,001	100.0

a. Future streams of benefits are evaluated by a 5.5-percent rate of interest and future streams of costs by a 4-percent rate of interest. See also footnote, Table 17.

crude way the degree of such inconsistency in the results of the tests. In 107 of the 147 projects, complete consistency was achieved. Of these projects, 62 were accepted by all of the criteria and 45 were rejected by all. In the remaining 40, the answers given by the proposed criteria are not as neat. Individual projects are accepted by some of the criteria but rejected by others. By percent of Federal funds committed, however, the degree of consistency is somewhat clearer: 84 percent of the Federal funds committed were allocated to projects accepted or rejected by all of the criteria and only 16 percent were allocated to projects in which the answer was inconsistent.

The inconsistency present, however, is not limited to the situation in which marginal projects uniformly ranked are placed on different sides of an acceptance-rejection line by different criteria. This type of inconsistency can occur simply because of the higher standard of justification required by some criteria as compared to others; i.e., some criteria may simply be willing to move further

TABLE 23

Number of Rejections Out of Five Tests for Each of the Projects Constructed in Ten Southern States from 1946 to 1962

Number of Rejections	Number of Projects	Federal Funds Committed, Thousands of Dollars	Percent of Total Federal Funds Committed
0	62	1,109,944	41.98
1	6	196,299	7.42
2	16	168,830	6.39
3	10	36,612	1.38
4	8	23,971	.91
5	45	1,108,345	41.98
	147	2,644,001	100.0

down a list of monotonically ranked projects than others. Such a situation is obviously present, but an inconsistency of a higher order also exists. When some projects accepted by criteria x are rejected by criteria y, while other projects accepted by criteria y are rejected by criteria x, such higher level inconsistency is present. This inconsistency appears as a disparity in the actual ranking of the projects and its extent is expressed in Table 24.[43]

Thus, for example, in comparing the results of the Eckstein test with the results of the proposal by Eckstein-Krutilla, a substantial overlap is seen to exist. Among the 90 projects accepted by the Eckstein test, there were 6 that were rejected by the Eckstein-Krutilla formulation (row C, column B). Conversely, of the 87 projects accepted by the Eckstein-Krutilla proposal, 4 possessed benefit-cost ratios below 1.4 when evaluated at a 2.5 percent rate

43. Although two different criteria may rank two projects inversely, there is nevertheless a relatively similar ordering of the projects taken as a whole. As the following table shows, the rank correlation between any of the criteria taken two at a time is extremely high.

Criteria	A	B	C	D	E
A	—	+.975	+.967	+.977	+.957
B	—	—	+.997	+.997	+.986
C	—	—	—	+.979	+.986
D	—	—	—	—	+.984
E	—	—	—	—	—

TABLE 24

Degree of Inconsistency Among Six Criteria Caused by Non-Unique Ranking of Projects as Expressed in the Acceptance-Rejection Decisions

	Number Rejected By					
	A	B	C	D'	D	E
Number Accepted by Interest Rate Correction (A)	—	12	11	26	35	31
Number Accepted by Eckstein-Krutilla Proposal (B)	0	—	4	13	24	19
Number Accepted by Eckstein Proposal (C)	1	6	—	17	25	21
Number with Rate of Return of 5.5% or More (D')	0	0	1	—	10	5
Number with Rate of Return of 6% or More (D)	1	0	1	0	—	1
Number Accepted by Risk Correction Proposal (E)	0	0	0	0	8	—

of interest and were, therefore, not acceptable under the Eckstein test (row B, column C).

Table 24 yields yet another insight. In setting up his test, Eckstein realized that, because the ratio of operating costs to investment costs directly influenced the size of the benefit-cost ratio, the choice of a single value as a cut-off benefit-cost ratio would lead to the acceptance of some projects, namely those of low capital intensity, with a rate of return significantly below the desired rate and the rejection of some, namely those of high capital intensity, with a rate of return above the desired rate. In defense of his method, however, he makes the following assertions:

[T]he marginal projects which would be undertaken [under the proposed test] would not represent a misallocation of capital into a use in which it is incapable of earning a satisfactory rate of return.[44]

. . . .

[A]n interest rate of 2½ percent coupled with a ratio of 1.4 are combinations which will produce an average rate of return for the entire federal program of about 6 percent . . . .[45]

44. Eckstein, *op. cit.*, p. 101.
45. *Ibid.*, p. 104.

Both of these statements appear rather untenable. The evidence in Table 24 rather effectively illustrates the costs involved in choosing a single benefit-cost ratio as a cut-off. Although the ratio chosen by Eckstein (1.4) aimed at yielding a rate of return of 6 percent, it accepted 25 projects with a rate of return less than 6 percent (row C, column D), accepted 17 projects with a rate of return less than 5.5 percent (row C, column D'), and rejected 1 project with a rate greater than 6 percent (row D, column C). Consequently, in opposition to the first statement, it appears that marginal projects may well be accepted even if they do not yield a satisfactory rate of return. Of the projects accepted by the Eckstein test, for example, 2 had rates of return less than 4.5 percent.

As regards the second statement, there is no more reason for claiming that such a combination of interest rate and cut-off benefit-cost ratio will yield an average rate of return of 6 percent than claiming that the average return will be 7, 8, 9, or any other percent. The adoption of such a single benefit-cost ratio only assures that some projects bearing rates of return equal to or greater than the desired rate (6 percent in this case) will be rejected by the test, while other projects bearing rates of return less than the desired rate will be accepted. The average rate of return of the entire Federal program depends, then, upon the ability of the average rate of return of those accepted projects with a rate of return greater than 6 percent to outweigh the average rate of return of those accepted projects with a rate of return less than 6 percent. Consequently, the two statements in defense of the Eckstein test appear quite unwarranted.[46]

Estimate of Misallocation

From the evidence presented, one can hardly doubt that a great number of projects have been constructed which, if economic ef-

46. This criticism, it should be noted, is directed primarily at the expression of the proposal presented in Eckstein's early and rather formative 1958 study. To some extent, the proposal has been modified and elaborated upon in a more recent analysis. See Otto Eckstein, "A Survey of the Theory of Public Expenditure Criteria," in Universities—National Bureau Committee for Economic Research, *Public Finances: Needs, Sources and Utilization* (Princeton: Princeton University Press, 1961), pp. 439–505. A somewhat similar criticism is leveled at the Eckstein proposal by Hirshleifer *et al.* See Hershleifer, De Haven, and Milliman, *op. cit.*, p. 150.

ficiency had been the sole objective, would not have been constructed. Although each of the criteria have presented somewhat varied estimates of the misallocation of national resources (see Tables 18 to 22), it seems plausible that some acceptable estimate of the size of this misallocation is possible. Consequently, it will be assumed that any project that is rejected by three or more of the five tests should not have been constructed and that any project which is accepted by three or more of the five tests should have been constructed. For those projects in the latter category, it is presumed that national income is the greatest possible per dollar devoted to water resource development. For projects in the former category, the reverse is presumed true. According to this approach then, 63 of the 147 projects representing $1,169,000,000 of committed Federal funds or about 44 percent of the total are devoted to projects which should not have been undertaken; the construction of these projects has led to a misallocation of national resources and economic waste. Such misallocation of national resources must be minimized, if not eliminated, if national income is to be maximized and if a more rapid rate of national economic growth is to be secured. Surely, the adoption of appropriate criteria by those agencies involved in the evaluation of such investment would be a logical first step in such an elimination.

6

Economic Efficiency and the Distribution of Income

THUS FAR in the study, several important questions together with their equally important policy considerations have been discussed and analyzed. Theoretical and empirical analyses have been applied to both the concept of income redistribution and the concept of economic efficiency as they relate to a governmental expenditure program. In this chapter the previous results will be summarized, and an empirical analysis dealing with the inter-relationship of these two concepts will be presented.

Synopsis of Preceding Analysis

Up to this point, the study can be thought of as, first, an attempt to isolate and understand the motives or goals which determine the allocation of Federal rivers and harbors investment and, second, an attempt to evaluate the efficacy of those goals which are susceptible to economic measurement and analysis. In the first few chapters, these determinants of the allocation of water resource investment were isolated through an analysis of Congressional sentiment as expressed in floor speeches, hearings, and other publications. Essentially three, rather vague motives were distinguishable: political manipulation, regional aid or regional income redistribution, and economic efficiency. Moreover, it was noted that contemporary recommendations for modification of the allocation process view both economic efficiency and income redistribution as legitimate and acceptable goals for social policy and, consequently, urge the refinement of both of them for use in the future allocation of Federal investment funds.

From this background then, the following questions concerning both of these social goals were discussed: (1) Does the evidence on the projects actually constructed support the conclusion that economic efficiency and regional income redistribution have served as criteria for the allocation of past investment? (2) Has the past allocation of investment funds led to an increase or a decrease in the disparity of regional incomes? (3) In analyzing the Corps program in a particular low income region, the South, (a) how great has the redistributional impact been and (b) how efficient has the allocation of Federal expenditures been?

In Chapter Three, the first two of these questions were treated. From the evidence presented there it was concluded that both of the concepts have, in fact, played somewhat significant roles in the determination of investment allocation. Although weak and far from the economist's ideal, economic efficiency was present in the distinct preference for those projects either possessing high benefit-cost ratios or located in areas demonstrating a high degree of growth potential. Likewise, the relationship between the level of regional income and the volume of construction appropriations was both positive and rather close, demonstrating regional aid to be a rather well-defined and effective part of the entire, multifaceted criterion. Moreover, it was concluded that the movement of wealth caused by the Corps program has, without question, tended to equalize regional per capita incomes.

Both Chapters Four and Five were devoted to the third question. Through a detailed empirical analysis of the benefits received and the costs incurred by ten southern states through the postwar Corps program, the redistribution impact was treated. The results of the analysis led to the conclusion that the South experienced a net benefit of approximately 1.3 billion dollars from the program in the 17 years from 1946 to 1962. The analysis of allocative efficiency was handled through the application of a series of proposed efficiency tests to pre-construction data of the 163 southern projects. From this analysis, it was concluded that approximately 44 percent of the total committed investment in the southern phase of the program was devoted to projects which should not have been constructed.

These two studies then, suggest the following conclusion: even though both regional aid and allocative efficiency are criteria of Federal expenditure, a substantial share of the net benefit secured in the case of the South was secured through the construction of economically inefficient projects; i.e., only at the sacrifice of a substantial amount of additional national income (economic efficiency) did the nation secure such a sizable net benefit for one favored area of the country. The inference immediately arises that such investment is not only an inefficient means of securing maximum national income but also, and equally important, it may be an inefficient means of redistributing income toward a favored area. Because the construction of such economically inefficient projects necessarily means that income losses exceed income gains, it is clear that, in the absence of external economies, the sum of net regional income gains is smaller than the costs incurred by the rest of society in providing the regional benefit. Consequently, insofar as either economically efficient projects or pure income transfers exist as possibilities for regional aid, the redistribution of income by means of the construction of such economically inefficient projects is an inefficient means of effecting such redistribution.[1]

1. However, as Stephen Marglin has said in defense of such construction (assuming that these other alternatives do not exist), "Thus income must be redistributed through such means as development of water-resource projects, *with accompanying inefficiencies*, if desired income-redistribution goals are to be achieved without violating institutional and political arrangements valued by the community. Economists especially must avoid the temptation to dismiss as "irrational" institutional and political barriers to full realization of the economic potentialities of efficiency plus the desired distribution of income, which necessitates sacrifice of a bit of one to achieve some of the other."—See Maass, Hufschmidt, *et al.*, *Design of Water Resource Systems*, pp. 66–67. Emphasis added. It must, therefore, be emphasized that the construction of such projects becomes an inefficient means of redistributing income to a favored group only if (1) the sole objective is the maximization of the size of the national income pie and (2) superior techniques of redistribution are not available. For example, if the maximization of social *welfare* is the objective, the construction of such economically inefficient projects may well *not* be an inefficient means of securing the desired distribution. Under any circumstances, however, the most desirable condition would exist if an abundance of economically efficient projects are available in the favored region. For a further discussion of this problem and its implications for social policy, see Hirshleifer, De Haven, and Milliman, *Water Supply*, pp. 132–137, and the Epilogue to this study.

National Income Maximization and the Redistribution of Income

An attempt is now made to isolate the impact of such inefficient expenditures on the redistribution of income toward the ten southern states. What would have been the regional impact had the Federal government constructed only those projects which pass the economic efficiency tests?

In Chapter Four, the total regional impact of the 163 projects in the Corps General Construction program on ten southern states was presented in detail. The results of that analysis are summarized in Table 25. As seen in the table, approximately 1.5 billion dollars

TABLE 25

Appropriations and Returns to Ten Southern States From the Corps of Engineers General Construction Program, 1946 to 1962

State	Appropriations Received [a]	Median Gross Returns [b]	Median Net Returns [b]
	Thousands of Dollars		
Alabama	113,787	156,253	79,794
Arkansas	273,717	337,167	289,848
Florida	187,141	341,312	123,122
Georgia	178,380	232,799	125,681
Kentucky	327,278	494,651	396,639
Louisiana	113,415	307,134	194,442
Mississippi	6,580	15,160	−23,879
North Carolina	58,465	60,610	−55,784
South Carolina	87,011	127,070	78,925
Tennessee	161,179	229,794	131,210
Ten-State Region	1,506,953	2,301,950	1,339,998

a. Data taken from Table 11.
b. Data taken from Table 13.

was appropriated by the Federal government in the years 1946 to 1962 to projects in these states. The median estimate of gross benefits which accrued to the residents of these states from the projects is about 2.3 billion dollars. The median estimate of net benefits is about 1.3 billion dollars. The estimate of the gross effect was obtained by summing the present values of the expected project benefits represented by annual appropriations when discounted by a 4.5-percent rate of interest. The net effect was estimated by subtracting the necessary costs to the southern states from the estimate of gross returns. These necessary costs were expressed as (1) the sum of the present values of local operation, maintenance, and repair costs prorated by appropriation, (2) the sum of locally borne construction costs, (3) the share of total annual national construction costs of the program contributed by the residents of the ten states, and (4) the present value of future national operation, maintenance, and repair costs which must be borne by residents of these states.

To estimate the impact which would have occurred if only the efficient projects were constructed, those projects failing to pass the efficiency tests are now eliminated from the regional analysis. From the total amount of regional gross returns, the sum of the present value of expected benefits of the unproductive projects is subtracted. The local construction costs and the present value of locally borne operation, maintenance, and repair costs of these projects are likewise eliminated from their respective regional totals. Finally, the degree of inefficiency found in these 163 projects is assumed to approximate the degree of inefficiency of all projects constructed during the 17-year period in the entire nation, and the contribution of the ten southern states in the form of Federal taxes in support of the total Corps program is reduced in proportion to the decrease in appropriations received by the South due to the elimination of the inefficient projects.

It should be noted that several basic assumptions are implicitly posited in making these subtractions. First, the studies of regional impact and economic efficiency are assumed to accurately approximate the true regional impact of the program and correctly point out the truly inefficient projects. Also, it is assumed that the decrease in total Federal appropriations caused by the elimination of the inefficient projects is not reallocated to some other expenditure program but results in an equivalent decrease in taxes. Finally, the tax decreases are assumed to be passed along to the residents of states in proportion to the incidence of Federal taxes on the states' residents as determined in the previous regional impact analysis.

The results of eliminating the inefficient projects from the regional analysis are presented in Table 26. There it is seen that, whereas the economically efficient projects received about 56 percent of the total Federal funds committed, they provided 75 percent of the total net returns to the southern states. Conversely, the projects failing to pass the efficiency tests received 44 percent of the total Federal funds committed but yielded only 25 percent of the total net benefits. The data on gross benefits tell a similar but less pronounced story; the efficient projects here account for about 68 percent of gross benefits. Strange as it may seem, three states (Louisiana, Mississippi, and North Carolina) would have been better off (greater net returns or smaller net costs) with a smaller appropriation and smaller program devoted to only efficient projects than with the larger total appropriation and larger total program.

TABLE 26 [a]

Estimated Appropriations and Returns to Ten Southern States
Assuming Construction of Only the Efficient Projects of the
Corps of Engineers General Construction Program, 1946 to 1962

State	Appropriations Received		Median Gross Returns		Median Net Returns	
	Thousands of Dollars					
Alabama	24,930	(21.9)	52,101	(33.2)	8,917	(11.5)
Arkansas	83,032	(30.3)	114,328	(33.9)	90,110	(31.1)
Florida	111,740	(59.7)	250,137	(73.3)	113,636	(92.3)
Georgia	78,803	(44.2)	111,746	(48.0)	51,707	(41.1)
Kentucky	244,705	(74.8)	408,511	(82.9)	351,016	(88.5)
Louisiana	101,142	(89.2)	287,555	(93.6)	222,189	(114.3)
Mississippi	4,498	(68.4)	13,298	(87.7)	−10,757	(45)[b]
North Carolina	48,467	(82.9)	48,964	(80.8)	−16,765	(30.1)[b]
South Carolina	41,826	(48.1)	72,521	(57.1)	45,023	(57.0)
Tennessee	120,408	(74.7)	186,555	(81.1)	128,895	(98.2)
Ten-State Region	859,551	(57.0)	1,545,605	(67.7)	983,971	(74.5)

a. The numbers in parentheses are the percentages of the total values (in Table 25) represented by the efficient projects alone (the values in Table 26). For example, the appropriation which Alabama received for the efficient projects (24,930) is 21.9 percent of the total appropriation received by Alabama for all projects (113,787).
b. These percentages relate to minus values. Thus, the higher the percentage, the greater the fraction of total net loss incurred.

A comparison of Tables 25 and 26 illustrates the statement made previously concerning the relative inefficiency of redistributing income toward a favored region through the construction of economically inefficient projects. Of the total Federal expenditure of 1.5 billion dollars, approximately 640 million dollars or 44 percent was allocated to projects failing to pass three of the five economic efficiency tests. The net effect which accrued to the region because of this 640-million-dollar expenditure totaled only 340 million dollars. This evidence supports the claim that, had the government constructed only efficient projects in the South, national expenditures and tax revenues could have been cut by 640 million dollars, which expenditure led to only about 340 million dollars in net returns to the ten-state area. Compare this with the net returns of 980 million dollars which resulted from the 860-million-dollar Federal expenditure on southern projects passing the pure economic efficiency tests. The point then is quite clear: should either economically efficient projects or even pure income transfers exist as feasible alternatives in securing regional aid, the construction of economically inefficient projects in favored areas is an inefficient means of securing such income transfers.

Epilogue

The Measurement of Economic Welfare: An Empirical Experiment

THIS CONCLUDING section is both a candid examination of the essence and import of the study's method and conclusions and an experiment with that singularly knotty problem present in all economic analyses which attempt either to formulate or to evaluate economic changes affecting society, that is, the problem of the economist's relative inability to accurately measure the level of or changes in economic welfare. Indeed, an examination of the ability of the profession to identify changes in this variable appears to be quite in order if economic analysis is to be both relevant and understood.[1]

First, the nature of the problem which has plagued all efforts to evaluate the welfare impact of economic changes is investigated. In this discussion, the present effort is examined, and the grounds upon which it and other studies like it rest are stated and defended. Second, because the general approach and its defense are found to be hardly a counsel of perfection, the existence, nature, and empirical feasibility of some suggested alternative approaches to welfare evaluation are investigated in the hope that they may yield some clue for the development of a superior technique. One of

---

1. "The concept of maximum aggregate satisfaction is essentially quantitative. It refers to the maximization of a quantity of satisfactions to be enjoyed by the people of a society. Consequently, if the concept is to have practical significance—if it is not to be a mere phrase devoid of content—there must be some means whereby quantities of satisfaction can be made susceptible to measurement. Without the possibility of such measurement there would be no practicable way of determining the degree to which, in any given situation, maximum aggregate satisfaction is approached, or of ascertaining what particular use of resources would, in fact, lead to maximum satisfaction. Thus, the validity of any statement regarding the conditions that are necessary to the attainment of economy is dependent upon the availability of a suitable technique for reducing satisfactions to quantitative terms."—Howard R. Bowen, *Toward Social Economy*, p. 124.

these approaches is then tentatively accepted and applied empirically to our data in a pair of experiments in welfare evaluation. Through this approach, it is hoped both that the significance of the present study (and such like it) can be more adequately determined and that a superior approach for future work on similar questions can be distinguished.

A Brief Critique of Method and Conclusions

The study presented in the first six chapters lies in the mainstream of what could be called applied or empirical welfare economics. By seeking answers to questions concerning both the economic efficiency and the redistributive impact of a Federal expenditure program, concern for evaluating changes in economic welfare has been demonstrated and acceptance of the multidimensionality of the economic welfare function has been affirmed. Moreover, because the analysis of both of these welfare dimensions has been framed in terms of money income gains and losses to groups of individuals, the door has been left open for the drawing of economic welfare implications.

In fact, the ease by which such changes in a group's income often become improperly equated with equivalent changes in the group's economic welfare has led to a most cautious interpretation of evidence and statement of conclusions. For example, consider Chapters Three and Four of the study in which the regional impact of the Corps program was analyzed. In these analyses, the estimates of regional impact were obtained by comparing the money income losses and gains experienced by the residents of individual states or groups of states. Because the evidence was based on the money unit as a measuring rod, when it was demonstrated that New York had a net loss of x dollars and Alabama had a net gain of y dollars, the conclusion was not made, for example, that national welfare had increased because a rich state had, in some sense, subsidized a poor state. Likewise, the demonstration that New Yorkers suffered a net loss of income carried no conclusion that the loss necessarily entailed a decrease in their welfare. In the same vein, it was not concluded that the economic welfare of the people of Alabama was necessarily augmented because they experienced a net dollar gain.

Moreover, when the evidence demonstrated that the program had tended to equalize the per capita distribution of income among states, again no concrete welfare conclusions were drawn on either the state or national level. And in Chapter Four, when the ten southern states were demonstrated to be rather large dollar beneficiaries of the program, no claim was made concerning the impact of the program on the welfare of the residents of these states.

A similar situation exists in Chapter Five. In that chapter, several decision criteria were applied to the benefit-cost data of Corps projects in an attempt to evaluate the degree to which these projects satisfied the goal of economic efficiency. Each of the criteria applied in that study was concerned with but one of the dimensions of economic welfare, the size of the national income, and each of them, therefore, attempted to maximize only this dimension. Consequently, the only projects which were rejected by the criteria were those projects which implied an actual decrease in national income, i.e., those projects in which the present value of expected dollar costs exceeded the present value of expected dollar benefits. When it was concluded, then, that a substantial proportion of the projects would, in all probability, decrease future national income, no claim was made concerning the impact of these projects on future national welfare. The same statement applies to those projects which were expected to increase national income. Again future national welfare could be increased, decreased, or remain unchanged, even though it is estimated that future national income will be increased. In other words, it is quite conceivable that a project which is expected to increase national income may well cause a decrease in national economic welfare because of the resultant equity considerations, and conversely, a project which is expected to decrease national income may well, for the same reasons, cause national economic welfare to be augmented.

If these propositions are true, then how is this analysis to be viewed? If it is possible that a positive regional impact may entail a decrease in the economic welfare of the region's residents, or if an economically efficient water resource project may, in reality, decrease national economic welfare, then of what relevance are either the numbers or the conclusions? The economists' answers to such questions have, in general, been most equivocal. Only by fortifying their analyses with rather heroic (and usually implicit) assumptions which posit the existence of rather patently unreal worlds, have they been able to form their welfare statements. That is to say, conclusions on changes in national or regional welfare have been identified with conclusions on changes in national income only by assuming the existence of a naive welfare function which weights increments of income to each and every recipient equally, i.e., by assuming that the marginal utility of income is equal and constant for every individual.[2]

In evaluating this study, then, this tenuous assumption must either be accepted or rejected. If it is accepted, the estimated income changes are claimed to be, in fact, welfare changes. If it is not accepted, no welfare statements can be made.

Although the money unit is admittedly inadequate as a welfare guage, it is nevertheless tentatively accepted, and through its acceptance, a cautious relevance and importance for the tacit welfare implications of the data is posited.[3] Because the profession has not yet developed and therefore does not admit the existence of any welfare guage superior to the money income unit, and moreover, because there is no "superman" (to use Professor Little's metaphor) at hand to decree a welfare function bearing the real value of money income to different individuals, the money income unit provides the only and, therefore, the best empirical welfare measurement available. This fact, combined with the desire (indeed, need) to make some judgment on the welfare impact of economic

2. See, for example, Eckstein, *Water Resource Development*, pp. 24 ff. and McKean, *Efficiency in Government*, pp. 127–133. Stephen Marglin has put this point in a slightly different way: "Identifying national welfare with the size of national income not only excludes non-economic dimensions of welfare but also implies . . . that society is totally indifferent to the recipient of the income generated . . . . Social indifference to the distribution of income generated . . . suggests that the marginal social significance of income is the same regardless of who receives it; a dollar of extra income to Jones is no more socially desirable than a dollar to Smith, despite differences in initial incomes, employment opportunities and the like."—See Maass, Hufschmidt, *et al.*, *Design of Water Resource Systems*, p. 17.

3. "We are interested in the distribution of money only because we believe that there is a very good correlation between money incomes . . . and real income."—See I. M. D. Little, *A Critique of Welfare Economics*, p. 57.

change makes its immediately obvious that a welfare estimate based on such a yardstick, although inadequate, is substantially more valuable than no estimate at all.[4] It is in this sense, then, that the empirical results of this volume are offered.

However, because the assumption required to weld money income units into equality with units of economic welfare is so inadequate and because no welfare statements can be made in the absence of this assumption, some new effort must be made to secure a superior technique for evaluating changes in economic welfare. Perhaps by scanning the suggestions of the theoretical welfare economists, some clue will be found which contains the seed of such an empirically feasible technique.

The Empirical Relevancy of Some Welfare Suggestions[5]

As the new welfare economics would suggest, adequate theoretical yardsticks for measuring the changes in social economic welfare attributable to an economic change are indeed available. In briefly perusing the suggestions of the new welfare economists, the positions of Professors Pareto, Kaldor, Hicks, and Little are specifically considered.

Pareto, without question, has suggested the most rigorous test of increases in economic welfare outside the requirement that an economic change must make all individuals in the society better off. According to Pareto, if an economic change has caused at least one person to be made better off without having caused anyone else to be made worse off, then the change is to be accepted as improving welfare.[6] Although this proposition is theoretically sound, it

4. Or even more strongly, "Since the alternative is not to retire to inactivity but, rather, to reach decisions in the absence of analysis, we may take some comfort from the belief that thinking systematically about problems and basing decisions on such analysis are likely to produce consequences superior to those that would result from purely random behavior."—John V. Krutilla, "Welfare Aspects of Benefit-Cost Analysis," *Journal of Political Economy,* LXIX (June, 1961), 234.

5. This section, it should be noted, draws heavily upon an essay by Otto Eckstein.. See Otto Eckstein, "A Survey of the Theory of Public Expenditure Criteria," Universities—National Bureau Committee for Economic Research, *Public Finances; Needs, Sources and Utilization* (Princeton University Press, 1961), pp. 439–505.

6. Vilfredo Pareto, *Manuel d'Economie Politique,* pp. 617 ff.

is, nevertheless, unacceptable for the present purposes. Because each of the economic changes that have been discussed and in fact, almost every economic change conceivable, causes some economic sacrifice to at least one individual, this suggesstion provides no empirical help.

Recognizing the restrictive nature of this proposition, Professors Kaldor and Hicks have suggested a technique which appears far more promising.[7] According to their proposal, if the individuals who experience a net gain from an economic change would be willing to compensate those individuals who experience a net loss, rather than forego the impact of the change, then the change has increased social economic welfare. This suggestion, although promising in that it covers a much wider range of situations, is still far too restrictive. Not only is it impossible to imagine the compensation actually being made (which is, in fact, not an absolute require- ment) but also it is equally impossible to imagine the formation of a list of losers and gainers together with their real gains and losses, which would be essential for such an evaluation. Again, no real help can be expected from this source.

However, there is one final suggestion. Clearly recognizing the impossibility of divorcing welfare conclusions from specific ethical judgments, Professor Little has posited a still less restrictive yet appropriate welfare criterion for evaluating any two alternative situations.

We can thus say that an economic change is desirable (and increases welfare) if it causes a good redistribution of wealth, and if the potential losers could not profitably bribe the potential gainers to oppose it— always assuming that no still better change is therefore prejudiced.[8]

Even though this criterion permits judgment on the basis of what is probably a minimum of restrictions, it is obvious that the need remains unfulfilled. Besides being unable to frame an em- pirical evaluation in terms of a comparison between pairs of

7. N. Kaldor, "Welfare Propositions of Economics and Interpersonal Com- parisons of Utility," *Economic Journal,* IL (September, 1939), 549–552; J. R. Hicks, "The Foundations of Welfare Economics," *Economic Journal,* IL (December, 1939), 696–712; and J. R. Hicks, "The Valuation of the Social Income," *Economica,* VII (May, 1940), 105–124.

8. Little, *op. cit.,* p. 109.

alternatives (which the Little criterion requires), the telling problem is that economists acting as economists have no right to declare any distribution to be either good or bad. As Eckstein states, they have no right "to attach social weights to individual welfare in the social welfare function." Besides the drawbacks of these suggestions which have already been mentioned, it should be added that none of these proposals is free from the rather serious conceptual problem of assessing the external effects of consumption. That is to say, even if they were found to be empirically feasible, they would still not necessarily be reliable estimators. As Baumol pessimistically states in appraising the nature of this problem:

Is there any hope of further progress based on empirical investigation and analysis of the problem of the interdependence of activities of economic units? I cannot pretend to offer even tentative answers. It seems to me, however, that if the subject is to achieve primary importance for practical men, this question must be faced and answered.[9]

Finding, then, but little encouragement in the suggestions of the new welfare economists, is there any option left? Perhaps there is. Taking ". . . the rather casually dispensed advice of the critics of welfare economics . . . seriously," [10] Eckstein has suggested an approach which, although not permitting the economist to solve the ethical problem, does allow him to perform legitimate experiments in welfare evaluation. Through this approach, the economist acquires the ability to formulate statements concerning the welfare impact of economic changes even though as economist he does not possess the policy-maker's prerogative of assigning unequal weights to the dollars of gain and loss to different individuals. Such experiments, Eckstein suggests, become possible for the economist by accepting out of hand the judgments of the policy-makers whom he serves and by embodying them in an objective function which he then maximizes. In his own words:

The economist can . . . feel free to perform experiments in policy evaluation using specific objective functions, treating the results as free of absolute normative significance. For example, he can assume a certain shape for the marginal utility of income function . . . or he may

9. William Baumol, *Welfare Economics and the Theory of the State*, p. 167.
10. Eckstein, "A Survey of the Theory of Public Expenditure Criteria," *op. cit.*, p. 445.

choose to use a form of the function that has been implicitly produced by the political process. The effective marginal rates of the personal income tax at different income levels can be interpreted as implying a marginal utility of income curve. If the government is assumed to act on the principle of equimarginal sacrifice, then marginal effective tax rates can be the basis for deriving a measure of the government's notion of marginal utilities of income.

The kind of question that could be posed when such a function is applied to the analysis of a policy is of the following form: assuming the values placed by the government on marginal income of different income classes in its personal tax legislation, will a policy raise or lower total national economic welfare? [11]

Because such an approach appears to be not only a solution to the economist's ethical problem but also empirically feasible in that it allows real weights to be attached to increments of income to different individuals, it is tentatively accepted as being a superior approach and used in a series of experiments in welfare evaluation.

The Determination of an Empirical Welfare Gauge

To make this approach and its conceptual framework empirically workable, however, the policy-maker's evaluation of the marginal utility of increments of income to individuals of different income levels (i.e., the marginal utility of income function) must first be secured. Then, from this function a series of defensible weights must be devised to be used as evaluators of the welfare impact of money income flows to individuals of different income levels. Finally, with the function secured and the series of weights devised, the experiments in policy evaluation can be performed.

The policy-maker's estimate of the marginal utility of income

11. *Ibid.*, pp. 447–448. It should be noted that this position is based on the assumption that the reactions of all individuals in a society to changes in money income are identical. As Joan Robinson has stated: "To a strictly logical mind any discussion of utility to more than one individual is repugnant. It is not really justifiable to talk about maximum satisfaction to a whole population. But common sense protests that if we treat all individuals as being exactly alike it is then permissable to sum their satisfactions, and that human beings, in their economic needs, are sufficiently alike to make the discussion of aggregate satisfaction interesting. Upon this basis we may say that if any two individuals have the same real income they derive the same satisfaction from it. We may further say that if one individual has a larger real income than another the marginal utility of income to him is less."—Joan Robinson, *The Economics of Imperfect Competition,* p. 318.

function is itself an ethical judgment. It is, nevertheless, adopted in the following analysis as being an appropriate means by which to determine an adequate welfare gauge.

Although the procurement of this estimate appears to be straightforward in principle, in reality it becomes most problematic. Because there is no single policy-maker who is both rational and consistent, but rather a transient group of policy-makers, who, acting as a group, are neither rational nor consistent, any attempt to secure an estimate of their evaluation must rest on evidence which is largely inadequate. In fact, there are those who would claim that such a procurement is neither relevant nor possible.[12] These doubts notwithstanding, there appears to be substantial evidence that Congress does, in fact, value income flows to individuals of varying wealth positions differently. Moreover, the vast bulk of this evidence lies in the direction of higher weights placed on increments of income to low income groups and lower weights placed on increments of income to high income groups. By accepting an important instance of such weighting (namely, the personal income tax) as representative of general Congressional evaluation, such an estimate of the marginal utility of income function can be formed. Assuming that Congress, in establishing the Federal personal in-

---

12. Professor Lerner would consider the entire attempt to be irrelevant. This position would stem from his apparent belief that the only feasible indicator of welfare is the money income unit no matter who the recipient might be. He states: "But we have no way of directly comparing the well-being of different consumers. Our only objective general indication is their money income . . . . We may have good reason for believing that one consumer is better off than he was before and that another is not as well off as he was before, but we have no more reason for supposing that the old situation is better than the new one . . . than from supposing that the new one is better than the old one."—Abba P. Lerner, *The Economics of Control*, p. 24. Professor Little also objects, but his objection rests on substantially different grounds. He does not doubt the relevancy of working with such an objective function; rather he questions the possibility of securing an adequate estimate of the policy-maker's evaluation. His position is expressed in the following statement: "But what does this concept of an ideal distribution really mean? We have seen that the ideal distribution was to be defined by 'superman' . . . . Could 'superman' be interpreted, for instance, as public opinion? . . . [In] a democratic state, it seems absurd to suppose that public opinion could define an ideal distribution. Could 'superman' be interpreted as Parliament or the Cabinet . . . ? [This] suggestion also rests on the highly undemocratic idea that the government always knows what is best—or that it alone can say what is in the public interest."—Little, *op. cit.*, pp. 121–122.

come tax structure, acted on the principle of equimarginal sacrifice, its evaluation of the relative marginal utilities of income of individuals of different income levels can be estimated from the *inverse* of the effective marginal tax rates at these levels.[13] In Figure 4, the actual marginal tax rates for the years 1950 and 1958 are presented by income class.[14]

From this general form of the politically determined marginal utility of income function, a series of weights must be devised by which to evaluate the welfare impact of increments of income to individuals of different income levels. By defining the implied marginal utility of income of an individual receiving the average annual gross income level to be equal to unity, that is, to accept it as *numeraire*, the marginal utility of income of an individual receiving any annual gross income level can be stated in terms of it. Thus, for example, if the marginal effective tax rate of the average gross income level was found to be .2, the marginal utility of income attached to this income level would be assigned a value of unity and all other implied marginal utilities of income would be valued relative to it. The gross income level bearing a marginal tax rate of .4 would be judged to possess a marginal utility of income equal to one half that of the average gross income level, and consequently, increments of income to individuals of this income level would be weighted by a value of .5. By the same process, increments of income to individuals with a gross income level bearing a marginal tax rate of .1 would be weighted by a value of 2.[15] In Table 27, these welfare equivalent weights are presented for the years 1950 and 1958 by income class.

13. If, for example, at a gross income level of $5,000, the marginal effective tax rate was .25 and at a gross income level of $20,000, the marginal tax rate was .5, then, given the assumption that Congress acted on the principle of equimarginal sacrifice, it could be estimated that Congress valued the marginal utility of an additional dollar of income to an individual in the lower income class to be equal to twice the marginal utility of an additional dollar of income to an individual in the higher income class.

14. These rates were calculated by dividing the change in income tax paid per return by bracket by the change in adjusted gross income per return for both 1950 and 1958. The data necessary for the calculation was obtained from U.S. Treasury Department, Internal Revenue Service, *Statistics of Income for 1950,* pp. 35–37 and U.S. Treasury Department, Internal Revenue Service, *Statistics of Income for 1958,* p. 27.

15. The average gross income levels per return were found to be $3,420 in

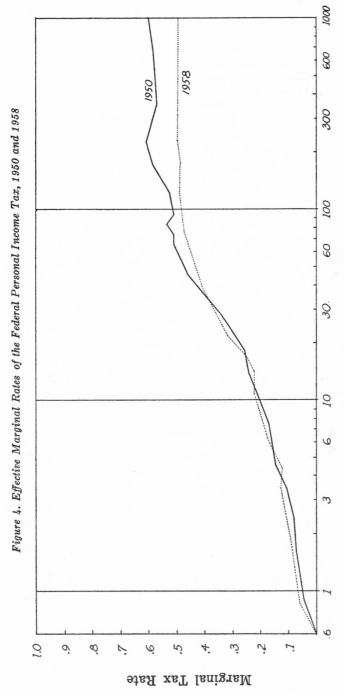

Figure 4. Effective Marginal Rates of the Federal Personal Income Tax, 1950 and 1958

TABLE 27

Welfare Equivalent Weights by Income Class for 1950 and 1958

1950		1958	
Gross Income, Thousands of Dollars	Welfare Equivalent Weights	Gross Income, Thousands of Dollars	Welfare Equivalent Weights
Under 1	2.28	Under 1	2.65
1–2	1.50	1–2	1.71
2–3	1.30	2–3	1.34
3–4	.99	3–4	1.07
4–5	.75	4–5	1.03
5–10	.59	5–6	.94
10–15	.46	6–7	.80
15–20	.41	7–8	.73
20–25	.34	8–9	.69
25–30	.31	9–10	.65
30–40	.26	10–15	.61
40–50	.23	15–20	.52
50–60	.21	20–25	.42
60–70	.20	25–50	.33
70–80	.20	50–100	.28
80–90	.19	100–150	.27
90–100	.20	150–200	.27
100–150	.19	200–500	.27
150–200	.18	500–1,000	.28
200–250	.17	1,000 or more	.27
250–500	.18		
500–1,000	.18		
1,000 or more	.17		

Thus, the weight attached to any income level becomes a type of welfare equivalent. That is, an additional dollar of income to an individual whose income level bears a weight of 2 would elicit an increase in his welfare which is equivalent to the increase elicited by two additional dollars to an individual of the average income level. In general, then, if an additional dollar of income to an individual of the average income level could be said to increase his welfare by a certain amount, say x, then an additional dollar of income to an individual possessing an income less than that of the

---

1950 and $4,810 in 1958, and the marginal tax rates attached to these income levels, .105 and .135, respectively. Accepting the relative marginal utilities of income implied by the inverse of these rates as *numeraire* for each of the years, the welfare equivalents for each income class were calculated in terms of the *numeraire*.

average individual will increase his welfare by more than x, and an additional dollar of income to an individual possessing an income greater than the average will increase his welfare by less than x. In each case the increment to welfare will be equal to the product of x times the welfare weight attached to that income class.[16]

This system of raw welfare weights, however, is by itself not sufficient for the empirical task at hand. Because detailed data is not available on the recipients of the benefits of Corps projects, it is not possible to treat the Corps program as one which, in essence, allocates small additional amounts of income to individuals of different income levels. Rather, the program must be thought of as one which allocates sizable amounts of additional income to large groups of individuals with the distribution of the increments of income to the members of the group largely unknown. For example, instead of it being claimed that y dollars of benefits from project x accrue to individuals of income class $2,000 to $3,000 and z dollars of benefits of the project accrue to individuals of income class $3,000 to $4,000 and so on, all that can be claimed is that the entire benefit flow accrues to group m [17] with no accurate evidence concerning its distribution among the individuals of the group. Given this situation, then, the raw weights must be modified to allow an evaluation of the welfare impact of dollar gains and losses to dif-

16. As Professor Meade has claimed: "[A] system of indices would enable one to say of any policy which made marginal changes in outputs and incomes whether from the point of view of economic equity as well as economic efficiency, the change added to economic welfare or not. . . . [I]t is not suggested that such marginal utility indices are objective facts which can be objectively measured. They are bound to be political or moral assessments which the economist as such must accept as given by the policy-makers. The economist's job can only be on the basis of any given schedule of distributional weights to say whether an economic policy would then lead to a greater economic welfare or not." Again, "we, therefore, need some apparatus for judging simultaneously the efficiency and equity aspects of economic changes which are brought about by economic policy. Moreover, because of the difficulties of redistributing income without introducing inefficiencies—if for no other reason—we need an apparatus which will help us to choose between two policies even though neither one gives us utopian economic efficiency."— J. E. Meade, "The Theory of International Economic Policy," *Trade and Welfare,* II, 70 and 79. It should be noted that this position is considered by some observers to be "frankly ascientific." See Krutilla, "Welfare Aspects of Benefit-Cost Analysis," *op. cit.,* p. 231.

17. Even this rather limited statement requires a rather strong set of assumptions. See the discussion in Chapter Four, pp. 85-87.

ferent groups rather than different individuals. More precisely, because the groups of individuals to be dealt with are differentiated primarily by geographical region rather than by income level, this revised series of weights must, in effect, allow evaluation of the welfare impact of income flows to different geographical regions, which flows are distributed to residents of the regions according to certain assumptions.[18]

Consequently, a set of three alternative welfare weights is formed for each state; each weight is based upon a different assumption concerning the distribution of the incremental income gains and losses within the state. First, it is assumed that state income gains are distributed among the state's residents in proportion to the existing state income distribution, and second, it is assumed that they are distributed equally among the state's residents. It is assumed that income outflows from the state (in the form of Federal taxes) are borne in proportion to the existing state distribution of the total Federal tax burden by income classes.

To calculate the weights based on these assumptions, the following distributions must be obtained: (1) the percent of state income in each income class by state,[19] (2) the percent of state population in each income class by state,[20] and (3) the percent of

18. Since the welfare impact of such flows depends not only upon the average income level of the region to which they accrue but also upon the distribution of the flow within the region, the modified weights must consider both of these variables. Thus, for example, the weight attached to an income flow into a poor region must be higher than the weight attached to an income flow into a rich region even if an identical pattern of distribution of the flow among the residents of each region is assumed. Likewise, the weight attached to a flow of income into a region which is distributed in proportion to the existing regional income distribution would be quite different from the weight attached to a flow of income into that same region distributed equally among the region's residents.

19. This distribution for each of the 50 states was calculated from data on adjusted gross income by state by income class for 1950 and 1958. The data was secured from U.S. Treasury Department, Internal Revenue Service, *Statistics of Income for 1950*, pp. 119–131 and *Statistics of Income for 1958*, pp. 67–70.

20. The percent of state personal income tax returns in each income class was used as an estimate of the percent of state population in each income class. The data on tax returns by income class by state for 1950 and 1958 was secured from U.S. Treasury, Internal Revenue Service, *ibid.* This procedure was necessary to maintain comparability of state income classes essential to securing the regional weights. See Selma F. Goldsmith, "The Relation of Census In-

the total state Federal tax burden which is carried by each income class by state.[21] With these relative frequencies used as weights, a weighted average equivalent value is computed for each state for each of the three assumptions. These welfare weights can then be interpreted as Congress's relative evaluation of the welfare impact of incremental money income flows out of and into each of the states when the flows are distributed among the state's residents as posited by the assumptions. For example, a welfare weight attached to a state under one of the distribution assumptions of .9 would imply a Congressional estimate of the welfare impact of an additional dollar of income to that group (distributed as assumed) as equal to nine-tenths the welfare impact of an additional dollar of income to an individual of the average income level, the weight attached to this latter individual being used as *numeraire*. This set of weights is presented for each of the fifty states in Table 28.

Two Experiments in Welfare Evaluation

This set of state welfare equivalent weights derived from the social estimate of the marginal utility of income function is used in this section in two experiments in welfare evaluation. First, the

come Distribution Statistics to Other Income Data," in National Bureau of Economic Research, *An Appraisal of the 1950 Census Income Data* (Princeton: Princeton University Press, 1958), pp. 65–107.

21. This distribution for each of the 50 states was obtained by allocating each state's Federal tax burden for 1950 and 1958 to the various income classes in that state in proportion to the national burden of total Federal taxes by income class. The method of estimating the state Federal tax burden is presented in Appendix A and the results are displayed in Table 7. The estimate of the burden of total Federal taxes by income class for each state was calculated by multiplying the amount of total Federal tax per income tax return in each income class on a national basis by the number of returns in each income class for each state. The amount of total Federal tax per income tax return in each income class nationally was calculated from the estimate of total Federal tax liability by income class as presented by Musgrave. For 1950, Musgrave's estimate of the liability for the year 1948 was used. R. A. Musgrave, J. J. Carroll, L. D. Cook, and L. Frane, "Distribution of Tax Payments by Income Groups: A Case Study for 1948," *National Tax Journal*, IV (March, 1951), 1–54. For 1958, Musgrave's estimate of the liability for the year 1954 was used. U.S. Congress, Joint Economic Committee, *Federal Tax Policy for Economic Growth and Stability*, Joint Committee Print, 84th Congress, 1st Session, November 9, 1955, article by R. A. Musgrave, "The Incidence of the Tax Structure and Its Effects on Consumption," pp. 96–114. In each case the liability of the income classes above $10,000 was distributed in proportion to the personal income tax.

TABLE 28

Weighted Welfare Equivalent Weights by State, 1946 to 1962 [a]

State	Welfare Equivalent Weights When Income In(De)crements Are Distributed as		
	Income	Population	Federal Tax Burden
Alabama	.95	1.35	.83
Alaska	.77	1.13	.71
Arizona	.86	1.25	.74
Arkansas	1.00	1.44	.85
California	.81	1.18	.69
Colorado	.88	1.26	.75
Connecticut	.82	1.20	.68
Delaware	.75	1.21	.53
Florida	.90	1.32	.75
Georgia	.94	1.34	.81
Hawaii	.96	1.31	.80
Idaho	.94	1.31	.83
Illinois	.83	1.20	.70
Indiana	.90	1.25	.79
Iowa	.94	1.31	.83
Kansas	.91	1.32	.80
Kentucky	.96	1.37	.83
Louisiana	.90	1.29	.77
Maine	1.00	1.40	.88
Maryland	.87	1.24	.75
Massachusetts	.89	1.27	.75
Michigan	.84	1.20	.73
Minnesota	.91	1.31	.79
Mississippi	1.00	1.43	.86
Missouri	.89	1.30	.76
Montana	.91	1.31	.81
Nebraska	.94	1.34	.82
Nevada	.80	1.16	.66
New Hampshire	.98	1.33	.87
New Jersey	.85	1.18	.72
New Mexico	.87	1.27	.77
New York	.82	1.21	.67
North Carolina	.99	1.38	.85
North Dakota	1.00	1.40	.88
Ohio	.86	1.22	.75
Oklahoma	.92	1.32	.79
Oregon	.85	1.23	.74
Pennsylvania	.90	1.25	.76
Rhode Island	.91	1.27	.77
South Carolina	.99	1.37	.87
South Dakota	1.03	1.45	.91

TABLE 28 (Continued)

State	Welfare Equivalent Weights When Income In (De) crements Are Distributed as		
	Income	Population	Federal Tax Burden
Tennessee	.96	1.39	.81
Texas	.87	1.28	.72
Utah	.91	1.26	.82
Vermont	1.00	1.35	.89
Virginia	.94	1.32	.81
Washington	.85	1.20	.75
West Virginia	.97	1.35	.87
Wisconsin	.90	1.28	.79
Wyoming	.88	1.25	.77
United States	.87	1.26	.74

a. Each of the values listed is the median of the 1950 and 1958 computed values.

direction and magnitude of the change in national economic welfare resulting from the allocation of postwar Corps appropriations will be estimated through the application of these state welfare weights and, second, the southern projects evaluated in Chapter Five by the pure efficiency criteria will be re-evaluated by a welfare maximization criterion based on a multidimensional welfare function which combines both the efficiency and the equity (redistribution of income) aspects of economic welfare.

Changes in economic welfare are most properly viewed as some positive function of both changes in the size of the income pie and changes in its distribution. Indeed, in the real world any economic phenomenon which results in observable changes in society's welfare invariably operates through changes in both of these welfare determinants. It would be helpful, therefore, if through an experiment one of these variables could be held constant, and the change in welfare caused by a change in the other could be estimated. In this first experiment, the size of the income pie is arbitrarily held constant, and an attempt is made to estimate the welfare change resulting from a particular change in the distribution of the pie. The question posed is the following: what has been the direction and magnitude of the change in economic welfare resulting from the redistribution of income caused by the postwar Corps program?

That is, abstracting from any change in the size of the income pie caused by the projects constructed, what, if anything, can be claimed concerning the welfare impact of the fiscal transactions represented by the Corps program?

Application of our postulated welfare function to the previous state-by-state analysis of program costs and appropriations [22] appears to be a feasible approach in attempting to arrive at some estimate of the change in national welfare which resulted from these transactions. That is, if both the appropriations to Corps projects in a state and the costs to the state's residents in support of the Corps program can be considered adequate surrogates of money income gains and losses to the state's residents, then, by application of welfare weights derived from an appropriate marginal utility of income function to these values, an estimate of the net change in welfare experienced by each state can be secured. Further, with this figure for each state, both the direction of the change in national welfare can be determined and, with substantially less confidence, the magnitude of this change can be estimated.

To accurately estimate the welfare impact of taxing and re-distributing some 8.25 billion dollars (the amount of postwar Corps appropriations), the distribution of the cost (Federal tax collections) and the distribution of gains (Federal appropriations) among individuals of different income groups must be known. Because it is not possible to ascertain this latter concept, two alternative assumptions which yield two different estimates of the welfare impact of the appropriation are made. First, it is assumed that the money income increment for each state in the form of Federal appropriation equals the present value of the benefits of Corps projects and is distributed among the state's residents in proportion to the present state distribution of money income by income class. Second, it is assumed that this money income increment for each state is distributed equally among the state's residents.[23] With respect to

22. See Chapter Three, pp. 59-66.
23. Given a diminishing marginal utility of income function, these two assumptions can be considered, for all practical purposes, to yield a minimum and a maximum estimate of the resulting change in welfare. The theoretical minimum and maximum would be obtained by assuming that the entire appropriation was distributed to the highest and the lowest income classes, respectively.

the distribution of costs, it is assumed that the state's Federal tax burden in support of the Corps appropriation equals the present value of total program costs to the state and is allocated to the state's residents in proportion to the existing state distribution of the total Federal tax by income class.[24]

Thus, in performing the calculations appropriate to these assumptions, the state appropriation figures will be weighted alternately by the state welfare weights found in the income and population columns of Table 28. Similarly, the state cost figures will be weighted by the state welfare weights found in the Federal tax burden column of Table 28. By subtracting the weighted cost values from each of the alternative weighted gain values, a practical minimum and maximum estimate of the direction and magnitude of the change in welfare can be made for each state. The results of this application of welfare weights to the flow-of-funds data is expressed in Table 29.

TABLE 29

Net Welfare Impact of Corps Program Under Two Alternative Assumptions Concerning the Distribution of Money Income Gains by State, 1946 to 1962

State	Net Welfare Impact When Income Gains Are	
	Distributed as Present Income, Thousands of Dollars	Distributed Equally, Thousands of Dollars
Oregon	458,859	688,368
Washington	427,377	641,422
South Dakota	421,958	601,312
North Dakota	414,396	591,326
Arkansas	372,656	549,305
Kentucky	291,282	443,013
Louisiana	289,666	445,209
Oklahoma	238,427	368,689
Tennessee	183,086	298,958
Kansas	164,338	267,478
Mississippi	132,136	202,682
West Virginia	101,055	157,448
Texas	92,766	256,445
Georgia	87,346	157,271
Nebraska	63,263	111,143
Missouri	52,259	146,237

24. See footnote 23, Chapter Three.

TABLE 29 (Continued)

State	Net Welfare Impact When Income Gains Are	
	Distributed as Present Income, Thousands of Dollars	Distributed Equally, Thousands of Dollars
Alabama	50,925	95,416
Florida	45,570	124,544
South Carolina	43,513	77,012
Iowa	31,074	79,152
Vermont	28,357	42,535
Idaho	27,345	46,085
New Mexico	17,314	34,095
Montana	11,829	26,378
Alaska	8,741	15,234
New Hampshire	6,969	17,126
Hawaii	−3,549	1,056
Arizona	−6,586	2,131
Nevada	−8,469	−7,699
Wyoming	−8,617	−7,383
Virginia	−9,557	25,494
Utah	−19,495	−18,611
Delaware	−19,513	−16,083
Maine	−24,058	−21,885
Rhode Island	−24,322	−20,620
North Carolina	−39,680	−16,528
Colorado	−55,118	−47,765
Indiana	−56,331	−43,912
California	−59,004	165,093
Minnesota	−68,799	−51,189
Connecticut	−77,044	−61,861
Wisconsin	−131,649	−130,466
Michigan	−132,381	−71,128
Maryland	−143,612	−130,932
Massachusetts	−146,998	−116,436
New Jersey	−153,681	−131,439
Ohio	−165,763	−88,903
Pennsylvania	−245,011	−162,680
Illinois	−268,227	−194,789
New York	−728,072	−671,619
United States	1,466,971	4,665,729

What conclusions can be drawn from the results of this experiment? First of all, given the assumptions and accepted utility function, it appears likely that the net welfare impact of the postwar Corps program has been both positive and rather sizable. More precisely, because the assumptions concerning the intra-regional distribution of the money income increment are, in some sense, limiting cases, the redistribution of income caused by the regional allocation of Federal appropriations and taxes has likely resulted in an increase in national welfare equal to that which would have occurred if from 1 to 5 billion dollars had been distributed among a group of individuals of the average gross income level.[25]

The significance of this conclusion is that, in distinction to the preceding net flow-of-funds analysis, this sort of experiment is at least capable of supporting, albeit weakly, some statement concerning the national welfare impact of the redistribution of money income caused by a Federal expenditure program.[26] That is, by accepting a particular socially determined marginal utility of income function and by positing seemingly reasonable limiting assumptions concerning the intra-regional distribution of the money income increment, the resulting statement appears to be both more helpful and more satisfying than the rather sterile conclusion of the earlier analysis.

In addition to this national impact, it is also interesting to note the disparate effect of the welfare weights on individual states. Thus, for example, when it is assumed that the state money income gains are distributed equally among the state's residents, four states (Hawaii, Arizona, Virginia, and California) which experienced a net loss of money income demonstrate a positive net welfare impact. Indeed, because of the shape of the accepted marginal utility of income function, the greater the degree to which the intra-regional distribution of money income gains favors low-income groups, the more states which will demonstrate a positive welfare impact and the larger will be the estimated national welfare impact.

25. It will be recalled that the implied marginal utility of income of the average gross income level was taken to be the *numeraire* on which the welfare weights are based.

26. Because the size of the total Federal Corps appropriation equaled the size of the Federal tax collections which supported it, the results of the previous analysis on the national level were required to demonstrate a national net flow of money income effect equal to zero. Consequently, no judgment concerning the welfare impact of the program on a national level could be drawn. Our claim in that analysis was limited to the statement that the impact simply tended to equalize state per capita incomes.

Finally, although obvious if the general nature of the posited marginal utility of income function is given, it would perhaps be helpful to delineate those factors which determine the magnitude of the welfare impact which results from the simple redistributional consequences of Federal fiscal transactions. If economic growth consequences of the transactions are abstracted from, such a welfare impact is a positive function of some combination of (1) the degree of progressivity of the entire Federal tax structure, (2) the degree to which the regional allocation of the budget favors low income areas, and (3) the degree to which the intra-regional distribution of the benefits of the Federal appropriation favors low income groups within the regions.

As a second experiment in welfare evaluation, an attempt is made to evaluate the efficacy of the southern Corps program in securing the goal of maximum economic welfare by applying a welfare maximization criterion to the benefit-cost data of the projects constructed in this region during the postwar period. Through such an experiment not only will a direct evaluation of the efficacy of the program in securing a welfare maximum be obtained but also an additional evaluation of the social worth of each of the projects. The conclusions yielded by this sort of experiment can in no way be considered normative; nevertheless, its results are of rather unique interest. This is so because such an experiment is capable of clearly isolating the effect of including in the welfare function that primary, though often ignored, determinant of the welfare impact of an economic change, namely, the redistributive impact of such a change. Stated somewhat differently, if a set of projects is evaluated by a criterion which is based on a naive welfare function which values increments of expected income to different individuals equally (i.e., a function which defines social economic welfare as a single-valued function of the size of the income pie), and then these projects are evaluated by the same criterion but based on a welfare function which values additional dollars of expected income to different individuals differently (i.e., a function which, recognizing that increments of income to different people yield different changes in social welfare, modifies the value of income flows depending upon the recipient), the effect of such equity considerations on project evaluation can be clearly seen. Moreover, by extrapolating the results obtained in the re-evaluation of southern projects, and therefore low income area projects, to projects whose created income streams accrue to high income areas, insight can be gained into the effect of the income position of project beneficiaries on the allocation of Federal expenditures.

The essence of this experiment could be described as the re-evaluation of all visible flows of project costs and benefits according the estimated welfare losses and gains of the individuals affected by these flows.[27] Conceptually, these individuals can be divided into two, non-mutually exclusive categories for any given project: (1) those individuals who are the beneficiaries of the stream of project outputs and (2) those individuals who bear the cost of constructing and maintaining the project. The individuals in the second of these groups can be further distinguished on the basis of the channel through which their contribution is made, i.e., (1) those individuals who bear the local project costs and (2) those individuals who bear the Federal project costs.

In treating the beneficiaries of a project's benefits, it is first assumed that the entire list of a project's beneficiaries is composed of the residents of the state in which the project is located. In addition, it is assumed that the benefit stream is distributed among the state's residents in proportion to the existing distribution of state income by income classes.[28] With these two assumptions, the welfare weight attached to the present value of the benefit stream for any given project is that weight found in the income column of Table 28 corresponding to the state in which the project is located.

In dealing with the locally borne costs, it is assumed that the total burden is carried by the residents of the state in which the project is located and further that the burden of these costs falls on the state's residents in proportion to the distribution of the total Federal tax burden by income class. That is to say, it is assumed that the local tax collections in support of a Corps project

27. The welfare gains and losses are expressed in terms of the welfare impact of dollars of gain or loss to an individual of the average gross income level.

28. For other necessary assumptions relating to the project data see Chapter Five, pp. 106-107.

are spread over a state's residents with the same degree of progressivity as the total Federal tax structure. Thus, for any given project the welfare weight attached to the present value of the local cost stream is that weight found in the Federal tax burden column of Table 28 corresponding to the state in which the project is located.

The remaining costs are those borne by the Federal government. Because these expenditures are appropriated by Congress out of the general fund of the treasury, they are borne by all of the taxpayers of the nation. Moreover, because the general fund of the treasury is composed of the tax receipts of the entire Federal tax structure, these Federal project costs are borne by United States residents in proportion to the distribution of the total Federal tax burden by income class. Thus, for any given project, the welfare weight attached to the present value of the Federal cost stream is that weight found in the Federal tax burden column of Table 28 corresponding to the United States.

The criterion by which this set of weighted benefit and cost variables for each project is evaluated in this experiment is the benefit-cost ratio.[29] The parameters used in the criterion, namely the interest rate and the length of project life, are specified to be 5.5 percent and 50 years, respectively. The results of the experiment for the southern Corps projects are presented in Table 30.

A comparison of the results in this table with those presented earlier shows that a substantial number of the projects which failed to satisfy the benefit-cost criterion when maximum national income or economic efficiency was the sole objective do, in fact, satisfy it when the objective is multidimensional. In Chapter Five it was shown that 72 of the 147 southern projects bearing 50 percent of the total Federal funds committed failed to satisfy the same criterion when maximum national income was the goal and when welfare weights were not attached to the costs and benefits.[30] When the redistributive impact is used to revalue the pure income variables, i.e., when the goal becomes multidimensional, only 25 of the projects representing 18 percent of the Federal funds committed

29. See Chapter Five, pp. 101-102.
30. See Chapter Five, p. 112.

TABLE 30

*Benefit-Cost Ratios of Projects Constructed in Ten Southern States
From 1946 to 1962 When Welfare Equivalent Weights Are Attached to
Benefits and Costs* [a]

Benefit-Cost Ratio	Number of Projects	Federal Funds Committed, Thousands of Dollars	Percent of Total Federal Funds Committed
.60– .79	0	—	—
.80– .99	25	472,184	17.86
1.00–1.19	34	674,498	25.50
1.20–1.39	32	646,744	24.45
1.40–1.59	13	123,150	4.66
1.60–1.79	8	145,867	5.52
1.80–1.99	9	319,099	12.07
2.00–2.49	11	116,486	4.41
2.50–2.99	5	126,882	4.80
3.00–4.99	6	5,969	.23
5.00– or more	4	13,123	.50
	147	2,644,001	100.0

a. Future streams are evaluated by a 5.5-percent rate of interest. See also the first footnote of Table 17.

are rejected by the criterion. Thus, it is estimated that 47 of the projects representing 32 percent of the Federal funds committed will result in both a decrease in the expected size of the national income and a concurrent increase in expected total social welfare, while 25 of the projects accounting for 18 percent of the Federal funds committed will result in a decrease of both expected national income and social welfare.

In explanation of this result, it is clear that the above-average welfare weights attached to the benefits of projects whose beneficiaries are low income groups permits such projects to be accepted for construction even though they fail to pass the pure income (economic efficiency) test, i.e., permits them to meet a less stringent dollar test than projects whose beneficiaries are higher income groups. Extrapolating this result, one can see that if this form of criterion were used on a national scale, those projects whose beneficiaries are of the below average income groups would be substantially favored in the allocation of appropriations. On the other hand, those projects whose beneficiaries are of the above average income groups would be forced to meet a more stringent dollar test. Thus, the effect of including the redistributive impact in the welfare function would be to restrict project construction in high income regions and expand it in low income regions. Those regions of rather average income levels would remain relatively unaffected by such an inclusion.[31]

Moreover, from these results a further insight into the feasibility of redistributing income through such a Federal investment program can be gained. In Chapter Six, it will be recalled, it was suggested that the redistribution of income through the construction of economically inefficient projects in favored areas was, because of the resulting decrease in national income, an inefficient means of

31. This extrapolation was, in fact, indirectly made in an analysis which treated all of the new Corps projects started in the period 1958 to 1962. By re-evaluating all 240 of these projects (representing some $2.73 billion dollars in Federal funds committed) by both an effective pure efficiency criterion (the benefit-cost ratio with a 5.5 percent rate of interest and a length of project life of 50 years) and the multifaceted welfare criterion discussed previously, an attempt was made to determine which of these criteria could better explain the actual allocation of committed Federal funds, i.e., to ascertain whether or not the inclusion of additional welfare considerations besides efficiency into the criterion would yield a superior approximation of the actual allocation of Federal funds. In this analysis, the actual state allocation of Federal funds committed expressed in relative terms was compared to the relative state allocation which would have occurred if (1) the effective pure efficiency criterion and (2) the welfare criterion were used by Congress as sole guides for the allocation of Federal funds. Although use of both the pure efficiency and the welfare criterion would have resulted in a reduced total program (total Federal funds committed of 1.71 billion dollars or 63 percent of the total in the case of the pure efficiency criterion and 2.23 billion dollars or 82 percent of the total in the case of the welfare criterion), the welfare criterion yielded a substantially closer approximation to the actual allocation than did the pure efficiency criterion. In the study, the measurement of the degree to which the experimental relative allocations approximated the actual relative allocation was accomplished through the traditional Chi-square based "goodness of fit" technique which yielded a value of 26.9 when the pure efficiency allocation was compared with the actual and a value of 8.3, signifying a substantially closer fit, when the welfare allocation was compared with the actual. Thus, not only does this experiment allow conclusions to be drawn on the allocation criteria actually used by the Congress (namely, that Congress does react to welfare considerations other than pure efficiency, that projects in low income areas are, in fact, favored relative to projects in high income regions) but also allows an evaluation of the reallocative effect of making sole use of a multifaceted welfare criterion as opposed to exclusive use of an effective pure efficiency test. By comparing the relative geographical distribution of Federal funds committed to those of the 240 projects passing

securing the desired income distribution.[32] Through this experiment, however, a somewhat modified position becomes apparent. By substituting a multidimensional welfare function for the single-valued national income function, the results of Table 30 demonstrate that the redistribution of income through the construction of some economically inefficient projects may well be a desirable technique. Because the expected welfare gains of those 32 projects which are accepted by the welfare criterion but rejected by the efficiency criterion exceed the expected welfare losses, it is clear that expected total social economic welfare has increased. Thus, given the multidimensional welfare function based upon the estimate of the marginal utility of income function which was adopted from the policy-makers, construction of the 32 economically inefficient projects may well be an efficient means of securing the desired redistribution. Again, however, it is clear that a rather more desirable situation would exist if an abundance of economically efficient projects are available in the favored region, i.e., if the desired income redistribution could be achieved with no expected decrease in the size of the national income.

Finally, because this criterion, which overtly favors a low income region such as the South, nevertheless rejects a substantial number of projects which passed the rather nondiscriminating efficiency test used by the Corps, additional doubt concerning the appropriateness of the present Corps approach cannot help but arise.

---

the pure efficiency test with the relative geographical distribution when the same size budget was allocated by means of the welfare criterion, it was observed that the program was restricted in the higher income states and expanded in the lower income regions. Whereas the twenty states with the lowest weights received 54 percent of the budget when the efficiency criterion was applied, these states received only 37 percent of the budget when the welfare criterion was applied. On the other hand, the twenty states with the highest weights received 43 percent of the budget when the welfare criterion was applied but only 31 percent when the efficiency criterion was applied. Thus the extrapolation cited in the text does appear verified.

32. See Chapter Six, pp. 120-124.

Appendix A

An Estimate of the State Incidence of Federal Taxes

To ESTIMATE the share of the taxes paid by the residents of each of the 50 states for the Federal rivers and harbors and flood control budget, three steps are necessary: (1) total Federal appropriations to the program must be determined, (2) the incidence of total Federal taxes paid by the residents of each state must be estimated, and (3) the amount of the total program appropriation must be distributed among the states in proportion to the total Federal taxes paid. This procedure assumes that the residents of a given state will help to finance any given Federal expenditure program in proportion to their contribution to total Federal tax revenue. In Table 9 the first step of this procedure was accomplished, and total program appropriations were listed in that table by year.

The second step is somewhat more rigorous. Primarily, it involves the determination of a method to estimate the state incidence of Federal taxes and then the determination of what years to be used in such an estimation. The method used in this study is derived basically from a 1943 study by Professor Harold M. Groves,[1] in

1. Harold M. Groves, *Federal, State and Local Government Fiscal Relations,* Senate Document 69, 78th Congress, 1st Session, pp. 207–220. The basic method and especially the assumptions used in both this study and Groves's study have been widely used. See Twentieth Century Fund, *Studies in Current Tax Problems,* pp. 1–52; Temporary National Economic Committee, *Who Pays the Taxes?,* Monograph 3 (Washington, D.C.: Government Printing Office, 1940); Social Security Board, *Fiscal Capacity of the States,* Bureau of Research and Statistics Memorandum No. 43 (Washington, D.C.: 1941), pp. I. 43–I. 47; Schaller, "Federal Grants-in-Aid and Differences in State Per Capita Incomes, 1929, 1939, and 1949," *National Tax Journal,* and J. Wilner Sundelson and Selma J. Mushkin, *The Measurement of State and Local Tax Effort.*

which he estimated the state distribution of Federal tax incidence for fiscal year 1940. The years which are used in this study for such an estimate are 1950 and 1958.[2]

The individual Federal taxes presented in Table 31 are placed in four classifications depending on the assumptions made in their allocation. First, the individual income tax is allocated to the states on the basis of collection. The assumption is that the taxpayer files his return in the state in which he resides.[3] Second, the corporate taxes—income, capital stock, and excess profits—are distributed in proportion to income from dividends and interest.[4] Third, the estate and gift taxes and the admissions taxes are allocated accord-

2. The reason for not forming such a distribution for each of the 17 years is that the proportion of total Federal taxes paid by any given state changes only slowly over time. The proportion is, because of the predominance of the progressive income tax, largely determined by the level of per capita income and the size of the population, and these variables have changed very slowly over time. Of the ten states, only Florida's share of total Federal taxes changed by as much as .5 percent between 1950 and 1958. The 1950 distribution was used to estimate taxes for the years 1946 to 1954, and the 1958 distribution was used for the years 1955 to 1962.

3. It is assumed that personal income taxes are not shifted. Nevertheless, because taxpayers may file returns in either the state in which they live or the state in which they work, collections do not necessarily portray incidence. A sample of 1936 tax returns, however, showed that only 3.3 percent of the returns, accounting for 3.4 percent of statutory income, were not filed in the state of residence and that by far the majority of these occurred in the Washington, D.C., and the New York City areas. U.S. Treasury Department, *Treasury Department Bulletin* (October, 1941), p. 52. The data for 1950 total income taxes and the state in which the returns were filed were secured from U.S. Commissioner of Internal Revenue, *Annual Report of the Commissioner of Internal Revenue, 1950,* pp. 66 ff.; that for 1958 from *ibid.,* 1958, pp. 84 ff.

4. This procedure is based on the orthodox assumption that these corporate taxes affect the corporation directly and thus reduce dividend payments by the amount of tax collected. Moreover, it is assumed that this reduction was proportionate to the size of the dividend and interest payment received. See Groves, *op. cit.,* p. 208. Note that this orthodox theory has been challenged by the hypothesis that some part of this tax may be shifted forward to the consumer, J. Fred Weston, "The Incidence and Effects of the Corporate Income Tax," *National Tax Journal,* II (December, 1949), 300–315. The solution to the problem appears, at present, to be statistically unsolvable. The data on the corporate taxes paid were secured from U.S. Commissioner of Internal Revenue, *op. cit.,* 1950, pp. 66 ff. and *ibid.,* 1958, pp. 84 ff. The state distributions of total interest and dividend payments were secured from U.S. Department of Commerce, *Survey of Current Business* (August, 1951), p. 20 for fiscal year 1950 and *ibid.* (August, 1959), p. 21 for fiscal year 1958.

ing to the state of collection.[5] Finally, all of the remaining taxes listed in Table 31 are distributed on the assumption that incidence of the tax falls on the final consumer.[6]

TABLE 31

Total Federal Taxes Paid, 1950 and 1958 [a]

Revenue Source	1950 [b]	1958 [b]
	Millions of Dollars	
Individual Income Tax	17,153	38,569
Corporate Taxes [c]	10,854	20,533
Estate Tax	657	1,277
Gift Tax	49	134
Admissions Tax	413	98
Motor Vehicle Excises [d]	1,421	3,624
Alcohol Taxes	2,219	2,946
Electrical Energy Taxes	86	—
Others:	3,889	4,954
Tobacco Taxes	1,328	1,734
Stamp Taxes [e]	85	109
Manufacturers' Excises [f]	330	465
Retailers' Excises	409	342
Miscellaneous [g]	1,308	1,504
Customs	429	800
Total	36,741	72,135

a. See footnotes 3, 4, 5, and 6 of Appendix A for sources of tax data.
b. The data are for fiscal years 1950 and 1958.
c. Includes corporate income, excess profits, and capital stock taxes.
d. See footnote 6 of Appendix A.
e. Includes stamp tax on playing cards.
f. Excludes motor vehicle excise taxes.
g. Includes taxes on sugar, communications, transportation, use of safe deposit boxes, coconut and other processed vegetable oils, narcotics and marihuana, club dues, initiation fees, coin-operated games, bowling alleys, gambling, adulterated or processed butter, cheese or oleomargerine, firearms, transfers, etc.

5. The data on these taxes were secured from U.S. Commissioner of Internal Revenue, *op. cit.*, 1950, pp. 70 and 96 and *ibid.*, 1958, pp. 86-87 and 94-95.
6. The motor vehicle taxes (including gasoline, lubricating oil, tires, motor vehicles, oil by pipeline, and the use taxes) are allocated to the states in proportion to motor vehicle registrations. The data on the total payment of these taxes were obtained from U.S. Commissioner of Internal Revenue, *op. cit.*, 1950, pp. 84-86 and *ibid.*, 1958, pp. 92-93. Data on motor vehicle registration (minus publicly owned vehicles and net of re-registration) were obtained from U.S. Bureau of the Census, *Statistical Abstract of the United States*, 1952, p. 497 and *ibid.*, 1960, p. 513.
The alcoholic beverage taxes are allocated in proportion to the state distribution of total sales of retail package liquor stores and drinking places. Total

Through the resulting statistical series, the proportion of the total Federal tax bill paid by each of the 50 states can be estimated. The results of this procedure are presented in Table 7 for an average of the years 1950 and 1958. The total Federal program appropriation for each of the 17 years was then allocated to each state on the basis of these proportions.

---

alcohol tax data were secured from U.S. Commissioner of Internal Revenue, *op. cit.*, 1950, p. 80 and *ibid.*, 1958, pp. 86–87. The liquor sales data are from U.S. Bureau of the Census, *Census of Business*, 1948, Vol. I, pp. 1.46 and 1.51 and *ibid.*, 1958, Vol. II, pp. 1.57 and 1.59. An average of the 1948 and 1954 data was used to estimate 1950 sales.

The electrical energy tax (1950 only) was allocated in proportion to electrical energy production. Data on the tax were secured from U.S. Commissioner of Internal Revenue, *op. cit.*, 1950, p. 86. Data on electrical energy production were secured from *Statistical Abstract of the United States*, 1952, p. 481. There was no Federal electrical energy tax in 1958.

The remaining taxes, which are mainly tobacco, manufacturers' and retailers' excise taxes plus customs collections (See footnotes to Table 31 for complete breakdown), are allocated to the states in proportion to total retail sales. Data on the taxes were secured from U.S. Commissioner of Internal Revenue, *op. cit.*, 1950, pp. 82, 84, 86–92 and *ibid.*, 1958, pp. 90–91, 103–105, and (for customs collections) U.S. Treasury Department, *Annual Report of the Secretary of the Treasury*, 1950, p. 66 and *ibid.*, 1958, p. 74. Data on the sales of retail stores were secured from U.S. Bureau of the Census, *op. cit.*, 1948, Vol. I, p. 1.07; *ibid.*, Vol. I, p. 1.41 and *ibid.*, Vol. II, p. 1.11. Again sales data for 1950 are an average of 1948 and 1954 retail sales.

Risk, Uncertainty, and Water Resource Investment Decisions

THE DECISION to appropriate funds for the construction of water resource projects involves an evaluation of the same types of evidence as the decision to invest in additional capital equipment on the part of the firm or the decision to purchase a new car on the part of the individual consumer. Because of the entrepreneur's lack of perfect foreknowledge, such a decision to invest waits upon his evaluation of uncertain anticipated returns attributable to the investment and a comparison of these anticipations with uncertain estimated costs. The same situation exists with the individual consumer. In both of these cases, decisions are made by imperfect mechanisms (individuals) which evaluate imperfect evidence (the anticipations of uncertain returns and costs).

A similar situation exists in the decision-making framework employed by the Federal government in evaluating alternative proposed investments in rivers and harbors projects. However, the decision mechanism, in this case, is not an individual but rather the body corporate of the Congress, and, as such, the imperfectness of the mechanism may well be compounded. As described in Chapter Two, the evidence in this situation is that presented by the U.S. Army Corps of Engineers to the Congress and is based upon Corps estimates of both the costs and the benefits expected in each individual project. Thus, as in the case of private decisions, public choice is also performed under conditions of risk and uncertainty.

The General Nature of Risk and Uncertainty

To both social scientists and decision-makers the treatment of uncertain expectations remains somewhat nebulous. In their analyses (both theoretical and practical) one repeatedly finds the existence of imperfect foreknowledge impounded in the box of *ceteris paribus* and uncertainty of outcome treated, in Frank Knight's words, "as if it were a gamble on a known mathematical chance." However, certain of the key issues have been dealt with and a body of acceptable doctrine has evolved.

The first of these definitive statements was made by Knight in *Risk, Uncertainty and Profit*, where he was the first to explicitly set forth the dichotomy between different varieties of uncertainty. That type of uncertainty associated with an isomorphic mechanism which is capable of turning out mutually exclusive sets of alternatives, each with an objective probability *measurement*, he named risk. Its opposite, that type of uncertainty in which ". . . there is *no valid basis of any kind* for classifying instances" or for which ". . . there is no possibility of forming *in any way* groups of instances of sufficient homogeneity to make possible a quantitative determination of true probability," [1] he called true uncertainty.

Another major clarification came some years later in the work of Nicholas Georgescu-Roegen. In a rather unique analysis, Georgescu pointed out that the Knightian dichotomy transformed the concept of expectations into two completely separate and extreme categories ". . . which, strictly speaking, cannot represent expectations common in real life." [2] In reality, that is, decisions must be made on anticipations which form an infinite continuum between these two extremes. More significantly, Georgescu proceeded to demonstrate that neither ordinal nor cardinal numerical values can be applied to any point on this range of expectations except the extreme point of true risk. Expectation, then, becomes ". . . 'the state of the mind [of a given individual] with respect to an assertion, a coming event, or any other matter on which absolute knowledge does not [necessarily] exist.' " [3]

As a consequence of this pair of contributions,[4] the generally

1. Frank Knight, *Risk, Uncertainty and Profit*, pp. 225 and 231.
2. Nicholas Georgescu-Roegen, "The Nature of Expectation and Uncertainty," *Expectations, Uncertainty and Business Behavior*, Mary Jean Bowman, ed., p. 25.
3. *Ibid.*, p. 12. (Brackets are in the original.)
4. Nearly all of the discussion of subjective probability and decision theory between the contributions of Knight and Georgescu has been ignored in this brief discussion. In a rather more complete discussion of uncertainty in the

accepted theory of risk and uncertainty has abandoned its early reliance on the concept of the probability distribution of expectations concerning any given event. Decision-making is now viewed as being dependent upon expectations which lie along this continuum from pure risk to pure uncertainty, expectations which by their very nature are neither cardinally nor ordinally measurable.

It should be noted, however, that although expectations are neither cardinally nor ordinally measurable, they are comparable. To paraphrase Georgescu: because of the existence of common elements in the evidence, it is possible for the decision-maker to establish various hierarchies among expectations upon which to base a rational decision. Among the common elements which form the basis for such comparability are: (1) the importance of past observations, (2) the credibility of each piece of information, and (3) the logical relation between each piece of evidence and its corresponding prediction. In his words,

[T]he hierarchy in each direction can be established by any rational individual according to that theory of probability connected with the particular facet of expectation: past observations, credibility, logical relation.[5]

After each expectation is ranked according to these criteria, the decision is made. But if, as usually is true, these ranked hierarchies are contradictory, to make a choice will involve the assigning of weights to the various and opposing hierarchies in a largely subjective and arbitrary manner.

Decisions regarding expectations of this type involve mainly intuition and good judgment in weighing the evidence and scarcely any numerical operations.[6]

Concepts of Risk and Uncertainty in Water Resource Projects

As with all evidence which underlies decision-making under conditions of uncertainty, so too the Corps estimated values of

---

area of water resource decisions, Robert Dorfman discusses these contributions and states that ". . . at the present state of development . . . [their] conclusions cannot be applied to decisions in the water-resource field." See Maass Hufschmidt, *et al., Design of Water Resource Systems,* pp. 129–145.

5. Georgescu-Roegen, *op. cit.,* p. 27.
6. *Ibid.,* p. 27.

project costs and benefits are simply best guesses. Admittedly, these best guesses or expectations are a significant factor in the formation of an investment decision. However, just as the arithmetic mean is but a single moment out of an infinity of moments needed to completely describe a frequency distribution, so these estimated values are incomplete (and often misleading) descriptions of the distribution of possible benefits and costs. Because of the varying degrees of uncertainty involved in these estimates, specific allowance must, if possible, be introduced into the decision-making process. For analytical purposes, the risk and uncertainty elements contained in water resource projects can be separated into three categories. They are: (1) uncertainties peculiar to the concepts in which all projects are evaluated, i.e., costs and benefits, (2) uncertainties associated with particular types of projects, and (3) uncertainties peculiar to individual projects.

UNCERTAINTIES PECULIAR TO THE CONCEPTS OF PROJECT COSTS AND BENEFITS. In addition to dealing with separate and unique phenomena, the concepts of project costs and benefits differ with respect to several important characteristics. Significantly, all of these differences appear to result in a substantial divergence in the degree of uncertainty included in the estimates of each of them. That is to say, because of both the estimation techniques used and the essential characteristics of the concept itself, estimates of project benefits must, generally, be viewed as possessing a substantially different degree of credibility than estimates of project costs. To more fully understand the meaning of this statement as well as the reasoning upon which it is based, the causes of some of these differences are investigated by comparing both the nature of several characteristics of the two concepts and the techniques by which they are estimated. Those attributes to be briefly evaluated are the following: (1) the possibility of the continuous reappraisal of estimate accuracy, (2) the degree to which the variables are deferred or immediate, (3) the nature of the components upon which the real estimates are based, (4) the relative importance and accuracy of future price projections, and (5) the relative insurability of project costs and benefits.

First, because of the ease of *ex post* measurement in the case of project costs, it is possible and relatively easy to continually reappraise the magnitude of the margin of error between the actual and the estimated values. As both construction costs and operating, repair, and maintenance costs are actually experienced in completed projects and can be compared to their estimated counterparts, the Corps of Engineers can continually adjust its estimation procedures to yield more accurate predictions. As regards the concept of benefits, however, attempts to secure such *ex post* measurement are extremely difficult. Because the value of actual flood damage without a project can never be experienced once the project is constructed, actual flood control benefits, for example, are neither easily nor accurately compared with preconstruction estimates of flood damage to be averted by the project. The absence of this characteristic in the benefit concept forces the Corps to estimate anew in each case without the advantage of being able to discover and correct overt bias in the estimation procedure.

The second distinguishing characteristic concerns the degree to which project costs and benefits are deferred rather than immediate variables. Because deferred effects involve a greater degree of uncertainty than do immediate effects, this too is a relevant distinction. In the process of project evaluation, the concept of costs has been divided into two categories: those costs which are deferred (operation, maintenance, and repair costs) and those costs which are borne immediately (investment costs). The importance of time-related uncertainty involved in the concept of costs is thus determined by the ratio of annual deferred costs to immediate costs. According to Eckstein the effective range of this ratio is .01 to .1.[7] On the other hand, the benefits which accrue to a project are all deferred, and moreover, if the level of benefits depends on the degree of economic development of a region, the bulk of the benefits will occur late in the life of a project; i.e., they are deferred far into the future. Thus, because of this characteristic, the concept of project benefits appears to be subject to a relatively greater burden of those uncertainties related to the passage of time than is the concept of project costs.

In the third place, the variables upon which real benefit esti-

7. Eckstein, *Water Resource Development*, pp. 58 and 85.

mates are based differ, by their very nature, so widely from the variables which form the basis of real cost estimates that the analyses to which they give rise must be viewed with different degrees of reservation. Thus, whereas real benefits depend primarily upon variables of an evolutionary and, hence, relatively unpredictable nature, real costs depend upon the semi-static principles of engineering theory. The rate and trend of regional economic development, the degree to which navigation will be superseded by other modes of transportation during the next century, and the nature and extent of property development along river frontage are examples of the type of variables involved in the estimation of real benefits. Cost estimates, on the other hand, are based on physical and engineering data which are quantitatively measurable. The number of tons of earth to be moved, the number of tons of concrete to be poured, the number of personnel required to operate an installation, and the length of life of replaceable equipment exemplify the variables upon which cost estimates are based. Thus, because the variables underlying the estimation of real costs appear to be more amenable to accurate *ex ante* measurement than the variables underlying benefit estimation, it seems reasonable to again view cost estimates with less skepticism than estimates of benefits.

A fourth relevant difference concerns the relative importance and accuracy of future price projections in the transformation of real benefit and cost estimates into their monetary counterparts. First, because all benefits accrue in the future while most costs are immediate, the projection of future prices to be attached to predicted real benefits is extremely important. The diminishing credibility of far distant projections again forces the concept of project benefits to be viewed with a relatively greater degree of skepticism than the cost concept. In addition, it seems plausible to claim that to some extent the variables upon which future cost estimates are based are somewhat more susceptible to accurate price projection than are the variables underlying benefit estimates. Surely, for example, the trend in wage rates paid to operating personnel is less difficult to anticipate than the trend in local real estate values.

The final difference in these two concepts lies in the relative presence (or absence) of a repeatable process which permits the determination of some measurement of objective probability. Because of the actual repetition of the process of cost estimation over a long period of time and the possibility of checking estimated with actual values, the concept of project costs appears to be most closely associated with such a process. By comparing the estimated cost with the actual cost, a distribution of prediction error could be formed and an observed relative frequency (probability) for each size of error could be determined. Because of the possibility of such a distribution, some image of a repeatable, measurable process is present. In the case of benefits, however, the time element and the difficulty of accurately measuring *ex post* results nearly eliminate all possibility of creating such a repeatable, probability-producing process. That is, because of the previously mentioned differences in the nature of cost and benefit estimates, it appears that costs are substantially more insurable than are benefits.

The framework of uncertainty theory is applied by locating the concepts of expected project benefits and costs on the Map of Expectations—a concept developed by Georgescu-Roegen to allow given sets of multifaceted expectations to be labeled more credible or less credible.[8] In this analysis, two criteria are used to locate these concepts on the Map: the Knight criterion and the Georgescu criterion. With respect to the Knight criterion, a concept is positioned somewhere on the continuum between pure risk and true uncertainty by determining whether or not there is any sort of isomorphic mechanism present which will enable the computation of objective, numerical probabilities for the outcomes involved. Those variables which obviously possess this sort of mechanism will be located at the extreme of pure risk: those variables in which there is complete absence of such a mechanism will be located at the extreme of true uncertainty. In Figure 5, the continuum of all possible points between these two extremes is defined by the line *AB* on the Map of Expectations. Thus, the more evident it is that such a mechanism may be present, that is, the more insurable and predictable is the estimated outcome of a variable, the closer will it lie to point *A* on the continuum.

8. The Map of Expectations presented here is a modification of the map presented by Georgescu. See Georgescu-Roegen, *op. cit.,* p. 23.

The Georgescu criterion for locating concepts on the Map, i.e., for determining the credibility of outcomes, also embodies the idea of a continuum. In this case, however, the continuum ranges from absolute certainty, *C*, to absolute impossibility, *I*,[9] with an infinite number of paths between the two. In the case of the unique

Figure 5. Map of Expectations

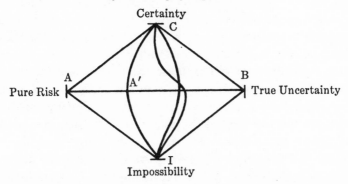

path *CAI*, that is, the path which passes through the pure risk extremum on the Knightian continuum (*AB*), expectations concerning any concept are placed higher or lower on this path depending upon the numerical value of the objective probability measurement attached to them. An expectation with a probability of unity, for example, would lie at the certainty extremum of *CAI*.

9. Note that two terms are used on the Map which appear to be antonyms: absolute certainty (the term used by Georgescu) and true uncertainty (the term used by Knight). In fact, they are not. Georgescu's absolute certainty connotes the idea of perfect foreknowledge or probability = 1 and its opposite, absolute impossibility, bears the connotation of zero degree of foreknowledge or probability = O. Knightian true uncertainty, rather than being the opposite of absolute certainty, is defined as the impossibility ". . . of either calculating . . . a probability *a priori* or of determining it empirically by studying a large number of instances." (Knight, *op. cit.*, p. 226). Georgescu, it appears, misinterprets this concept of true uncertainty when he writes in description of the Knightian concept ". . . *uncertainty expectations,* whose evidence includes no information about the predicted event." (Georgescu-Roegen, *op. cit.*, p. 25). The point is that uncertainty expectations may well possess large amounts of information about the predicted event but not that type of information which enables the computation of the objective probability of the event. "The essential and outstanding fact is that the 'instance' in question is so entirely unique that there are no others or not a sufficient number to make it possible to tabulate enough like it to form a basis for any inference of value about any real probability in the case we are interested in." (Knight, *op. cit.*, p. 226).

Eastward along the Knightian continuum, paths are reached representing more realistic concepts whose expected result cannot be determined exclusively by objective probability, that is, concepts whose expectations are based on progressively smaller degrees of risk-type or insurable evidence. In these cases, other more subjective information must be introduced into the decision-making process. That is, expectations which lie on paths other than CAI are placed higher or lower on these paths by evidence which may not be ordinally measurable or even comparable. Nevertheless, although the simple numerical probability determination present in the pure risk case is absent in these cases, it is possible for a rational individual to establish a decision hierarchy in any direction if he is given certain kinds of information. Following Georgescu, once the north-south path of these intermediate concepts has been determined by the degree of probabilistic evidence which they possess, they will be placed higher or lower on the path depending upon "the importance of past observations, . . . the credibility of each piece of evidence, . . . [and] the various logical connections between each E[vidence] and the corresponding P[rediction]." [10]

Within this framework then, the concepts of benefits and costs are first located on the east-west continuum by means of the Knight criterion, and the vertical path upon which each will lie is thereby determined. Because of the possibility of conceptualizing the existence of a repeatable process in the case of project costs as well as the relative ease of insuring these results in comparison with benefits, the concept of project costs lies to the west of the benefit concept on the Knight continuum. Stated alternatively, because it is a concept which possesses a relatively more uncertain nature, the vertical path of benefits lies to the east of the path of the cost concept.

To locate each of these concepts vertically, i.e., to establish various hierarchies among these expectations, they must be subjected to the appraisal of Georgescu's three guides. When held up to the scrutiny of the first of these criteria, i.e., the importance of past observations, it is clear that the concept of costs must be ranked

10. Georgescu-Roegen, *op. cit.,* p. 27.

above that of benefits. Because of the relative ease of *ex post* measurement and therefore the possibility of continually reappraising error margins, cost estimates appear to make substantially better use of the corrective value of past observations than do estimates of benefits.

The judgment yielded by the second criterion, i.e., the credibility of evidence, is similar to that yielded by the first. Because of the difficulty of *ex post* reappraisal of estimate accuracy, the additional contingencies associated with events expected far in the future, the heavier reliance on uncertain, far-distant price projections as well as the very nature of the real variables upon which estimation depends, the concept of benefits appears to possess evidence which is substantially less credible than that of project costs. Again, estimates of cost rank higher than benefit estimates.

The logical relation between evidence and prediction, the third Georgescu variable, also favors the concept of project costs. The technique of cost computations from the evidence of measurable physical and engineering data possesses a high degree of logical causality. Being based upon the measurement of existent realities, the path from evidence to prediction appears much more airtight in the case of costs than in the case of benefits. Again, project costs appear more credible and rank higher than the concept of project benefits.

In summary then, it appears to be a reasonable assertion that on the Map of Expectations the concept of project benefits lies both to the east and to the south of the concept of project costs; in Knight's terminology, benefits are more uncertain and less predictable and insurable than are costs and, in Georgescu's terminology, predictions of benefits rank lower in the subjective hierarchy of credibility, as judged by all three criteria, than similar predictions concerning project costs. If an index of credibility could be established, the conclusion of this analysis would be that, in general, the expected value of benefits for any given project possesses a lower index of credibility than the expected value of costs and, concurrently, the distribution of possible project benefits reveals a larger variance than the distribution of project costs. Figure 6 depicts such a project whose expected benefit-cost ratio, computed by these methods, equals unity. The distributions shown are subjective evaluations with no necessary measurement present. The points which the analysis makes, therefore, are that the degree of credibility associated with the expected value of benefits is smaller than that associated with the expected value of costs, and at the

Figure 6. Distributions of Benefits and Costs of a Project Whose Benefit-Cost Ratio Equals Unity

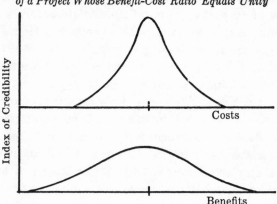

extremes, possible project benefits appear more credible than corresponding costs. Consequently, because in such a situation the variance of the distribution of benefits is greater than the variance of the distribution of costs, the claim that the degree of risk and uncertainty associated with the concept of benefits exceeds that associated with the concept of costs is accepted.[11]

UNCERTAINTIES PECULIAR TO VARIOUS PROJECT TYPES. Up to this point, the only form of project uncertainty dealt with has been concerned with the diverse nature of expectations associated with differences

11. Without explicit discussion or defense, this disparity between the uncertainty components of project benefits and costs has been noted elsewhere in the literature. In a theoretical analysis of project design, Robert Dorfman states, "Since the outputs particularly are not exactly predictable. . . ." See Maass, Hufschmidt, *et al., op. cit.,* p. 104. In 1956, Fred A. Seaton, then the Secretary of the Interior, said in appraising benefit-cost analysis, "Costs can be measured with reasonable accuracy. Benefits are much more difficult to estimate even if the analysis is confined to primary benefits. . . . [T]heir estimation involves a large element of uncertainty." U.S. Congress, Joint Economic Committee, *Federal Expenditure Policy for Economic Growth and Stability,* article by Fred A. Seaton, "Federal Expenditures and Programs for the Development of Natural Resources," p. 655.

between the concepts of benefits and costs. Uncertainty of a different form appears when projects of different purposes are compared. In each of the functional project types (navigation, flood control, and power) the procedures used to estimate both benefits and costs introduce additional uncertainties. For each project type, computations are based on unique assumptions, are dependent for their outcome on unique variables, and consequently, the estimates possess varying degrees of risk and uncertainty. For example, some of the project types produce a marketable product; some do not. The benefits of some projects can be calculated with the help of mathematical expectation; i.e., Knightian pure risk is present to some degree. The benefits of some projects are in no way related to the existence of a repeatable random-creating mechanism. A similar situation exists with respect to project costs. The expected costs of some project types are accurately measurable and obtainable; the costs of others (those based more on hydrological and meteorological uncertainties) are more difficult to obtain and measure and, therefore, less credible.

In general, then, different types of projects possess different degrees of risk and uncertainty which, in the process of project evaluation, should be neither ignored nor neglected. After these various project types are subjectively evaluated by the Georgescu and Knight criteria, each project type could be placed in a general location on the Map of Expectations. The judgments involved here, however, do not appear to be as distinct as those between the degree of uncertainty related to the concepts of project costs and benefits. Project types held up to the various criteria would not fall into consistent hierarchies, and the actual determination of credibility would depend upon the subjective weighting of the alternative Georgescu criteria. Nevertheless, it appears that these project types can, in general, be assigned areas on the Map of Expectations, areas which may not be mutually exclusive but, rather, overlapping.

Because of this problem of non-mutual exclusiveness, the development of a general and precise criterion for project evaluation must await the formation of economic tools which will allow more precise distinctions to be made between project types and which will permit considerations attributable to the differences in uncertainty among project types to be introduced into the criterion. Some recognition, however, should be made of the problem, and available information concerning uncertainty variation among project types should become part of the general evaluation presented to Congress. For example, Congress should be enabled to say, when presented with two projects bearing the same benefit-cost ratio, "Project A is for flood control and project B is for navigation. Because our expectations concerning estimated benefits appear much more certain in the case of flood control than they do in the case of navigation,[12] we should pick project A if additional uncertainty is a disutility."

RISK AND UNCERTAINTY BETWEEN INDIVIDUAL PROJECTS OF THE SAME TYPE. The third type of uncertainty comparison which must be mentioned concerns the existence of varying degrees of credibility which can be attached to the expected outcomes of projects of the same type in different situations. Project A and project B, for example, both of which are flood control projects, both of which have the same benefit-cost ratio but which are in different localities possess, in all likelihood, different possible ranges of outcome and different degrees of credibility in both their expected costs and benefits. The location of the alternatives on the Map of Expectations is again essential when these projects are evaluated. Consequently, the decision-maker should possess sufficient information on credibility of expected outcome to enable him to choose, given his reactions to risk and uncertainty, either project A or project B. Although individual projects may also occupy overlapping areas on the Map, information as to range of outcomes and evidence relevant to the various credibility criteria should be available to the decision-maker.

Suggested Treatment of Uncertain Expectations in Water Resource Project Evaluation

The treatment of uncertain expectations proposed here, although far from a complete treatment, nevertheless, does focus attention

---

12. Edward F. Renshaw, *Toward Responsible Government*, p. 61. "The conjectural and hypothetical nature of navigation benefits would make these benefits about as uncertain as any benefit imaginable."

on a phase of the problem which has thus far been neglected, namely, the existence of disparate elements of risk and uncertainty present in project costs and benefits. The device proposed to make allowance for this disparity takes the form of an uncertainty premium (discount) included in an appropriate interest rate in the discounting of both project benefits and costs. Because both the concepts of costs and benefits involve risks and uncertainties, it is argued that an uncertainty allowance should be included in the interest rates used in discounting both of them. However, because project benefits appear substantially more uncertain than do project costs, the allowance made in the discounting of expected costs should be smaller than the allowance made in the discounting of expected benefits. Finally, because of the basic dissimilarity of the concepts of benefits and costs, it is argued that they must be adjusted in opposite directions.

Before this proposal is analyzed, the following rather basic assumptions upon which it is based are discussed: (1) The problem of evaluating certain types of uncertainty can be handled by a criterion yielding a single-valued result, (2) the concept of certainty equivalent serves adequately as a first approximation, and (3) the government's role as agent for the public necessitates the treatment of more uncertain outcomes as a disutility.

A SINGLE-VALUED CRITERION. As defined, the role of a criterion is to serve as a standard by which facts and information can be organized and evaluated and by which choices between alternative proposals can be made. It, therefore, follows that the more complete the criterion, that is, the more information which it is prepared to evaluate, the more valuable it will be in the process of decision-making. Certain forms of risk and uncertainty appear to be eligible for inclusion in such a criterion. In particular, the difference in the degree of credibility which surrounds expectations of project costs and benefits, discussed earlier in detail, seems to warrant such inclusion.

This is not, then, a claim that all uncertainty is capable of treatment in such a general criterion. Rather, it is a suggestion that, if the criterion concept is to be most helpful in the decision-making process, it should include as many as possible of those variables which it is capable of handling. To be eligible for inclusion in a criterion, a concept must fulfill at least one requirement—it must be of a form which is common to all the alternatives. Although, those uncertainties which are peculiar to various types of projects or peculiar to individual projects cannot be included in a unique criterion applied to all projects, that type of risk and uncertainty which is common to all projects, such as the difference in the degree of uncertainty between costs (in general) and benefits (in general), is eligible for inclusion.

CERTAINTY EQUIVALENT CONCEPT. The "certainty equivalent" concept has been widely used in analyses which attempt to explain behavior under non-static conditions. In most of the classical discussions of this concept, the problem of buyers' and sellers' expectations toward future prices has formed the background of analysis. In these analyses, it was hypothesized that a most probable future price expected with a degree of uncertainty could be replaced by a (subjectively) certain price. As Lange has stated, "[W]e can substitute for the most probable prices actually expected with uncertainty equivalent prices expected with certainty." [13] For the buyer, the substituted price was taken to be higher than the expected, though uncertain, price; for the seller, the substituted price was taken to be lower than the expected price. The magnitude of the difference between the expected uncertain price and its equivalent certain counterpart was determined by the effective range of expectations or, as Hicks has stated, ". . . an increased dispersion will have the same effect as a reduction of the expected price, in cases where the individual plans to sell." [14]

More recently, this same concept has been applied to the analysis of private investment. As entrepreneurs, to maximize profits, carry investment expenditure up to the point where the rate of return on capital is equal to the market rate of interest, some attempt is made to allow for the uncertainty connected with the rate of return on capital in a non-static world. This attempt

13. Oscar Lange, *Price Flexibility and Employment*, p. 31.
14. John R. Hicks, *Value and Capital*, p. 125. Hicks goes on to say, "If we are to allow for uncertainty of expectations, . . . we must not take the most probable price as the representative expected price but the most probable price $\mp$ an allowance for risk." *Ibid.*, pp. 125–126. See also Lange, *op. cit.*, p. 29.

takes the form of a risk discount or risk premium added to the appropriate rate. "Investment decisions are then supposed to be based on a comparison of this 'risk adjusted' or 'certainty equivalent' yield with the market rate of interest." [15] Because of the similarity between private investment alternatives and those in the public sphere, it will be assumed that this approach is also acceptable in the formulation of government investment decisions.

Although it has been shown that uncertainty can introduce a qualitatively new dimension into the behavior of economic variables which cannot be duplicated by any certain alternative, this does not appear to be the case in dealing with such investment behavior. The situation present here is not qualitatively different from one described by Friedman in defending the use of certainty equivalents:

To exemplify phenomena explainable in terms of certainty equivalents, consider an entrepreneur committed to producing a perishable product, and suppose that a substantial period must elapse between the final decision how large a cost to incur in producing it and the sale of the product. There may be uncertainty about both the price at which he can sell the product and the output he will get for a given cost. Yet, in analyzing the entrepreneur's decision how much to produce, we should be inclined—and I think correctly—to suppose that we could replace the uncertain future situation with certainty equivalents.[16]

ATTITUDE OF FEDERAL GOVERNMENT. The position taken in this proposed treatment of risk and uncertainty is that the degree of disutility should be treated as a positive function of the degree of uncertainty and that more certain outcomes are to be preferred by the Federal government to less certain outcomes. Because of its very nature, a representative government in the investment of public funds should serve as a reflector of the attitude of the populace. And, as Lange has stated: "Entrepreneurs and consumers prefer as a rule more definite to less definite expectations." [17] Although in the real world we can observe individuals who both place

15. Franco Modigliani and Merton H. Miller, "The Cost of Capital, Corporation Finance and the Theory of Investment," *American Economic Review,* XLVIII (June, 1958), 262.
16. Milton Friedman, "Discussion," *American Economic Review,* IXL (May, 1949), 196.
17. Lange, *op. cit.,* p. 30.

a premium on risky situations (gamble) and take action to eliminate risk (buy insurance), it is clear that ". . . the great majority of market transactions are carried on in amounts that there is definitely a preference for greater certainty of expectations." [18] Also, to the other large group of investors in the country, private industrialists, uncertainty is something to be avoided rather than courted. The general use of short payoff periods and high minimum rates of return illustrate this attitude on the part of private business.[19]

The Proposal

Based on the more uncertain nature of benefits as opposed to costs, the goal of this proposal is to attempt to reach a quasi-certainty equivalent figure for both estimated costs and benefits.[20] It is proposed, therefore, that a dual premium (discount) be incorporated into the appropriate interest rate used in discounting both future benefits and costs: the higher of the two rates to be used in the discounting of expected benefits and the lower, in the discounting of deferred costs.[21]

18. Lange, op. cit., p. 30, footnote and A. C. Pigou, The Economics of Welfare, p. 776. See also Milton Friedman and L. J. Savage, "The Utility Analysis of Choices Involving Risk," Journal of Political Economy, LVI (August, 1948), 279–304.

19. Joel Dean, "Measuring the Productivity of Capital," Harvard Business Review, XXXII (January, 1954), 120-130.

20. The term quasi-certainty is used to avoid the misconception that this modification attempts to make allowance for all forms of risk and uncertainty. Its goal is to treat only that type of risk and uncertainty which is capable of being treated in a single-valued criterion, i.e., uncertainty related to all costs and benefits and illustrated by the more uncertain nature of benefits as opposed to costs.

21. In general, four different approaches to the treatment of risk and uncertainty in expectations can be distinguished: (1) the application of a correction factor to each of the future expected values of revenues and costs (i.e., raising each year's cost estimate and reducing each year's benefit estimate), (2) the inclusion of a risk premium (discount) into the rate of interest used to discount future benefits (costs), (3) a reduction of the expected length of economic life, and (4) a flat reduction in the final benefit-cost ratio. See Friedrich and Vera Lutz, The Theory of Investment of the Firm, pp. 179–192. Because the uncertainty present in both the concepts of future benefits and future costs is not independent of the passage of time (i.e., the values more remote in time are more problematical) the more distant expected values must receive a greater correction than those expected in the near future. See Eckstein, op. cit., p. 88. This correction is built into the risk premium ap-

The first of the two considerations which determine the size of this net premium centers about the dual role played by the government as it evaluates costs and benefits. As it evaluates costs, the government plays the role of a buyer—a buyer of resources to construct, operate, and maintain its projects. The certainty equivalent value for a buyer who finds greater uncertainty to be a disutility will be greater than the expected value with uncertainty. As Lange states: "[B]uyers consider a price [or cost] expected with greater uncertainty as equivalent to a *higher* most probable price [or cost] expected with less uncertainty." [22] To achieve this result by an interest rate adjustment necessitates the injection of a *discount* into the appropriate base interest rate.

In its role as an analyzer and estimator of benefits, however, the government acts as a seller. Its role here is like that of a large corporation whose stockholders are the taxpayers and whose revenue from operations is similar to benefits from investment projects. Project benefits thus resemble sales, and as a producer of benefits, the government's role is that of a seller. In the case of a seller who is faced with uncertain expectations, the certainty equivalent value will be less than the expected value under conditions of uncertainty. "[A]n increased dispersion will have the same effect as a reduction of the expected price, in cases where the individual plans to sell." [23] Again, this directional change can be achieved through an adjustment of the rate of interest. The modification in this case, however, will have to be the injection of a *premium* into the interest rate. Consequently, to achieve a quasi-certainty equivalent for deferred costs and benefits, the two expected uncertain values are adjusted in opposite directions. "For sellers the risk premium is positive, for buyers it is negative." [24] To

---

proach, and it is, therefore, the one used in this study. None of the other approaches mentioned bear this characteristic. As Dorfman puts it: "This device has the effect of sharply reducing the present value of net benefits expected with uncertainty in the remote future while it reduces the present value of early-maturing benefits only mildly."—Maass, Hufschmidt, *et al.*, *op. cit.*, p. 149. For a further defense of this approach, see also J. Steindl, "On Risk," *Oxford Economic Papers*, V (June, 1941), 43–53.

22. Lange, *op. cit.*, p. 30. Compare also Hicks, *op. cit.*, p. 125.
23. Hicks, *op. cit.*, p. 125.
24. Lange, *op. cit.*, p. 31.

approximate the quasi-certain values, deferred costs are discounted by a rate which is smaller than the beginning pure interest rate, and benefits are discounted at a rate which is larger than this rate.[25]

The second consideration which causes a net premium is the presumption that benefits involve a larger degree of uncertainty than do costs. "As more definite expectations are preferred to less definite ones, the risk premium is the greater the greater the degree of uncertainty of the actual expectation." [26] For this analysis, then, the interest rate used to discount benefits deviates positively from the original appropriate rate more than the interest rate used to discount deferred costs deviates negatively from the original rate.[27] The existence of greater uncertainty in the concept of benefits as opposed to costs leads, therefore, to a greater *net* premium than would otherwise have existed.[28]

The effect of this technique is to decrease the unadjusted benefit-cost ratio for all projects. Those projects experiencing benefits and costs which accrue far in the future receive a heavier penalty than those whose deferred effects occur sooner. Projects which possess a relatively heavy capital structure are penalized less than those which have relatively less capital. Both of these are adjustments which point in the right direction; effects which are deferred far

25. This base rate is taken to be 4.5 percent, representing an estimate of the social cost of capital. For a defense of this rate, see Chapter Four, footnote 19 and Chapter Five, footnote 21.

26. Lange, *op. cit.*, p. 31.

27. Eckstein's detailed treatment of uncertainty by means of an adjustment in the rate of interest, it should be noticed, fails to consider both the need of including a discount in the rate used in evaluating costs and the existence of a substantial difference in the degree of uncertainty between costs and benefits. See Eckstein, *op. cit.*, pp. 86–90. By the use of an interest rate bloated by the inclusion of a positive risk premium to discount both deferred benefits and costs, Eckstein is adjusting the concept of costs in the wrong direction. By the use of but a single interest rate, the intrinsic difference in the uncertain nature of expectations associated with costs and benefits is ignored. The argument of this analysis is that an allowance for risk and uncertainty can be approximated in a single-valued criterion only through a recognition of both of these factors.

28. In the study, a premium of 1 percent was added to the 4.5 percent base rate in the discounting of benefits. For deferred costs, a discount of .5 percent was subtracted from the 4.5 percent base. The net premium is therefore 1.5 percent. In defense of the size of the premium or discount chosen see Eckstein, *op. cit.*, pp. 86–90 and Miller, *op. cit.*, pp. 354–356.

into the future are more uncertain as are the projects with a larger proportion of costs deferred and thus subject to the uncertainties which accrue with time, i.e., the projects with a lower capital intensity.

Given that the benefit-cost ratio (Z) is expressed by the equation:

$$Z = \frac{\Sigma \frac{B}{(1+i)^t}}{K + \Sigma \frac{O}{(1+i)^t}} = \frac{B}{O + A_{1t}K}$$

in which B is the annual flow of benefits, O is the annual flow of operation, repair, and maintenance costs, K is the fixed investment cost, i is the interest rate, A_{1t} is the annual capital charge per dollar of fixed investment, and t is the period of amortization, the injection of the certainty equivalent proposal modifies the criterion as follows:

$$Z = \frac{\Sigma \frac{B}{(1+i_2)^t}}{K + \Sigma \frac{O}{(1+i_1)^t}}$$

where i_2 is the interest rate plus risk premium and i_1 is the interest rate plus risk discount.

TABLE 32

Effect of Uncertainty Adjustment
On Projects of Different Economic Lives With O/K = .1 [a]

Time	B [b]	O [c]	K [d]	B(3½) [e]	O(2) [f]	Z' [g]
0	100	4.55	45.45	100.00	4.55	2.00
10	100	23.90	239.00	831.66	214.68	1.83
20	100	30.47	304.70	1421.24	498.18	1.77
30	100	33.83	338.29	1839.20	757.80	1.68
40	100	35.77	357.65	2135.51	978.67	1.60
50	100	36.96	369.55	2345.56	1161.28	1.53
60	100	37.76	377.64	2494.47	1312.54	1.48
70	100	38.34	383.44	2600.00	1437.75	1.43
80	100	38.76	387.60	2674.88	1540.32	1.39
90	100	39.06	390.63	2727.93	1624.50	1.35
100	100	39.28	392.77	2765.54	1692.97	1.33

a. A premium of 1 percent was added to the base rate of 2.5 percent in evaluating benefits and a discount of .5 percent was subtracted from this rate in evaluating deferred costs. All of the projects bear a benefit-cost ratio of 2 in the absence of the uncertainty adjustment.
b. B=an assumed annual benefit flow.
c. O=the necessary annual operation, maintenance, and repair costs given that B=100, i=2.5 percent, Z=2, and O/K=.1. This value was found by using
$$Z = B/(O + A_{1t}K)$$

and finding numerical values for A_{it} for different years from a table "Annuity whose Present Value is 1."

   d. K=the necessary investment cost given B=100, i=2.5 percent, Z=2, and O/K=.1.

   e. B(3½)=the present value of total benefit for projects of different lives discounted at a rate of 3.5 percent. Numerical values for $(1+i_2)$ found in a table "Present Value of an Annuity."

   f. O(2)=the present value of operation, maintenance, and repair cost stream given in column O for projects of different lives discounted at a rate of 2 percent.

   g. Z'=the benefit-cost ratio after injecting the premium and discount factors to allow for uncertainty.

By using an interest rate of 2.5 percent, a typical agency rate, as the base interest rate and by assuming different sizes of premiums and discounts, the effect of the proposal can be shown on any typical benefit-cost ratio not yet adjusted for uncertainty. Tables 32 and 33 and Figures 7 and 8 depict the effect of different size premiums and discounts upon projects of varying lives with a benefit-cost ratio equal to 2 and with capital structures (O/K) equal to .1 and to .01.

TABLE 33

*Results of Varying Uncertainty Adjustments Applied
to Projects of Different Economic Lives and Capital Structures*

Time	I [a]	II [b]	III [c]
0	2.00	2.00	2.00
10	1.90	1.95	1.89
20	1.81	1.90	1.86
30	1.73	1.86	1.82
40	1.67	1.83	1.79
50	1.62	1.80	1.75
60	1.57	1.77	1.71
70	1.53	1.74	1.68
80	1.49	1.72	1.66
90	1.46	1.70	1.64
100	1.44	1.69	1.62

   a. Z' for projects which possess Z=2 when i=2.5 percent, O/K=.01 with i_2=3.5 percent, i_1=2 percent.

   b. Z' for projects which possess Z=2 when i=2.5 percent, O/K=.01 with i_2=3 percent, i_1=2.25 percent.

   c. Z' for projects which possess Z=2 when i=2.5 percent, O/K=.1 with i_2=3 percent, i_1=2.25 percent.

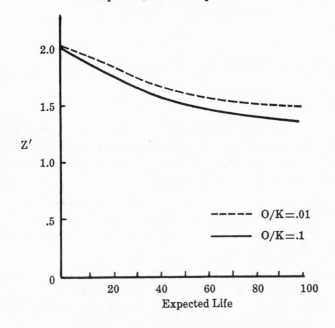

Figure 7. Uncertainty Adjustment
When $i_1 = 3.5$ percent and $i_2 = 2$ percent

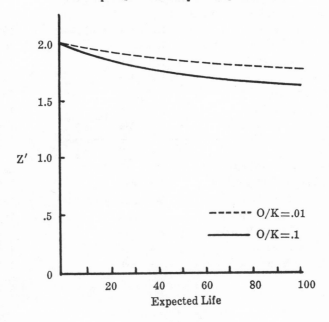

Figure 8. Uncertainty Adjustment
When $i_1 = 3$ percent and $i_2 = 2.25$ percent

Appendix C

Data on Southern Corps Projects

The following data provide some relevant information on the 163 projects in the South which make up the present study. In nearly all cases, the data were obtained from district offices of the U.S. Army Corps of Engineers.

Project	Type [1]	States Involved	Construction Dates
ALABAMA			
Apalachicola, Flint, and			
Chattahoochee Rivers	MP	Ala., Fla., Ga.	1947——
Gen. River Work	MP	Ala., Fla., Ga.	1946
Buford Dam	MP	Ala., Fla., Ga.	1950–57
Columbia Lock and Dam	MP	Ala., Fla., Ga.	1959——
Ft. Gaines Lock and Dam [2]	MP	Ala., Fla., Ga.	1956——
Jim Woodruff Lock and Dam	MP	Ala., Fla., Ga.	1949–60
Apalachicola River Channel			
Improvement	RH	Ala., Fla., Ga.	1957–58
Demopolis Lock and Dam	RH	Ala.	1950–55
Holt Lock and Dam	RH	Ala.	1962——
Jackson Lock and Dam	RH	Ala.	1957——
Mobile Harbor	RH	Ala.	1947, 1956–57
Paint Rock River	FC	Ala.	1962——
Warrior Lock and Dam	RH	Ala.	1955–58
ARKANSAS			
Arkansas River and Tributaries	MP	Ark., Okla.	1950——
Bank Stabilization	MP	Ark., Okla.	1950——
Dardanelle Dam	MP	Ark., Okla.	1956——
Augusta to Clarendon	FC	Ark.	1947
Bayou Bodcau Reservoir	FC	Ark., La.	1946–50
Beaver Reservoir	MP	Ark.	1959——
Blakely Mountain Reservoir	MP	Ark.	1946–55

Project	Type [1]	States Involved	Construction Dates
Blue Mountain Reservoir	FC	Ark.	1939–50
Bull Shoals Reservoir	MP	Ark., Mo.	1946–54
Bull Shoals Reservoir units 5 and 6	MP	Ark., Mo.	1958–62
Bull Shoals Reservoir units 7 and 8	MP	Ark., Mo.	1961——
Calion	FC	Ark.	1957–58
Cardens Bottoms Levee District No. 2	FC	Ark.	1948–50
Conway County Levee Districts Nos. 1, 2, and 8	FC	Ark.	1947–50
Conway County Levee District No. 6	FC	Ark.	1947–50
Crawford County Levee District	FC	Ark.	1947–50
De Gray Reservoir	MP	Ark.	1962——
Fort Smith	FC	Ark.	1946
Greers Ferry Reservoir	FC	Ark.	1957——
Little Missouri River below Murfreesboro	FC	Ark.	1955
Little Rock	FC	Ark.	1946–49
Little Rock to Pine Bluff	FC	Ark.	1947–50
McKinney Bayou and Barkman Creek	FC	Ark.	1959–61
McLean Bottom Levee District No. 3	FC	Ark.	1947–48
Millwood Reservoir	FC	Ark.	1961——
Narrows Reservoir	MP	Ark.	1946–52
Near Dardenelle	FC	Ark.	1947–48
Nimrod Reservoir	FC	Ark.	1939–50
Norfork Reservoir	FC	Ark., Mo.	1940–50
North Little Rock to Gillette	FC	Ark.	1939–47
Pine Bluff	FC	Ark.	1952
Red River at Garland City	FC	Ark.	1961
Red River below Denison Dam	FC	Ark., La., Okla., Tex.	1948——
Roland Drainage District	FC	Ark.	1947–48
Table Rock Reservoir	MP	Ark., Mo.	1956–61
Terre Noire Creek	FC	Ark.	1946
Van Buren	FC	Ark.	1947–48
Walnut Bayou	FC	Ark.	1958–59

Project	Type [1]	States Involved	Construction Dates
West of Morrilton	FC	Ark.	1949–50
FLORIDA			
Apalachicola Bay Channel St. Georges Sound	RH	Fla.	1956–57
Apalachicola, Flint, and Chattahoochee Rivers [3]			
Caloosahatchie River and Lake Okeechobee	RH	Fla.	1946–48
Canaveral Harbor: Jetties	RH	Fla.	1947
Central and Southern	FC	Fla.	1950——
Hollywood Harbor	RH	Fla.	1948–49
Horseshoe Cove	RH	Fla.	1958
Intra-Coastal Waterway Caloosahatchie River to Anclote River	RH	Fla.	1960——
Jacksonville Harbor	RH	Fla.	1951–52
Jacksonville to Miami Waterway	RH	Fla.	1951——
Key West (Reimbursement)	BE	Fla.	1962——
Lake Worth Inlet	RH	Fla.	1947–48, 1952
Lake Worth Inlet (Reimbursement)	BE	Fla.	1961——
Port Everglades Harbor	RH	Fla.	1961——
St. Andrew Bay	RH	Fla.	1950
St. Augustine Harbor	RH	Fla.	1956–58
St. Johns River Jacksonville to Lake Harney	RH	Fla.	1947–49
St. Josephs Bay	RH	Fla.	1949
St. Josephs Bay	RH	Fla.	1959–60
St. Lucie Inlet	RH	Fla.	1948
St. Marks River	RH	Fla.	1946, 1962
St. Petersburg Harbor	RH	Fla.	1957
Tampa Harbor	RH	Fla.	1947–51 1956–61
GEORGIA			
Alatoonah Reservoir	MP	Ga.	1946–50
Apalachicola, Flint, and Chattahoochee Rivers [3]			
Brunswick Harbor	RH	Ga.	1959–62

Project	Type [1]	States Involved	Construction Dates
Clark Hill Reservoir [4]			
Hartwell Reservoir [4]			
Macon	FC	Ga.	1949–50
Savannah Harbor	RH	Ga.	1947–52
Savannah Harbor	RH	Ga.	1957
Savannah River below Augusta	RH	Ga.	1958
KENTUCKY			
Ashland	FC	Ky.	1949–53
Barbourville	FC	Ky.	1955–58
Barkley Dam	MP	Ky., Tenn.	1957——
Buckhorn Reservoir	FC	Ky.	1957–60
Cannelton Locks and Dam	RH	Ky., Ind.	1962——
Catlettsburg	FC	Ky.	1956–59
Covington	FC	Ky.	1948–54
Dale Hollow Reservoir [5]			
Dewey Reservoir	FC	Ky.	1939–50
Fishtrap Reservoir	FC	Ky.	1962——
Green River Locks and Dam	RH	Ky.	1955–56
Greenup Locks and Dam	RH	Ky., Ohio	1957–61
Hawesville	FC	Ky.	1949–52
Jackson	FC	Ky.	1956
Louisville	FC	Ky.	1948–56
Markland Locks and Dam	RH	Ky., Ind.	1956——
Maysville	FC	Ky.	1949–56
McAlpine Lock and Dam	RH	Ky., Ind.	1957——
Meldahl Locks and Dam	RH	Ky., Ohio	1958——
Newport	FC	Ky.	1946–50
Nolin Reservoir	FC	Ky.	1959——
Ohio River Open Channel	RH	Ky., Ohio	1946–50
Pineville	FC	Ky.	1953–56
Rough River Reservoir and Channels	FC	Ky.	1957–60
Russell	FC	Ky.	1950
Taylorsville	FC	Ky.	1948–50
Uniontown	FC	Ky.	1948–50
Wolf Creek Reservoir	MP	Ky.	1940–48
LOUISIANA			
Aloha and Rigolette Area	FC	La.	1947–50

Project	Type [1]	States Involved	Construction Dates
Amite River and Tributaries	FC	La.	1957–60
Barataria Bay Waterway	RH	La.	1960–61
Bayou Bodcau, Red Chute, and Loggy Bayou	FC	La.	1946–49
Bayou Bodcau Reservoir [6]			
Bayou Chevreuil	FC	La.	1961
Bayou La Fourche and Jump Waterway	RH	La.	1962——
Bayous Petite, Anse, Tigre, and Carlin	FC	La.	1947
Bayou Pierre in vicinity of Shreveport	FC	La.	1948
Bayou Segnette Waterway	RH	La.	1957
Bayou Teche and Vermilion River	RH	La.	1939–51
Boeuf, Tensas Rivers and Bayou Macon	FC	La.	1947
Calcasieu River and Pass	RH	La.	1948–52
Freshwater Bayou	RH	La.	1962——
Gulf Intra-Coastal Waterway Lock and Dam at Algiers	RH	La.	1947–52
Plaquemine-Morgan City Alternate Route	RH	La.	1955–61
Jonesville	FC	La.	1949–50
Lake Pontchartrain	FC	La.	1949–50
Mermentau River	RH	La.	1949–53
Mississippi River Baton Rouge to Gulf	RH	La.	1959——
Mississippi River Gulf Outlet	RH	La.	1958——
Natchitoches Parish	FC	La.	1952–54
Pearl River	RH	La., Miss.	1946–52
Pineville	FC	La.	1947–49
Red River below Denison Dam [6]			
Red River in vicinity of Shreveport	FC	La.	1946–51
Wallace Lake Reservoir	FC	La.	1937–46
Waterway from Empire to Gulf	RH	La.	1948–50

MISSISSIPPI

Harrison County Shore Protection	FC	Miss.	1951–52

Project	Type [1]	States Involved	Construction Dates
Pascagoula Harbor	RH	Miss.	1953–54
Pearl River [7]			

NORTH CAROLINA

Project	Type [1]	States Involved	Construction Dates
Atlantic Intra-Coastal Waterway near Masonboro	RH	N.C.	1957–58
Buggs Island Reservoir [8]	MP	N.C., Va.	1946–54
Cape Fear River	RH	N.C.	1962
Cape Fear River at and below Wilmington	RH	N.C.	1947–49
Channel from Pamlico Sound to Avon	RH	N.C.	1947
Goldsboro	RH	N.C.	1948
Far Creek	RH	N.C.	1957
Intra-Coastal Waterway between Norfolk and St. Johns River	RH	N.C.	1955
Manteo Bay	RH	N.C.	1956–59
Morehead City Harbor	RH	N.C.	1960–61
Ocracoke Inlet	RH	N.C.	1961——
Pantego and Cucklers Creek	FC	N.C.	1961
Rollinson Channel Breakwater	RH	N.C.	1956
Stumpy Point Bay	RH	N.C.	1950
Wilkesboro Reservoir	FC	N.C.	1960——
Wilmington Harbor	RH	N.C.	1956–57

SOUTH CAROLINA

Project	Type [1]	States Involved	Construction Dates
Charleston Harbor	RH	S.C.	1946, 1949, 1962
Clark Hill Reservoir	MP	S.C., Ga.	1946–55
Hartwell Reservoir	MP	S.C., Ga.	1956——
Shipyard River	RH	S.C.	1950
Port Royal Sound to Beaufort	RH	S.C.	1956–57
Winyah Bay and Georgetown Harbor	RH	S.C.	1947–51

TENNESSEE

Project	Type [1]	States Involved	Construction Dates
Barkley Dam [9]			
Center Hill Reservoir	MP	Tenn.	1946–53
Cheatham Lock and Dam	MP	Tenn.	1950–59
Dale Hollow Reservoir	MP	Tenn., Ky.	1946–54
Lake City	FC	Tenn.	1958–59

Project	Type [1]	States Involved	Construction Dates
Memphis, Wolf River, and Nonconnah Creek	FC	Tenn.	1946–58
Old Hickory Lock and Dam	MP	Tenn.	1952–58

1. MP is multipurpose; RH is rivers and harbors (navigation); FC is flood control.
2. Name was changed to Walter F. George Lock and Dam.
3. See Alabama for project information.
4. See South Carolina for project information.
5. See Tennessee for project information.
6. See Arkansas for project information.
7. See Louisiana for project information.
8. Name changed to John H. Kerr Reservoir.
9. See Kentucky for project information.

Bibliography

Alchian, A. A. "The Rate of Interest, Fisher's Rate of Return Over Costs and Keynes' Internal Rate of Return," *American Economic Review*, VL (December, 1955), 938–943.

Bain, J. S. "Criteria for Undertaking Water-Resource Developments," *American Economic Review*, L (May, 1960), 310–321.

Baumol, William J. *Welfare Economics and the Theory of the State.* Cambridge: Harvard University Press, 1962.

Bowen, H. R. *Toward Social Economy.* New York: Rinehart and Co., 1948.

Bowman, Mary Jean (ed.). *Expectations, Uncertainty and Business Behavior.* New York: Social Science Research Council, 1958.

Carter, C. F., G. P. Meredith, and G. L. S. Shackle, *Uncertainty and Business Decisions.* Liverpool: Liverpool University Press, 1957.

Ciriacy-Wantrup, S. V. "Benefit-Cost Analysis and Public Resource Development," *Journal of Farm Economics*, XXXVII (November, 1955), 676–689.

———. *Resource Conservation Economics and Policies.* Berkeley: University of California Press, 1952.

Dean, Joel. "Measuring the Productivity of Capital," *Harvard Business Review*, XXXII (January-February, 1954), 120-130.

De Haven, J. C., L. A. Gore, and Jack Hirshleifer. *A Brief Survey of the Technology and Economics of Water Supply.* The RAND Corporation, Report R-258-RC, October, 1953.

de Roos, R., and A. A. Maass. "The Lobby That Can't be Licked," *Harpers*, August, 1949, p. 50.

Douglas, P. H. *Economy in the National Government.* Chicago: University of Chicago Press, 1952.

Eckstein, Otto. *Water Resource Development: The Economics of Project Evaluation.* Cambridge: Harvard University Press, 1958.

Federal Inter-Agency River Basin Committee. Subcommittee on Benefits and Costs. *Measurement Aspects of Benefit-Cost Analysis.* Washington, D. C.: Government Printing Office, November, 1948.

———. *Proposed Practices for Economic Analysis of River Basin Projects.* Washington, D. C.: Government Printing Office, May, 1950.

———. *Qualitative Aspects of Benefit-Cost Practice.* Washington, D. C.: Government Printing Office, April, 1947.

Federal Inter-Agency Committee on Water Resources. Subcommittee on

Evaluation Standards. *Proposed Practices for Economic Analysis of River Basin Projects.* Washington, D. C.: Government Printing Office, May, 1958.

Fox, I., and O. C. Herfindahl. "Attainment of Efficiency in Satisfying Demands for Water Resources," *American Economic Review,* LIV (May, 1964), 198–206.

Frank, A. D. *The Development of the Federal Program of Flood Control in the Mississippi River.* New York: Columbia University Press, 1930.

Friedman, Milton. "Liquidity and Uncertainty: Discussion," *Papers and Proceedings, American Economic Review,* IXL (May, 1949), 196–199.

———, and L. J. Savage. "The Utility Analysis of Choices Involving Risk," *Journal of Political Economy,* LVI (August, 1948), 279–304.

Groves, H. M. *Federal, State and Local Government Fiscal Relations.* Senate Document 69. 78th Congress, 1st Session. Washington, D. C.: Government Printing Office, 1943.

Hamburger, William. "The Determinants of Aggregate Consumption," *Review of Economic Studies,* XXII (No. 1, 1954), 23–34.

Harris, Seymour E. *The Economics of New England.* Cambridge: Harvard University Press, 1952.

Haver, C. B. "History and Status of Federal Resource Development Activities," *Natural Resources Paper No. 4,* Paper No. 5512, Chicago: The University of Chicago Office of Agricultural Economics Research, September, 1955 (mimeographed).

Hicks, J. R. "The Foundations of Welfare Economics," *Economic Journal,* IL (December, 1939), 696–712.

———. "The Valuation of the Social Income," *Economica,* VII (May, 1940), 105–124.

———. *Value and Capital.* Oxford: Clarendon Press, 1939.

Hirshleifer, Jack. *An Isoquant Approach to Investment Decisions.* The RAND Corporation, Report P-1158, August, 1957.

———. "On the Theory of Optimal Investment Decision," *Journal of Political Economy,* LXVI (August, 1958), 329–352.

———, James C. De Haven, and Jerome Milliman. *Water Supply: Economics, Technology and Policy.* Chicago: University of Chicago Press, 1960.

Holt, W. S. *The Office of the Chief of Engineers of the Army.* Service Monograph of the United States Government. No. 27. Baltimore: Johns Hopkins Press, 1923.

Hoyt, W. G., and W. B. Langbein. *Floods.* Princeton: Princeton University Press, 1955.

Kaldor, Nicholas. "Welfare Propositions of Economics and Interpersonal Comparisons of Utility," *Economic Journal,* IL (September, 1939), 549–552.

Kavesh, R. A., and J. B. Jones. "Differential Regional Impacts of Federal Expenditures: An Application of the Input-Output Matrix to Federal Fiscal Policy," *Regional Science Association Proceedings,* II (1956), 152–167.

Keynes, J. M. *General Theory of Employment, Interest and Money.* New York: Harcourt, Brace Co., 1936.

Kneese, A. V. *Water Resources: Development and Use.* Kansas City: Federal Reserve Bank of Kansas City, 1959.

Knight, Frank H. *Risk, Uncertainty and Profit.* Reissue. London: The London School of Economics and Political Science, 1948.

Krutilla, J. V. "Criteria for Evaluating Regional Development Programs," *American Economic Review*, XLV (May, 1955), 120–132.

———, and Otto Eckstein. *Multiple Purpose River Development: Studies in Applied Economic Analysis.* Baltimore: Johns Hopkins Press, 1958.

———. *Sequence and Timing in River Basin Development.* Washington, D. C.: Resources for the Future, Inc., February, 1960.

———. "Some Recent Developments in River Basin Planning and Evaluation," *Journal of Farm Economics*, XL (December, 1958), 1674–1687.

———. "Welfare Aspects of Benefit-Cost Analysis," *Journal of Political Economy*, LXIX (June, 1961), 226–235.

Lange, Oscar R. *Price Flexibility and Employment.* Bloomington, Indiana: Principia Press, Inc., 1944.

Leopold, L. B., and T. Maddox, Jr. *The Flood Control Controversy.* New York: Ronald Press, 1954.

Lerner, A. P. *The Economics of Control.* New York: Macmillan and Co., 1944.

Little, I. M. D. *A Critique of Welfare Economics.* 2nd edition. London: Oxford University Press, 1960.

Lutz, Friedrich A. and Vera. *The Theory of Investment of the Firm.* Princeton: Princeton University Press. 1951.

Maass, Arthur. *Muddy Waters: The Army Engineers and the Nation's Rivers.* Cambridge: Harvard University Press, 1951.

———, M. Hufschmidt, *et al. Design of Water Resource Systems. ibid.,* 1962.

Margolis, Julius. "Secondary Benefits, External Economies, and the Justification of Public Investment," *Review of Economics and Statistics,* XXXIX (August, 1957), 284–291.

———. "The Economic Evaluation of Federal Water Resource Development," *American Economic Review*, XLIX (March, 1959), 96–111.

McKean, R. N. *Efficiency in Government Through Systems Analysis: with Emphasis on Water Resources Development.* New York: John Wiley and Sons, Inc., 1958.

Meade, J. E. "The Theory of International Economic Policy," *Trade and Welfare.* Vol. II. London, New York, Toronto: Oxford University Press, 1955.

Miller, William L. "The Magnitude of the Discount Rate for Government Projects," *Southern Economic Journal*, XLVIII (April, 1962), 348–356.

Modigliani, F., and M. H. Miller. "The Cost of Capital, Corporation Finance and the Theory of Investment," *American Economic Review*, IIL (June, 1958), 261–297.

Moreell, Ben. *Our Nation's Water Resources—Policies and Politics.* Chicago: University of Chicago Press, 1956.

Musgrave, R. A., J. J. Carroll, L. D. Cook, and L. Frane. "Distribution of Tax Payments by Income Groups: A Case Study for 1948," *National Tax Journal,* IV (March, 1951), 1–54.

National Bureau of Economic Research. *An Appraisal of the 1950 Census Income Data.* Princeton: Princeton University Press, 1958.

National Rivers and Harbors Congress. *National Rivers and Harbors Congress and Its Work.* Washington, D. C.: National Rivers and Harbors Congress, 1940.

Pareto, Vilfredo. *Manuel d'Economie Politique.* Paris: M. Giard, 1929.

Peterson, E. T. *Big Dam Foolishness.* New York: Devin-Adair Co., 1954.

Pigou, A. C. *The Economics of Welfare.* 8th edition. London: Macmillan and Co., 1952.

President's Advisory Committee on Water Resources Policy, The. *Water Resources Policy.* Washington, D. C.: Government Printing Office, December, 1955.

President's Water Resources Council, The. *Policies, Standards and Procedures in the Formulation, Evaluation, and Review of Plans for Use and Development of Water and Related Land Resources.* Senate Document 97. 87th Congress, 2nd Session. Washington, D. C.: Government Printing Office, 1962.

President's Water Resources Policy Commission, The. *A Water Policy for the American People.* Vol. I. Washington, D. C.: Government Printing Office, 1950.

Ransmeier, J. S. *The Tennessee Valley Authority.* Nashville: Vanderbilt University Press, 1942.

Ratchford, B. U. "Government Action or Private Enterprise in River Valley Development: An Economist's View," *American Economic Review,* XLI (May, 1951), 299–307.

Regan, M. M., and E. L. Greenshields. "Benefit-Cost Analysis of Resource Development Programs," *Journal of Farm Economics,* XXXIII (November, 1951), 866–878.

Renshaw, E. F. "Measurement of Benefits From Navigation Projects," *American Economic Review,* XLVII (September, 1957), 652–662.

———. *Toward Responsible Government.* Chicago: Idyia Press, 1957.

Reuber, G. L., and R. J. Wonnacott. *The Cost of Capital in Canada.* Washington, D. C.: Resources for the Future, Inc., 1961.

Robinson, Joan. *The Economics of Imperfect Competition.* London: Macmillan and Co., 1934.

Schaller, H. G. "Federal Grants-in-Aid and Differences in State Per Capita Incomes, 1929, 1939, and 1949," *National Tax Journal,* VIII (September, 1955), 287–299.

———. "Social Security Transfer Payments and Differences in State Per Capita Incomes, 1929, 1939, and 1949," *Review of Economics and Statistics,* XXXVII (February, 1955), 83–89.

———. "Veterans Transfer Payments and State Per Capita Incomes, 1929, 1939, and 1949," *ibid.,* XXXV (November, 1953), 325–332.

Scitovsky, Tibor. *Welfare and Competition.* Chicago: Irwin, 1951.

Solomon, Ezra (ed.). *The Management of Corporate Capital.* Glencoe, Ill.: Free Press, 1959.

Steindl, Joseph. "On Risk," *Oxford Economic Papers,* V (June, 1941), 43–53.

Steiner, P. O. "Choosing Among Alternative Public Investments in the Water Resource Field," *American Economic Review,* IL (December, 1959), 893–916.

Stigler, George J. *The Theory of Price.* New York: Macmillan and Co., 1946.

Strotz, R. H. "Discount Rates Appropriate to Public Investment," Paper delivered at Mid-West Economic Association meetings, 1964 (mimeographed).

Sundelson, J. W., and S. J. Mushkin. U.S. Department of Labor. Social Security Board. *The Measurement of State and Local Tax Effort.* Bureau of Research and Statistics Memorandum No. 58. Washington, D. C.: Government Printing Office, 1944.

Tintner, Gerhard. "The Theory of Choice Under Subjective Risk and Uncertainty," *Econometrica,* IX (July-October, 1941), 298–304.

Twentieth Century Fund. *Studies in Current Tax Problems.* New York: 1937.

Universities-National Bureau Committee for Economic Research. *Public Finances: Needs, Sources and Utilization.* Princeton: Princeton University Press, 1961.

U. S. Army, Corps of Engineers, *Annual Report of the Chief of Engineers, U. S. Army.* Washington, D. C.: Government Printing Office, 1917–1962.

————. *Engineering Manual for Civil Works* (mimeographed instructions in district offices of Corps of Engineers).

————. *Orders and Regulations* (mimeographed instructions in district offices of Corps of Engineers).

U. S. Bureau of the Budget, *Circular A-47.* December 31, 1952 (mimeographed pamphlet issued by the Bureau of the Budget).

————. *Standards and Criteria for Formulating and Evaluating Federal Water Resources Development.* Report of Panel of Consultants to the Bureau of the Budget. Washington, D. C.: 1961 (mimeographed pamphlet issued by the Bureau of the Budget).

————. *The Budget of the United States.* Washington, D. C.: Government Printing Office, 1946-1962.

U. S. Bureau of the Census. *Census of Business, 1948.* Vol. I. Washington, D. C.: Government Printing Office, 1948.

————. *Census of Business, 1954.* Vol. I. *ibid.,* 1954.

————. *Census of Business, 1958.* Vol. II. *ibid.,* 1958.

————. *Statistical Abstract of the United States, 1952. ibid.,* 1952.

————. *Statistical Abstract of the United States, 1961. ibid.,* 1961.

————. *Statistical Abstract of the United States, 1962. ibid.,* 1962.

U. S. Commission on Organization of the Executive Branch of the

Government (1955). *Task Force Report on Water Resources and Power*. 3 vols. Washington, D. C.: Government Printing Office, June, 1955.

U. S. Commissioner of Internal Revenue. *Annual Report of the Commissioner of Internal Revenue, 1950*. Washington, D. C.: Government Printing Office, 1950.

——. *Annual Report of the Commissioner of Internal Revenue, 1958*. *ibid.*, 1958.

U. S. Congress, House. *House Report 7634*. 86th Congress, 2nd Session. Washington, D. C.: Government Printing Office, 1961.

——. *House Report 9076*. 87th Congress, 1st Session. *ibid.*, 1962.

——. *House Report 541*. 86th Congress, 1st Session. *ibid.*, 1960.

——. *House Report 1634*. 87th Congress, 1st Session. *ibid.*, 1962.

——. *House Report 2064*. 86th Congress, 2nd Session. *ibid.*, 1961.

——. *House Report 2181*. 87th Congress, 1st Session. *ibid.*, 1962.

——. *Report on Amite River and Tributaries, La.* House Document 419. 84th Congress, 2nd Session. *ibid.*, 1956.

——. *Report on Barataria Bay Waterway, La.* House Document 82. 85th Congress, 1st Session. *ibid.*, 1957.

——. *Report on Bayou Chevreuil, La.* House Document 347. 84th Congress, 2nd Session. *ibid.*, 1956.

——. *Report on Bayou Pierre in vicinity of Shreveport, La.* House Document 285. 79th Congress, 1st Session. *ibid.*, 1945.

——. *Report on Bayou Segnette Waterway, La.* House Document 413. 83rd Congress, 2nd Session. *ibid.*, 1954.

——. *Report on Channel from Hatteras Inlet to Hatteras, and Rollinson Channel, N. C.* House Document 411. 83rd Congress, 2nd Session. *ibid.*, 1954.

——. *Report on Freshwater Bayou and vicinity, La.* House Document 435. 86th Congress, 2nd Session. *ibid.*, 1960.

——. *Report on Lake Pontchartrain, La.* House Document 691. 79th Congress, 2nd Session. *ibid.*, 1946.

——. *Report on Mississippi River—Gulf Outlet.* House Document 245. 82nd Congress, 1st Session. *ibid.*, 1951.

——. *Report on Red River at Garland City, Ark.* House Document 167. 87th Congress, 1st Session. *ibid.*, 1961.

——. *Report on Red River and Tributaries, Tex., Okla., Ark., and La.* House Document 488. 83rd Congress, 2nd Session. *ibid.*, 1954.

——. *Report on Re-examination of Norfolk Dam, North Fork River, Ark.* House Document 290. 77th Congress, 1st Session. *ibid.*, 1942.

——. *Report on Survey of Pearl River, Miss.* House Document 408. 75th Congress, 2nd Session. *ibid.*, 1938.

——. *Report on Survey of Red River in vicinity of Shreveport, La.* House Document 627. 78th Congress, 2nd Session. *ibid.*, 1944.

——. Committee on Flood Control, *Report on Flood Control Appropriations*. Committee Document No. 1. 70th Congress, 1st Session. *ibid.*, 1927.

U. S. Congress, House. Committee on Public Works. *Hearings of the Subcommittee to Study Civil Works.* 82nd Congress, 2nd Session. *ibid.,* 1952.

———. Committee on Public Works. *Report of the Subcommittee to Study Civil Works: The Civil Functions Program of the Corps of Engineers, U. S. Army.* House Committee Print No. 21. 82nd Congress, 2nd Session. *ibid.,* 1952.

———. Committee on Public Works. *Report of the Subcommittee to Study Public Works: Economic Evaluation of Federal Water Resource Development Projects.* House Committee Print No. 24. 82nd Congress, 2nd Session. *ibid.,* 1952.

———. Subcommittee of the Committee on Appropriations. *Hearings on Public Works Appropriations.* 79th Congress, 1st Session to 87th Congress, 2nd Session. *ibid.,* 1946-1962.

U. S. Congress, Joint Economic Committee. *Federal Expenditure Policy for Economic Growth and Stability.* Joint Committee Print. 85th Congress, 1st Session. Washington, D. C.: Government Printing Office, November, 1957.

———. *Federal Tax Policy for Economic Growth and Stability.* Joint Committee Print. 84th Congress, 1st Session. *ibid.,* November, 1955.

U. S. Congress, Senate. *Report on Bayou Teche, Teche-Vermilion Waterway, and Vermilion River, La.* Senate Document 93. 77th Congress, 1st Session. Washington, D. C.: Government Printing Office, 1942.

———. *Report on Boeuf and Tensas Rivers and Bayou Macon, Ark. and La.* Senate Document 151. 78th Congress, 2nd Session. *ibid.,* 1944.

———. *Report on Lake Charles Deep Water Channel, La.* Senate Document 190. 79th Congress, 2nd Session. *ibid.,* 1946.

———. *Senate Report 1524.* 86th Congress, 2nd Session. *ibid.,* 1961.

———. *Senate Report 1768.* 87th Congress, 1st Session. *ibid.,* 1962.

———. Committee on Appropriations. *Hearings, First Deficiency Appropriations Bill, 1946.* 79th Congress, 1st Session. *ibid.,* 1946.

———. Select Committee on National Water Resources. *Report of Select Committee on National Water Resources.* 87th Congress, 1st Session. *ibid.,* 1961.

———. Subcommittee of the Committee on Appropriations. *Hearings on Public Works Appropriations.* 79th Congress, 1st Session to 87th Congress, 2nd Session. *ibid.,* 1946-1962.

U. S. *Congressional Record.* 79th Congress, 1st Session to 87th Congress, 1st Session. Washington, D. C.: Government Printing Office, 1945-1962.

U. S. Department of Commerce. *Business Statistics, 1961.* Washington, D. C.: Government Printing Office, 1961.

———. *Survey of Current Business. ibid.,* August, 1951; August, 1959; August, 1961; March, 1963.

U. S. Department of Labor. Social Security Board. *Fiscal Capacity of the States.* Bureau of Research and Statistics Memorandum 43. Washington, D. C.: Government Printing Office, 1941.

U. S. Temporary National Economic Committee. *Who Pays the Taxes?* Monograph 3. Washington, D. C.: Government Printing Office, 1940.

U. S. Treasury Department. *Annual Report of the Secretary of the Treasury.* Washington, D. C.: Government Printing Office, 1950 and 1958.

————. *Treasury Department Bulletin. ibid.,* October, 1941.

————. Internal Revenue Service. *Statistics of Income for 1950. ibid.,* 1954.

————. Internal Revenue Service. *Statistics of Income for 1958. ibid.,* 1960.

Weston, J. F. "The Incidence and Effects of the Corporate Income Tax," *National Tax Journal,* II (December, 1949), 300–315.

White, G. F. *Human Adjustment to Floods.* Chicago: University of Chicago Press, 1945.

Index

Abernethy, Thomas G., 24
Aggregate demand curve for project outputs, 85–86
Aid to depressed areas: as program goal, 29–31
Allocation of appropriations: by project type, 1–9; objectives determining, 21–40 passim, 41, 119; among projects, 41–51 passim; requirements for efficient, 42; regional, 52–54, 58, 59–67, 69–79, 145; impact of welfare criterion on, 147; explanation of, 150n
Allocation of expenditures. See Allocation of appropriations
Allocation of investment. See Allocation of appropriations
Allocation of resources: requirements for efficient, 42; pattern of, within state, 82n
Allocative efficiency: analysis of, 68, 95–124
Alternative cost principle, 82
Amortization, 102
Apalachicola, Flint and Chattahoochee project, 107
Appropriations Bill. See Public Works Appropriations Bill
Arkansas River project, 54n, 107n
Aspinall, Wayne N., 19
Asset values: maximum growth of, 99, 103
Associated costs: definition of, by agencies, 23
Authorization of projects: requirements for, 97. See also Omnibus Authorization Bill
Average rate of return. See Rate of return
Average tax rate: assumed equal to marginal tax rate, 89

Bain, Joe S., 99, 103n

Baumol, William, 131
Beaver Reservoir project, 106
Benefits: project, 37–40 passim, 45, 85, 96, 106; secondary, 23, 40, 50n, 100n; overestimation of, 25, 50n, 100n; underestimation of, 26; present value of, equal to appropriation, 63, 72, 142; treatment of uncertainty in, 100, 105, 169, 172–177; marketable and non-marketable, 103n; intangible, 107; beneficiaries of, 137, 147; welfare weights applied to, 147; uncertain nature of, 156, 159–166; difficult to estimate in flood control projects, 160
—program: regional, 59–66, 72, 80, 81–83, 85, 91–94, 119–123, 139–146
Benefit-cost analysis: applied in project evaluation, 22, 86, 106–117, 150n; refinement of, 22–23, 95–105; theory of, 36, 42; deficiencies of present, 96–100. See also Benefit-cost ratio, Interest rate
Benefit-cost data: used in proposed tests, 105–112; obtained from Corps of Engineers, 108; welfare weights attached to, 146–149
Benefit-cost ratio, 15, 119; as criteria for choice, 10, 16, 17, 21, 43, 67; congressional reaction to, 24–27; refinement of, 24, 95–105; criticism of, 25, 37, 96–100; definition of, 42, 63n, 96, 102, 175; as guage of efficiency, 44–50, 101–116; marginal, 45; weighted average, 45–50 passim, 109–112 passim; and interest rate, 98–99, 101–102; cut-off, 103, 106, 111, 116; and adjustment for uncertainty, 104–105, 174–177; as multidimensional criterion, 148–150
Benefit-cost technique. See Benefit-cost analysis; Benefit-cost ratio

WATER RESOURCE INVESTMENT AND THE PUBLIC INTEREST
An Analysis of Federal Expenditures in Ten Southern States

Robert H. Haveman

Has the taxpayer been getting his money's worth from Federal appropriations to water resource projects? Data from 147 water resource projects in a ten-state area in the South from 1946 to 1962 have been used in this study of economic efficiency and income redistributional aspects of public expenditures. This applied or empirical welfare analysis is a direct descendant of other analyses in water resource development by Otto Eckstein and John Krutilla.

Two primary variables used to investigate the relationship between welfare determinants — the size of the national income (economic efficiency) and its distribution — are incorporated into a multidimensional welfare function in an experiment in welfare evaluation which will be of special interest and importance to economists. The estimates of misallocation, the criticism of the existing techniques of evaluating water resource expenditures, and the suggestions for improving these techniques will interest every thoughtful citizen who desires the maximum social benefit for each dollar of social cost.

In the Foreword, Senator Proxmire of Wisconsin says, "Professor Haveman, in this excellent book, has performed a valuable service in bringing clarity to the difficult process of evaluating alternative government investments and stimulating further discussion of this little-understood but extremely important question."